TUNE IN OR BUY IN?

Papers from the 27th University of Manchester Broadcasting Symposium, 1996

Editors:

Sue Ralph
School of Education
University of Manchester

Jo Langham Brown
University College, Warrington
University of Manchester

Tim Lees
School of Education
University of Manchester

TUNE IN OR BUY IN?

Papers from the 27th University of Manchester Broadcasting Symposium, 1996

Edited by

Sue Ralph
School of Education, University of Manchester

Jo Langham Brown
University College, Warrington, University of Manchester

Tim Lees
School of Education, University of Manchester

Published with the generous support of Channel 4 Television

Current Debates in Broadcasting: 6

UNIVERSITY of LUTON PRESS

British Library Cataloguing in Publication Data
A catalogue record for this book is available from the British Library

ISBN: 1 86020 528 3
ISSN: 0963-6544

Published by
John Libbey Media
Faculty of Humanities
University of Luton
75 Castle Street
Luton
Bedfordshire LU1 3AJ
United Kingdom
Telephone: +44 (0) 1582 743297; Fax: +44 (0) 1582 743298
e-mail: ulp@luton.ac.uk

Cover design: Derek Virtue, Datanet
Typeset in Palatino
Printed in Great Britain by Bookcraft Ltd, Midsomer Norton, UK

Contents

Sponsors and Committee

One of the objectives of the Symposium Steering Committee is to keep the cost of attending the event as low as possible. It is greatly assisted in achieving this objective by the generosity of its long-term supporters and sponsors. The Committee would like to express its gratitude to its 1996 supporters and sponsors, who were:

Action Time
BBC North
Border Television
Channel 4 Television
Granada Television
The Guardian
Independent Television Commission
NYNEX CableComms Ltd

In organising the Broadcasting Symposium, the School of Education of the University of Manchester was advised by a Steering Committee, the members of which were:

Colin Shaw, CBE, Broadcasting Standards Council (chair)
John Gray, independent consultant (honorary president)

Sue Ralph, University of Manchester (director)
Marjorie Burton, University of Manchester (co-ordinator)
Tim Lees, University of Manchester (administrator)

1996 Committee:

Steve Avery, Kirklees Council
Louise Bennett, Independent Television Commission
Jo Langham Brown, University College, Warrington, University of Manchester
Sue Caro, Channel 4 Television
Freda Chapman, BECTU
Phillip Drummond, University of London
Lynne Fredlund, independent producer
Amanda Hayne (Publicity Officer) University of Manchester
Helen Hutchinson, Border Television
Jerome Kuehl, Open Media
Roy Lockett, BECTU
Jane Luca, Granada Television Centre
John Mundy, University College, Warrington, University of Manchester
Philip Radcliffe, University of Manchester
Helen Read, The Guardian
Clare Reynolds, Broadcasting Standards Council
Brook Sinclair, Adcomm Ltd
Nick Smith, Independent Television Commission
Veronica Taylor, British Film Institute

The Symposium is very grateful to Professor Katharine Perera, Pro-Vice Chancellor, University of Manchester, for her support and her welcoming address.

Transcriptions by Judie Collins
Audio recordings by David Griffiths and Stephen Glasgow

The Symposium is grateful to the following who chaired the Paper Sessions: Jo Langham Brown, Marie Brown, John Gray, Bryan Luckham, John Mundy, Sue Ralph, Brook Sinclair

Foreword

'May you live in interesting times,' runs the ancient Chinese curse; and in broadcasting, the times are very interesting indeed. Since the industry's beginning, there has never been a period of such uncertainty and rapid transition. Broadcasting is experiencing an earthquake, the after-shock of which will affect the industry for many years to come. Analogue, the prevalent technology for fifty years, is giving way to digital, and the very foundation of broadcasting is set to change. The consequences of this in the long term are largely unknown, but this doesn't lessen the speculation; and, privately, many broadcasting executives admit that, in terms of costs, they wish the technology had never been invented. Almost every speaker at this year's Symposium reflected his or her anxiety about digitalisation and its implications for ownership, regulation, casualisation, multi-skilling, content and standards.

The consequences for the workforce are likely to be traumatic. An industry already destabilised by the repercussions of the 1990 Broadcasting Act (which relaxed public service obligations, especially for ITV, and spelt the end for the long-running duopoly of the BBC and independent companies) now finds itself competing for audiences with cable and satellite in a hostile multi-channel environment. The well-paid, well-resourced, privileged practitioners of the past who embarked on careers in broadcasting are now giving way to a much less stable workforce of harassed and uneasy freelances. As far as new practitioners are concerned, salaries are going down, hours are going up, and working in broadcasting is now a matter of short-term contracts with too-frequent 'breaks' between. Unions have lost much of their power, and the impact of all this on new entrants to the profession is a matter of grave concern. Such was the point of view expressed by many of the delegates at this year's Symposium – especially in the light of persistent reports that many newcomers are working for nothing more than 'job experience'.

Mindful of the profound effects of such upheavals, this year the Symposium itself took on a new direction. At its inception, over a quarter of a century ago in 1969, the annual event was intended to provide a forum for practitioners to discuss broadcasting and its role in society. Academics were involved in the organisation of the Symposium and participated in the general discussions, but the main spotlight fell on the way broadcasters interpreted their responsibilities within the generally accepted framework of broadcasting as a public service. As Colin Shaw pointed out this year in his farewell speech, the emphasis did, for many years, tend to prioritise the BBC. However, in the last decade, with its increasingly multi-channel environment, the Corporation's role – while always important – has become notably less significant in the totality of broadcasting, and the Symposium also had to move on to focus on broader issues. In 1996, a further change took place. Under the Symposium's new Director, Sue Ralph, and a newly-constituted Committee, the decision was taken to re-orientate the event and create a space where media practitioners and academics could meet on an equal footing to discuss the dilemmas and the opportunities posed for broadcasters by the new digital age.

Consequently, a new feature this year was an invitation to the broadcasting and academic communities to submit, in addition to the main sessions, research papers which would delve more deeply into the perplexities facing broadcasters in an age when audiences supposedly have the upper hand in the marketplace of broadcasting. These papers were discussed at smaller group meetings in between and around the main sessions, and the debates aired through them stimulated lively and informed discussions in the plenary gatherings.

The idea worked well. What was striking was the degree of 'convergence' in the issues which exercised the minds of broadcasters and academics about the future of the industry. Technological change will inevitably alter viewer patterns and behaviour, and market-driven notions of what the viewers want will pose problems for an industry which, in Europe at least, has traditionally always thought of its role as encompassing a large degree of social responsibility.

We hope that, by bringing together media practitioners, academics, researchers, commercial and workforce interests, we will provide for the Symposia of the future an anxiety-free climate in which participants can frankly discuss and try out new ideas in a creative and supportive environment. In the old public service past, new broadcasting practitioners had the luxury of learning from well-established long-standing professional teams. With so many changes in the industry, and so much financial pressure, this unique feature of British broadcasting is slipping away. The consequences of this loss for programme quality could be disastrous. The Symposium can provide the forum for newcomers and veterans to address these concerns. With creative continuity in danger of being lost, there has never been a better moment for broadcasters and academics to meet and explore ideas.

This Symposium would not have been possible without the many valuable contributions by speakers and delegates. We would like to express our gratitude to all participants and let their words speak for themselves.

Jo Langham Brown
Sue Ralph
Tim Lees

The 1996 Symposium: Keynote Address

Tune In or Buy In?

Rt Hon Dr Jack Cunningham MP

Shadow Secretary of State for National Heritage

Shortly after Easter, the House of Commons will debate the Broadcasting Bill for the first time. This conference gives me a welcome opportunity to set down my own thinking on the wide range of issues surrounding that Bill.

C.P. Scott once opined of television that 'no good will come of this device. The word is half Greek and half Latin.' The jury is still out on whether he was right or wrong. 'Television,' said David Frost, 'is an invention that permits you to be entertained in your living room by people you wouldn't have in your home.'

We live in an information age. As Commissioner Bangemann put it, 'The information society is about new ways of living and working together.' The development of information superhighways brings exciting new possibilities across the whole range of human activities. Rigid distinctions between telephony, computing, broadcasting and films are rapidly eroding. New delivery systems bring new commercial, industrial and employment prospects. Distillation will accelerate the pace of change, create new challenges, new opportunities.

This is a time of convergence of education, the arts, drama, the cultural industries, films, television – giving the potential to bring considerable wealth to those countries who make a success of the opportunities.

Technological convergence can bring together work and leisure – the home and the office – education and entertainment. Broadcasting is a key area of activity wherein news, sport, drama, music, cultural activities, education, business and commerce all come together. Public policy in broadcasting has always been and will continue to be of critical importance. The growth of multimedia industries, and their significance to all aspects of our lives, means that public policy must now address these challenges: the technological innovations, the ownership issues, the questions of content and standards.

The question for us all is: can we meet the challenge of change and turn it to our advantage? To commercial and economic success? The opportunities are enormous, not just to install the technology but to develop the huge range of new services the technology will facilitate. That is why the Broadcasting Bill is so important.

I believe we must address these issues knowing too that Britain's future is inextricably linked to developments in the European Union. Nor is there any escape from the realities of the global economy. We must compete and prosper by facing the future, not hiding from it.

We do, after all, have some considerable advantages. First the English language. 80% of the world's business is conducted in English. 80% of all electronic text is stored in English. 70% of all films are made in English. Over half of the world's television broadcasts are in English.

We have probably the best television industry in the world, even though we must all the time reflect on the wonderful comment of Harriet van Horne when she said, 'There are days when any electrical appliance in the house, including the vacuum cleaner, seems to offer more entertainment possibilities than the TV set.' Nevertheless, British television sets global standards in terms of factual programmes, documentaries, and dramas. The BBC is one of Britain's few – perhaps only – global brand names.

As confirmed again this week at the Oscar awards, we have outstanding talents on the stage and screen, in animation, acting and directing.

Britain is the second largest CD-ROM publisher in the world.

The Open University is the world's most experienced, respected and successful distance learning institution.

If, as many believe, and as Professor Charles Handy succinctly put it, 'intelligence is the new form of prosperity', then education and training will be the foundation of future society's economic and social well-being. The new information technologies, especially in broadcasting, have a crucial contribution to make to the more successful education and training of our people. Labour's proposal for a 'University for Industry' is one good example to illustrate that point.

Britain should be as well-placed as any country to grasp the opportunities. But – will we?

Ministers often bear an uncanny resemblance to Henri Thoreau who remarked that, 'It would be folly to build a telegraphic system across the USA before checking whether anyone in California had anything to say to anyone in New York!'

But as we look to the future we can learn from the past. The decision to create the BBC was a stroke of genius. Public service broadcasting, the setting of standards, benchmarks of quality, universal access – will all continue to have a crucial role. These things were not simply left to the market. Nor can they be in the future. State involvement in broadcasting will, I believe, continue to be essential for the public interest.

This is how I see the broad picture. What of the Broadcasting Bill in detail?

Many here will be following the progress of the Bill with great interest, not least the Chairman, Colin Shaw, whose own organisation, the Broadcasting Standards Council, is due to be merged with the Broadcasting Complaints Commission. I will cover some of the issues of most concern to us in the Bill, including digital terrestrial television, the broadcasting of live sport, conditional access, and regulation.

Technological change sometimes proceeds as a gradual progression; sometimes, in large steps. The development of broadcasting has exhibited both of these features. The expansion of terrestrial television from BBC1 through to Channel 5 has been gradual. The launch of satellite television and the acceleration of cable in the last decade are examples of more rapid change.

Today we stand at another point of change in broadcasting: the introduction of digital technology. Digital has the potential to deliver better quality television pictures, a much greater number of television channels, and a far more efficient use of spectrum. The single biggest unanswered question in my mind is whether the introduction of digital can be delivered quickly and effectively, or whether the conversion from analogue will be a slow and painful one – or, indeed, whether it will happen at all.

The Government intends to hold an 'auction' for the right to operate those multiplexes not allocated to the existing terrestrial broadcasters. The auction will be unconventional in that the Government is not asking for money but, instead, firm intentions, detailed plans on how the multiplex operators will encourage the take-up of digital terrestrial television.

The multiplex operators will have to develop and subsidise the new equipment, whether it is in the form of set-top boxes or televisions or through the distribution of vouchers. Everyone is agreed that this is the expensive part of the operation. But they have no product to sell. New broadcasters will wish to see an existing consumer base before they invest in programming. In effect, they have to double the revenue of conventional broadcasters; revenue to pay for their programming, and revenue to pay the multiplex operators for the right to broadcast.

One of the lessons to be learned from the development of BSkyB is that it is the rights holders who have the valuable product. The top sporting events and films are what bring in the audiences, and BSkyB (and others) have to pay handsomely for them. It is not the sporting bodies who have to pay the broadcaster to be seen or heard on the air. The BBC even pays Camelot to be allowed to broadcast the weekly National Lottery live.

What will drive digital terrestrial television forward? Existing terrestrial broadcasters have little incentive to put their own money into the development of digital broadcasting. They can sit back and wait for the new players to invest. The multiplex operators have the dubious pleasure of funding the new technology in order for the existing terrestrial channels to provide over the new delivery system a product that will almost certainly be superior to the one which they themselves are offering.

The valuable commodity in this equation is radio frequency spectrum. Not that given to the multiplex operators, but that to be liberated by the compression of digital channels into a smaller part of the spectrum. If there is a sensible way of realising the revenue potential of the spectrum then it could be possible to put that money towards the development of digital.

But to use that spectrum, the existing analogue transmissions must be switched off. Under the government's proposals, a date will be set after five years, or when fifty per cent of viewers have gone digital.

My only advice would be, not to hold your breath.

Digital terrestrial television could be made to work if those responsible for promoting it were also charged with the responsibility of disposing of or at least leasing out for a fixed period the liberated spectrum to a variety of providers. A switch-off date for analogue could then be set and digital broadcasting launched with all the existing channels as well as a number of new free to air and pay TV services.

The implications of such a move are great. They imply that every household or every television owner is provided with a set-top box and that there will be universal access. The costs are great and would have to be borne by a private sector consortium, if not with the financial backing, certainly with the political backing of the Government. If the present proposals for digital broadcasting prove to be unrealistic, and potential multiplex operators do not materialise, then I believe that this may be the only option that a future Government will be able to pursue.

An approach that does not leave the take-up of digital entirely to the market also has major implications for equipment suppliers. A fixed cut-off date for analogue transmissions will require the availability of set-top boxes manufactured to a standard specification and delivered on time in very large numbers to the consumer.

In the Lords debates on the Broadcasting Bill, Labour has stressed the importance of properly regulated conditional access systems, of must-carry and must-offer protection, and of universal access. I understand that the broadcasters and manufacturers are already sitting down together to consider how they will cooperate to deliver the necessary requirements. I am sure that this process will not be easy. The involvement of a lead player in the form that I have suggested would smooth this path.

Alongside the development of digital terrestrial television, digital satellite broadcasting should also flourish. It is argued that the guaranteed additional digital channels for existing broadcasters gives a market distortion, but I believe it is right that Government takes a lead in particular types of broadcasting. Government has a role in ensuring that as wide a range of people as possible can have access to a basic level of service at a reasonable cost. We have done this with analogue and we should continue to do so with digital broadcasting.

The multi-channel television environment with a multitude of programme providers might result in a move between delivery systems for different broadcasters. For example, a pay-per-view general sports channel may be more lucrative on terrestrial television, while a more specialist channel might be better suited to satellite.

The debate on the televising of sport that Labour initiated is a case in point. This issue was not about BSkyB, as some have suggested (particularly newspapers in rivalry to News International), but a wider point of principle. Sky has been bold, innovative and successful in its approach to live sport. Labour has no intention to exclude them.

There are a small number of events – and it is worth remembering that the listed events do not necessarily have to be sporting occasions – that the public rightly believe should be available free to air on the widest possible basis. I also accept that the sporting bodies – the rights holders – also have a legitimate right to maximise their revenue for their product.

This is why we support the case for the unbundling of broadcast rights for sport. The separate sale of live coverage, re-broadcast rights, highlights and radio coverage would allow the growth of a variety of sports coverage suited to particular types of delivery system. There is no evidence either that this would substantially diminish the overall value of rights; it could increase it. If we were to proceed in this direction, then the relevance of the limited list would also diminish. It may well be that the voluntary code of practice being formulated by the Sports Council will be sufficient to ensure unbundling. However, should there be failure to reach agreement, Labour will reintroduce amendments to the Bill to provide a statutory framework.

It seems to be increasingly apparent that the rights holders and programme providers will emerge with the upper hand in a world of multiple delivery systems. But we do not want a system where the viewer has to invest in a range of technology or separate boxes in order to watch programmes. The responsibility for ensuring that this does not occur will lie with Oftel and the Independent Television Commission (ITC) as the regulators. The Government has published its proposals for regulation of conditional access systems in a recent paper. The Government is also committed to the implementation of the European Union Television Standards Directive. However, we remain to be convinced that all the necessary steps are being put in place immediately and parliament should be debating the issues as part of the Broadcasting Bill. The Lords have spent some time considering the issues of conditional access and we will return to them again when the Bill undergoes detailed scrutiny in the Commons.

The regulation of broadcasting technology is only one half of the regulatory equation. Of equal if not greater importance is the regulation of broadcasting content. The emergence of a much wider range of television providers will not guarantee high quality. With a limited amount of advertiser and viewer revenue this must be a danger. I think we will have to define quality in different ways for different kinds of programming, depending on whether we are judging a small audience thematic channel or a high audience more generalist service.

The challenge will be to ensure that the high quality, high cost services that we currently enjoy are not reduced to the lowest common denominator. Few comments on quality can better that of Sam Goldwyn when he observed that, 'The wide screen makes a bad film twice as bad.'

The central responsibility to ensure that this quality is maintained will fall upon the ITC and the BBC Governors acting on behalf of Parliament and the public whose interests they serve. Labour welcomes the merger of the Broadcasting Standards Council and the Broadcasting Complaints Commission, but I believe that a further step could be taken. The ITC has the main role in considering issues of quality. I believe that we should consider whether it should deal with matters of standards and complaints.

In considering the question of content regulation you will be aware of the growing public debate on the possible introduction of V-chip technology. While I welcome a debate on how we ensure that children are protected from violent or disturbing images on our television screens, I share the ITC's concerns over the practicalities and value of the V-chip.

Even if every new television set were to be fitted with the chip from tomorrow, that would leave thirty six million television sets without it in every day use. Many of the older sets will survive for years and some inevitably find their way into children's bedrooms. This also neglects the problem of video recorders, which would also require V-chips, as probably would personal computers in the near future. There is also a legitimate argument that over-reliance on such end-user technology might lead to a lowering of standards in the general quality of material broadcast. The V-chip could easily erode the well-established principle of the nine o'clock watershed. However, the over-riding principle must be that the exercise of parental responsibility could only ever be supported by the V-chip and not replaced by it.

Last year, Labour published *Communicating Britain's Future*, a policy document on the information superhighway. We also considered the issue of the future of Oftel. It may be that if we are to have a super-regulator for the content of broadcasting, then we should also have a similar body for the broadcasting transmission which also embraces telecoms. An Ofcom could take on the technical aspects of the work of the ITC as well as that of the Radiocommunications Agency.

There seems little point to me in continuing with a multitude of regulators – a recent study by the Institute for Public Policy Research identified ten different media regulators – particularly when there is little public understanding of their respective roles. Our proposals would go some way towards relieving the confusion and leave us with two distinct bodies: one for content, or 'software', and one for the transmission and 'hardware' aspects of television broadcasting.

Perhaps the biggest problem with the current broadcasting technology has also been demonstrated in Europe. The European Parliament is currently considering amendments to the 1989 *Television Without Frontiers* directive. One of the areas of greatest contentions is over content quotas for video on demand services. The 1989 directive did not deal with this matter. A new directive on *New Audiovisual Services* has yet to be published. Any new regulatory framework must satisfy the legitimate aspirations of the European programming industry.

Some of the problems experienced in developing a satisfactory European regulatory framework have been the result of different Directorate-Generals being responsible for different aspects of broadcasting. In much the same way, in Britain we have dual responsibilities between the Departments of National Heritage and Trade and Industry. It is still not clear to me whether wholesale convergence of broadcasting and telecommunications will take place, but there is little doubt that some measure of convergence has already started and that it will continue. The debate on the regulation of that future environment has already started with Oftel's document *Beyond the Telephone, the Television and the PC*, as well as numerous academic publications.

We have to be prepared for a world in which entertainment and work use large volume video and data communications and a high degree of remote interactivity. Our current legislative and regulatory framework offers little hope of dealing with the prospect of moving images being transmitted on the Internet. This development is surely going to ignite fierce debate about censorship and freedom of expression in just the same way that it is already doing in the United States.

The legislative framework that Parliament is debating can only be a snapshot of a field that will continue to develop rapidly. It may be that digital terrestrial television will develop successfully and be with us for some considerable time. Alternatively, it could become outmoded before it has achieved any real penetration of the market. Legislation can only attempt to deal with major changes in broadcasting; in the long term, the regulatory regime we use is the only way in which continuous change can be effectively managed.

When we consider all these new opportunities we should be determined to maximise the industrial and commercial benefits for UK plc. As an American president once observed, 'Yesterday is not ours to recover, but tomorrow is ours to win or lose.'

Children and the Television Screen:

Modes of Participation in the Media Environment

Sonia Livingstone and George Gaskell
Media Research Group, London School of Economics and Political Science

The research described in this paper is conducted in association with the Broadcasting Standards Council and is financially supported by the British Broadcasting Corporation, the Independent Television Commission, Yorkshire/Tyne Tees Television, British Telecom and the Leverhulme Trust.

Despite the substantial academic literature concerned with children and television, little work has examined children's uses of the new media. In this paper, we consider the research issues which are raised by the new media to which children and young people are increasingly exposed. This sets a context to our current research project on the meanings, uses and impacts of different forms of media on children and young people. In the second half of the paper, we outline our design and methods for this new project, together with some very preliminary findings from the pilot research.

Our general approach makes a number of assumptions. First, that research should adopt a more integrative approach than hitherto, for the past research has tended to consider different media, or different categories of children, making broader comparisons or conclusions difficult. Second, that 'new media' should be studied both for themselves and because they are potentially changing the context within which children become involved with older or more familiar forms of media. Third, that comparisons can be productively made not only across different media forms or categories of children, but also across time. Specifically, a comparison with research conducted in the early days of television (Himmelweit, 1958; Schramm, 1961) is instructive for the conduct of research in the early days of new media, both for the similarities and differences between methods and findings from the 1950s and the 1990s.

Thus, our focus is on children and young people's involvement with the mass media in a time of rapid changes in domestic electronic media. Rather than simply focusing on media effects, the most heavily researched but also highly vexed topic in the field of children and media (Livingstone, 1996), we suggest that future research should focus on the broader concept of involvement or engagement with media. Thus, rather than add to a body of research which has, to be blunt, absorbed a lot of effort for rather little return, our focus adopts an integrated framework concerning everyday practices and habits, the socially constructed meanings which children and adults attach to different media/activities, the importance of media in socialization processes, and questions of impact or change following the introduction of new media forms. Put simply, the following kinds of questions need answers.

What increased diversity of media are becoming available to children and young people? How do children perceive the various opportunities available to them? What influences their choices, and what do they gain from their involvement with old and new media? What is the significance for children of the growing technological convergence between broadcasting, computing and telecommunications? Or the significance of the growing social convergences between home and work, leisure and education, public and private spaces? What further opportunities are associated with greater access to new media offerings and what are the disadvantages of limited access?

Before such questions can be pursued, let us look back forty years to the early research on the mass child television audience. In 1958, Himmelweit et al's seminal study of television and the child examined the ways in which the new medium television, a single channel at the start of her study, had affected children's lives. The project took a comprehensive look at a new technology entering children's lives, examining both immediate and longer term implications of television use. At the time, almost nothing was known about the likely impact of the medium on children, and consequently, the design and findings of the study were integral in framing the field of media research both in Britain and elsewhere, and in playing a role in informing broadcasting and educational policy.

Television and the Child systematically examined the impact of television on children and young people by comparing those with and without television (and for a subset of children, those before and after it entered their homes) in the early years of its introduction into Britain. Four main types of effect were considered: displacement effects (children's leisure choices); programme content effects (children's perceptions of meanings); effects on family life; and effects on children's emotions. The guiding assumption, which research both then and since has supported, was that television has a diverse range of extremely moderate effects on children, and these differ for different groups of children, with ability, gender, social class, age and personality all playing a part.

The main findings of this substantial and multimethod project were as follows. Television to some extent displaced reading and 'doing nothing' especially immediately after adoption, by providing functionally equivalent leisure possibilities, and this had little apparent detrimental effect on school work. The effects on beliefs and behaviour were few. Most significantly, while many children were frightened by television, they rather liked being frightened, and no effects of television aggression or violence could be clearly identified. This issue of television violence and aggression has been one of continual concern, despite the fact that Himmelweit's results more or less stand the test of time. There was some evidence that children became more ambitious and more middle class in aspirations as they saw middle class, comfortable situations being portrayed on television. There was evidence of the effects of sex stereotyping, with girls particularly becoming more likely to want to adopt a feminine role. In addition,

Himmelweit's results suggested that less informed or less critical children were most affected by the new medium of television. A central finding was that not only the social background of the children but also the measured intelligence of the children mediated many of the effects observed.

The Himmelweit project looked at the relationships within the family and showed the importance of the ways in which parents mediate children's relationship to television, with parental control and parental example proving important in determining the viewing habits of children. Moreover, immediately apparent in the 1950s was something which still gives concern today - the fact that however much we control and monitor children's programmes, children are actually watching all kinds of programmes including adult programmes.

The questions faced by the Himmelweit project seem, in retrospect, relatively straightforward when compared with the current situation. At that time, the key issue was what happens when a new medium 'television' enters children's lives; in the 1990s many changes are occurring in children's lives in terms of the different forms of technology which are increasingly available to mediate both leisure and education. Our present project is closely related to the Himmelweit project in the sense that we also feel that this is a defining moment in which children's lives are undergoing rapid change. In contrast to Himmelweit, however, we lack functionally equivalent comparisons to her study investigating those with and without access to television. Rather, we have a very complex set of patterns in which children almost invariably have access to many different kinds of media.

Specifically, what kinds of changes should be considered when we compare research in the 1950s and in the 1990s. Very obviously there is an increased range of channels available to children, a range which has grown on terrestrial television since the 1950s but most rapidly grown on cable/satellite television during the 1980s (and is now available to around a quarter of British children, ITC 1994). More recently, we are seeing a convergence of different forms of media and telecommunications, integrating television, education, computing and information. One might call the result a kind of 'technicization' of leisure, with children's leisure activities increasingly calling upon and making use of a particular kind of technology. How far, then, are the media involved in every part of children's lives? It seems that the media are present, sometimes in the background, sometimes in the foreground, in all kinds of activities – from their schoolwork, to what they do in their bedroom, to the way in which they behave as a family; but the importance and meaning of this is yet to be discovered through empirical research.

Closely linked to the increasing involvement of the media in everyday life is an increasing participation in the consumer society. Some talk about children nowadays as being more 'adult-like' and some are concerned about the way that children are conceived as a 'market' for whom products are developed and marketed. This concern reflects the greater interlinking between entertainment/leisure and consumption/economic participation in the market. Additionally, the growth of the media in children's and adults' lives introduces a cultural shift from that which was publicly organised or which occurred in public spaces and/or in the public interest, to something which has been increasingly privatised, occurring within the private sphere of the house and without public visibility or access.

Finally, in relation to children, one aspect which is of particular interest to us is the possibility of what we call the 'techno-generation gap': the idea that children are being drawn into new forms of media involvement, technological expertise and consumer participation, in a way that their parents may not be or may be less familiar with. One might ask therefore whether a gap is opening up in terms of awareness and interest, particularly in new media, between children and their parents.

In this introduction to our planned research, we have used the terms 'old' and 'new' media in a slightly cavalier fashion. However, we have tried to say what kinds of new media we are particularly interested in and why it is that they might be interestingly compared to older media (books, radio, terrestrial television). These different forms of media may be separated on a rough time dimension, reflecting when they were introduced into Britain, in order to bring out two parallel features which significantly discriminate these different kinds of media (see Table 1).

Table 1: Distinguishing 'Old'and 'New' Media

	Examples	Familiarity	Interactivity
'old' media	terrestrial television and radio	incorporated into domestic routines for a generation	standard forms, mass audience minimal choice (exposure, channel)
'new/ current' media	video recorder, satellite television, teletext	familiar for most households over the past 10+ years	additional choice, active control over access to information and/or entertainment
'new/ recent' media	cable television, camcorder, home computer	currently being adopted by a (growing) minority of households	broadcasting + narrowcasting; production and consumption of media, manipulation of info + entertainment
'new/ prospective media	interactive teletext, multimedia, home shopping, internet	may be adopted in coming decade, subject to development, access and availability	interactivity between medium and user, expanding individual choice/control

The first feature, which we are calling 'familiarity', identifies as 'new/current' a number of media which have been around for a while (the video recorder, satellite, teletext and so forth). Such media are familiar in aspects of life for children today but significantly were not familiar for the parents' generation – in other words, media which were introduced into the household between the two current generations. This allows us to raise questions about media with which children might be more familiar than their parents, reflecting differences between the generations in childhood experiences.

Next are the 'new/recent' media, media which are currently being adopted (cable television, camcorder, home computer). These media, while familiar as a concept, are still only available to a minority of households. Finally, most people's perceptions of what the 'new' media are, actually refer to what we have called 'prospective' media. Prospective media do not exist in any widespread form and yet are the subject of a great amount of concern (interactive teletext, multimedia, homeshopping, internet etc). While research on these media is much desired, it is impractical insofar as only early adopters, typically industry employees or experimental markets, have had any access to these as yet, and children in particular have little or no experience of these. In our present study we are, in a sense, researching the future!

Parallel with the dimension of familiarity is that of interactivity, a much used but rather ill-defined term which focuses attention on the relationship between the child and a medium. With 'old' media, standardised content was beamed out to a mass audience and relatively few opportunities for choice were available: they could choose which channel to watch and how much to watch but that was more or less it. However, through the recent introduction of the various new forms of media we can identify increasing amounts of choice, increasing amounts of active control available, and the increasing integration of entertainment and information functions in the media available to children and young people. We should note, however, that while we may talk about individuals choosing activities, this is a rather ambiguous area insofar as it sometimes means choosing to record a programme on video and at other times means investigating the depths (or maybe rather, breadth) of a CD-ROM. The kinds of interactional and communicative possibilities opened up by new media cannot be clearly outlined at the present point; here we simply wish to highlight some of the key issues raised by new media, and to hypothesise that these will differentiate among media in terms of correlated dimensions rather than any simple polar opposition between 'old' and 'new'.

How then, can we research children and new media, when at least the 'prospective', and most 'hyped' forms of new media are not available as yet on the domestic market? One approach is, following our suggestion of thematic dimensions which differentiate among media, to explore those forms of media which are different and yet are in place today, compared to those available several decades ago, focusing on the themes outlined above of familiarity, contextualisation, choice and agency and mode of engagement. What then, are the significant changes?

One recent and salient trend in the British context, which does not raise new technological questions about interactive media or new forms of media, is the rapidly increasing multiplicity of domestic media. The household in the 1950s acquired the one television set, placed in the living room, and everyone had to negotiate with each other about how they were going to engage with that set. Similarly, when the video recorder was first introduced, it was expected that each household might or might not buy one VCR. Yet, recent figures show that households, particularly those with children, are now acquiring multiple television sets and, in lesser proportion, multiple VCRs, multiple computers and multiple telephones. A little over half of all British children now have a television in their bedroom and this increases as children get older, and in households lower in socioeconomic class. A similar pattern is seen for the video (see Table 2).

Table 2: Percentage of Children having different media in bedroom *(Youngview Television Opinion Panel, January 1996)*

	Books	Radio	Stereo	TV	Computer	Game-boy	Video
ALL	89	72	59	54	38	23	15
Sex							
Boys	87	68	55	57	46	25	18
Girls	92	75	64	52	29	22	12
SES							
AB	92	71	59	32	22	23	6
C1	89	73	55	53	38	26	11
C2	90	72	66	59	41	22	24
DE	88	71	58	65	44	22	18
Age							
6-7	84	51	21	29	13	13	6
10-11	87	69	52	50	44	26	10
13-14	93	83	81	65	44	29	23
15-16	92	84	85	66	39	28	24

Thus, even simply looking at children's media in terms of the significant change in the numbers of goods available, quite different sorts of research questions begin to emerge. For example, children with televisions in their bedrooms may be able to view programmes in an unregulated manner in a private sphere 'invisible' to their parents as well as to those outside and, indeed, to each other. How, then, do family members share experiences, or even know what the others know? What do they talk about, and are the domains of conflict or negotiation changing?

Figure 1: Audience Ratings

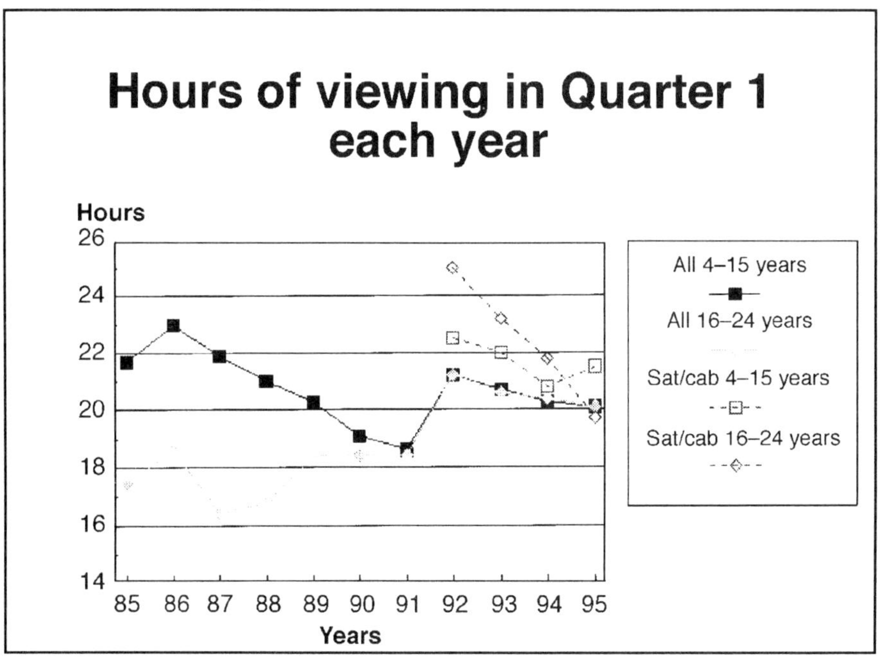

Current audience figures showing average television viewing by different age groups (see Figure 1) point to another change. One of the standard findings in the literature has always been that, while children watch television with a considerable amount of enthusiasm, teenagers tend to move away from television, significantly reducing their viewing, in favour of other activities. Yet Figure 1 shows the interesting finding that in just the ten years from 1985 to 1995 there is a very clear convergence of children aged 4–15 years (top line) with people aged 16–24 (bottom line). This suggests that although the standard finding in the literature was true ten years ago it is not so now as the teens and young adults are being brought back into that general pattern, and this is particularly true for those who have cable and satellite television. This suggests that increasing diversification in broadcast programmes, especially the emergence of 'youth programming' during the 1990s, together with the diversification of modes of television transmission (i.e. the advent of cable and satellite), is resulting in a trend by which audiences that were 'easily escaping' from the new mediated management of leisure are now being increasingly drawn in.

One of the approaches we have used in our pilot research is asking children about the future. For example, we have asked children to draw their ideal bedroom in the year 2000, which proved to be a very popular task. Figure 2 shows a picture drawn by a ten year old boy, a fairly typical drawing. What is interesting is the astonishing multiplicity of goods – lots of televisions, videos, and computer games. When asked, the child had explained the choice of so many sets, positioned all around the room, by pointing out that each would be tuned to a different channel; thus all possibilities are available to him at once! As with boys in our focus groups, the issue of what they might watch or what they might find out, was not so popular a topic of conversation and failed to elicit the same enthusiasm as discussions about which technologies are or could be available to them.

Figure 2: Child's drawing showing multiplicity of goods

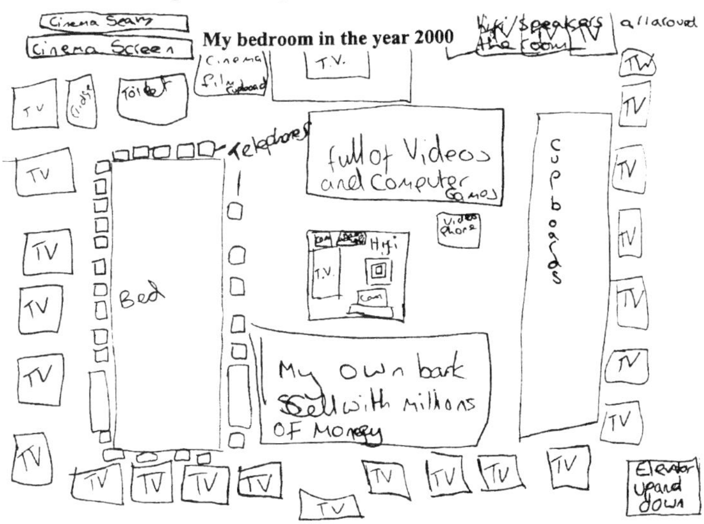

Thus, we have some initial sense of the possible changes occurring in children's lives, and of the ways in which we might access these. But much lies behind, and follows on from, the initial selection of research questions. The research agenda for media, children and young people, can be thought about in three main ways, or in terms of three sources for a research agenda, although undoubtedly, all have something to offer (Livingstone, in press). Without a clear grounding in the past research literature (Media Research Group, 1995), albeit that the concentration of this research is on children and 'old' media, research is likely to be highly specific and short-term, even short-sighted, in its focus.

For example, recent discussion of the so-called 'Violence chip' might suggest that researchers should rush out and investigate its likely effects even before its technical viability or social acceptability has been established, and we would have yet another study disconnected from others in a disconnected field. Such research is primarily motivated by what we might call the 'moral panic agenda' – a new social problem or political controversy is reframed in public discourse by identifying the media, typically the most recent technological development, as responsible. Media research is then commissioned in order to establish whether the panic has any basis in reality.

The moral panic agenda overlaps with, and to some extent forms, the public agenda. This identifies the questions people are concerned about as the basis of a research agenda. Unfortunately, both children and new media are controversial and emotive topics. The combination therefore arouses strong opinions about what the research questions should be. Yet, as has been documented in the history of the gradual introduction of the new media over the last century, it is clear that as each new medium was introduced it was accompanied by a moral panic about what social changes may follow (Drotner, 1992; Pearson, 1983). Currently, moral panics centre on the internet and access to pornography, and on video games and the putative aggressive and addictive effects on young boys. In many ways similar questions were asked about the introduction of the VCR fifteen years ago and about the introduction of television forty or fifty years ago.

Interestingly, it would seem that as each new medium is introduced, we simultaneously forget about, accept, and so stop questioning the previous medium, so that it becomes part of our normative culture (Drotner, 1992). The implication is that although the moral panic agenda may validly express public fears, it nevertheless tends to be quite conservative, resting on the assumption that change is dangerous and something to be feared. Put slightly more politically, a moral panic agenda is sometimes said to express respectable middle class fears about what other people, predominantly the working classes, are doing (Pearson, 1983). Perhaps more importantly from our point of view, the moral panic agenda has not necessarily been supported by empirical research. For instance, we do not find groups of teenagers turned by computer games into lonely, isolated addicts who are not able to communicate with each other (Durkin 1995). What is happening are new ways of forming peer networks around the new media. For example children might go round to each others' houses to talk about and play computer games, just as they might have visited and swapped comics a generation before. In brief, moral panic questions have not been productive of good academic research. The second set of concerns which direct empirical research focuses on technological change, a set of concerns which are inevitable given the rapid technological developments in domestic information and communication technologies. As each new technological change emerges, while attempting to sidestep the moral panics, there are a broad set of questions to be considered concerning their effects, their importance, their relation to previous technologies and practices and their accessibility and cost. Questions motivated in this way tend to focus not so much on the content of the media as on their form, asking in what new ways a new technology may facilitate or inhibit people's relationships to each other and to their work, education and leisure. For example, the Internet raises new possible forms of communication (discussion groups, anonymous interactions), new forms of relationship (virtual communities, relations which transcend spatial limitations), and may be transformative of older forms of practice (information search and access, education) (cf. 'The Net', Journal of Communication, Winter 1996, vol.46, No.1).

It can be problematic for the technological agenda that the questions regarding consequences are often conceived on the assumption that new forms of media displace old ones – television displaces books, cable/satellite displaces terrestrial broadcasting, etc. Any displacement, however small, may be of considerable concern to broadcasters. Yet, looking at the bigger picture, longer term historical evidence suggests that a more common pattern is that of supplementing rather than displacing. As new forms of media become available they supplement and diversify the leisure possibilities (Fischer, 1994). Thus our questions might better concern how people cope with the increasing diversity, and how new forms recontextualise or transform the use of older forms, rather than more simply how the new medium replaces older ones.

The last agenda draws critically but also constructively upon the theory and previous empirical research on children and older forms of media in order to frame how we might study the new media. In that respect we have also looked, not just at media and children, but also at the broader concerns that people have about the kinds of cultural shifts that children and the new media are themselves a part. Specifically, we have identified four key areas which we might use to ask about children and the new media (see Table 3): privatisation, individualism, globalisation and consumerism. Our aim is to relate these broad processes, which can be conceptualised as operating on several levels from the individual to society, as part of the specific process of socialising children and young people. In other words, we suggest that the media (information and communication technologies more generally) will affect children's lives both indirectly, through their role in modifying these broad processes (which in turn impact on socialising agencies such as school, home, community), and directly as a socialising agent in themselves.

Table 3: Applying theories of media change to the socialization of children and young poeple

Process	Questions relating to children/youth
Privatisation	* Relation between outside and inside home – loss of street corners, rise of shopping mall; visiting friends affected by media ownership * Relation between living room and bedroom cultures – visibility (regulability) of children to parents. * Duplication of goods demands that 'household' is inadequate unit of analysis – structured by gender and generation.
Individualisation	* Techno-generation gap? - as children are more expert in new media than parents or teachers (children develop new forms of media literacy, etc) * (Continued) Emergence of media-centred subcultures, increasing diversification and specialization possible
Globalisation	* New identities possible, cutting across national/community – virtual communities (may be very specialized), new forms of participation, European/global identification? * Homogenisation of youth cultures as all watch MTV/CNN/Disney channel, etc.
Consumerism	* Children as a market (as teens emerged as market during 50s, children are increasingly a market since 80s; downwards spread of consumerism) – for goods advertised via media – or media themselves * Particularly strong links between children's media and consumer goods – clothes, toy tie-ins, food, branded goods, etc. * Promotional concerns push media contents towards older children and towards boys * Peer relations – identity, acceptance – centre on possessions * Children/youth as negotiators in allocation of family income

The theme of privatisation raises questions of how leisure connects (or separates) spaces (with their rules and discourses) inside and outside the home. Concretely, one can ask whether children have less access to the street, what happens when they are collected from school and then stay indoors, or whether their conversations are quite different with their friends and family. Also, one can ask about the within-home privatisation process, as we see the change from 'living room culture' towards the growth of media-rich private 'bedroom cultures' (where teen, child and adult cultures, or masculine and feminine cultures, may all be separated rather than in competition).

Individualisation is commonly discussed both publically and academically, with a sense of the 1980s and the 1990s generating a 'me-generation', 'me-TV' etc. Are young people being brought up in an increasingly selfish way? More positively, it may be that the media might facilitate the construction of different kinds of sub-cultures, albeit more media-centred than hitherto. Such a process links with that of consumerism, as a major way in which people express both their individuality and their group membership through the consumption of certain goods (Lunt and Livingstone, 1992) – does every young child really worry about what kind of trainers they wear into school? It would appear that the age at which children may be seen as a valuable market and appealed to directly by advertisers is becoming ever younger, raising questions not only about children's understanding of these processes but also about their power within the household to negotiate over domestic resources (money, space and time).

We are particularly interested in the ways in which media as leisure/entertainment are increasingly integrated with consumerism (media as market/promotional culture). Kinder (1991) has suggested the influence of marketers and advertisers over media content is becoming ever greater, particularly in relation to the children's market. Thus, she observes that because boys are reluctant to watch girls' programmes and older children are reluctant to watch younger children's programmes, the successful consumer strategy is to broadcast programmes targeted to older boys all around the world so that a maximum audience (younger/older, male/female) will watch a single programme (and its associated toy tie-ins). This has consequences for public concerns about the growth of violence in children's media insofar as older boys programming is the most action-oriented and aggressive in content, and the least likely to contextualise this with moral messages or verbal explanation.

Turning finally to globalisation, it is clearly the case that the new media are more than likely to be global in character – whether through the common marketing of a single product around the world (popular music, games machines, CD-Rom software, Disney films and toy tie-ins) or through interlinking of media across countries (global/international TV channels/stations, the Internet). Once more, different possibilities become available to children (for leisure, identity, knowledge) if they consider themselves to be part of European youth, or MTV fans, or Internetters. These may be conceived positively in terms of transcending cultural prejudices, shared knowledge, new diverse (probably virtual or imagined) sub-cultures, or more negatively in terms of what Ritzer (1996) has called the 'McDonaldisation' of society in which everyone is increasingly drawn into a commodified mainstream.

We now turn to the development of the research and the methodologies to be used.

Across the social sciences there is a long history of trench wars between those who advocate qualitative and those who advocate quantitative research methods. Our position is to favour a multi-method approach. The social survey and quantitative methods are well indicated, to use a medical analogy, for some research questions; qualitative research methods are preferable for other types of research questions. Over the course of this study we intend to combine both qualitative and quantitative approaches in the pursuit of a comprehensive analytic description. The research can be divided into four overlapping phases, as shown below.

Research Design : A Multi-Method Approach

Phase 1

Individual and group interviews with children from all social categories aged 6-17 to provide an analytic description of children's media use and understandings.

Media biographies: technology and everyday life to look at the techno-generation gap and the privatisation of media and Leisure.

Preliminary surveys of children and parents, to test questions and concepts.

Phase 2

National sample of children and young people to quantify and extend insights from qualitative phase.

Targeted samples of special groups (e.g. info-rich, internetters, etc.).

Phase 3
Follow-up studies , both qualitative and quantitative, to explore further problematic results from the previous research phases.

Phase 4
A comparative international perspective with teams working in France, Denmark, Germany, Spain, Sweden, Switzerland, Israel, Italy, The Netherlands and possibly the USA.

Initially we are interested in talking to children and finding out about the uses, meanings and understandings of the media. We are covering an age range from 6-17 years, girls and boys, of diverse social and geographic backgrounds. Our preliminary studies are assessing the value of various ways of interviewing children of different ages, e.g. friendship pairs, focus groups in school and domestic contexts, and individual interviews. Does it make a difference if the interviewers are male or female? What terms do children use to describe domestic information and communication technologies? Can games, drawings, or other methods be used to supplement interviews?

These pilot studies are designed to fine tune our methods, to understand how children talk about the old and new media and to develop questions for the later research. Once this is completed we will embark on Phase One, the qual itative research. This will be followed by a national sample survey of children and some targeted surveys for particular groups. For example, there is an emerging, but small group of Internet users and computer buffs. A national survey would be unlikely to pick up sufficient numbers of these children to be able to conduct any interesting statistical comparisons. As such we feel that a combination of national survey and some target surveys of special interest groups will be valuable. It is likely that when Phases One and Two have been completed and the findings analyzed and interpreted, there will be parts of the picture where the detail is insufficient. We make allowances for this with Phase Three. Phase Four will involve international comparisons with the countries with which we are currently collaborating in the design of the research: France, Denmark, Germany, Spain, Sweden, Switzerland, Israel, Italy and the Netherlands.

Finally, let us discuss some of the preliminary findings from both qualitative research and surveys aimed at testing methods and questions. Figure 3 comes from a BBC panel survey in which we experimented, amongst other techniques, with drawings. In response to the question; draw yourself watching television, we can see the child sitting on her bed. Although she looks riveted by the programme, a rather large number of children who completed this questionnaire said, in response to another question, that boredom was the main reason why they watched television. Television appears to be used as a way of avoiding tedium. Despite this, there were also quite a number of children who said that they watched television because it was educational and interesting. But the prevalence of comments about boredom and the number of drawings of children watching alone characterise the loneliness and aimlessness of some contemporary television viewers.

Figure 3: Child's drawing of herself in bedroom

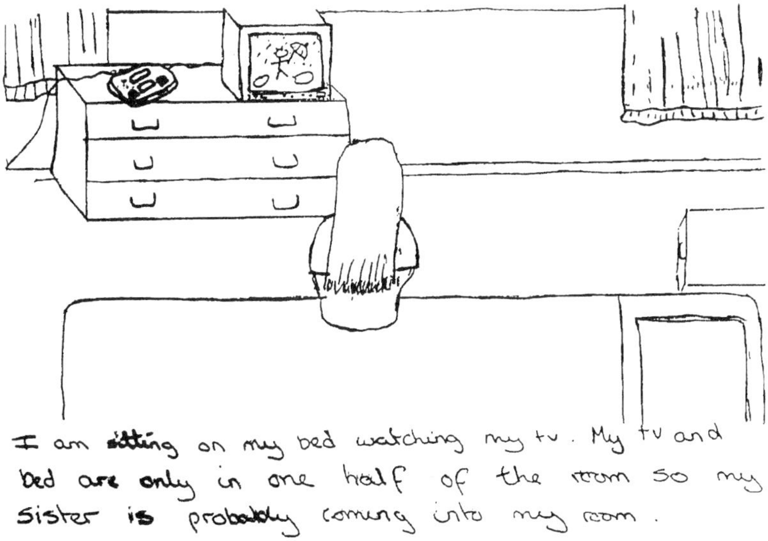

As a counterpoint, Figure 4 shows a more traditional picture of a child in the bosom of the family watching EastEnders, one of the most popular shows.

Figure 4: Child watching **EastEnders** *with family*

Figure 5 shows the percentage of parents following various pastimes with their child at least once a day, taken from the BBC's Television Opinion Panel. It is clear that watching TV and videos is a dominant activity which parents share with their children, whilst a walk in the country is the least shared activity. This finding illustrates the importance of television in contemporary British culture, especially for parent-child interactions.

Figure 5: Percentage of parents following various pastimes with their child

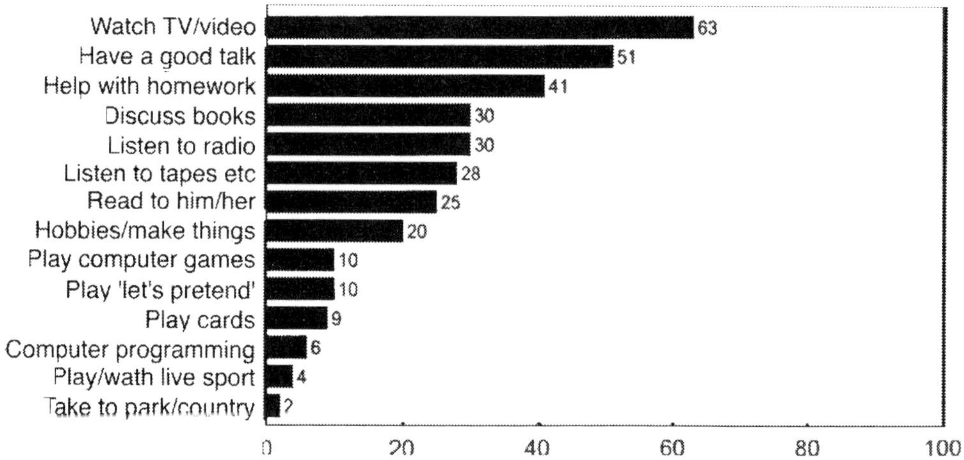

Figure 6 shows the results of the standard question about how much time children spend watching television, as reported by their parents. It is important to remember that there is always a problem with the reliability of such reports due to social desirability, memory errors and daily variations in viewings. But as can seen, there is an increasing amount of viewing as we progress down the sociodemographic categories. This is also related to parental viewing, for the children of heavier viewing parents tend to watch more television.

Parents in the Television Opinion Panel were also asked what they thought about children having television sets in their bedrooms. We can see from Figure 7 that as we move down the social class categories fewer and fewer parents thought that it is a bad thing. This is again reflected in the level of parental viewing with heavy viewers being less inclined to think that children having a TV in their room is a 'bad thing'.

Figure 6: Parental reports of children's viewing time

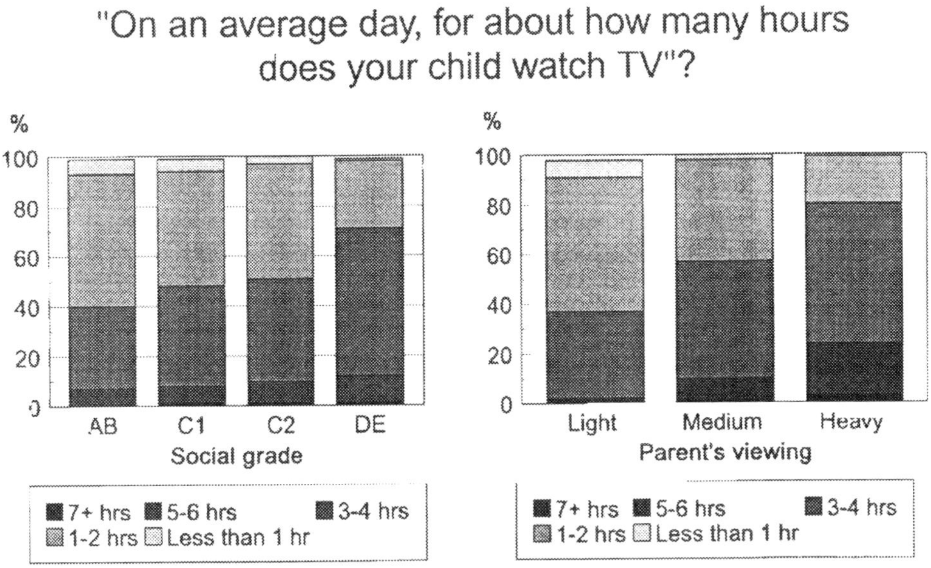

Figure 7: Parental reports about TV sets in child's bedroom

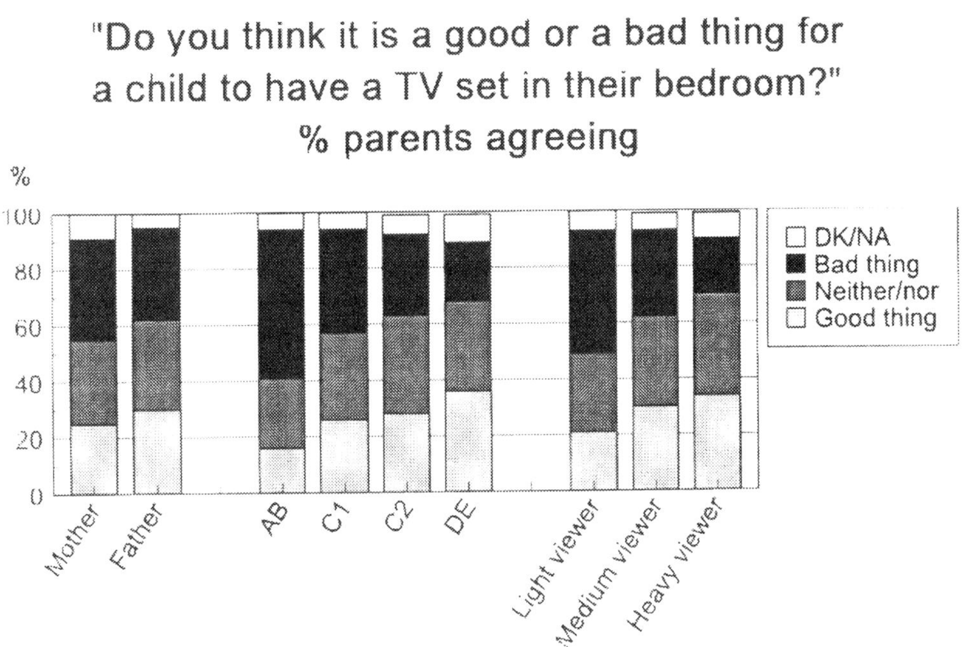

Figure 8 shows parents' responses to the question 'Which reason best describes how you come to watch television with your child?' It seems that mothers more than fathers claimed that they 'liked to know what their child watches', while for more fathers than mothers the claim is that he 'happens to be in the room' or 'likes the same programmes'. This raises some interesting questions about interviewing in families, such as who should be regarded as the adult informant and who is involved in parental mediation.

Figure 8: How parents come to watch TV with their children

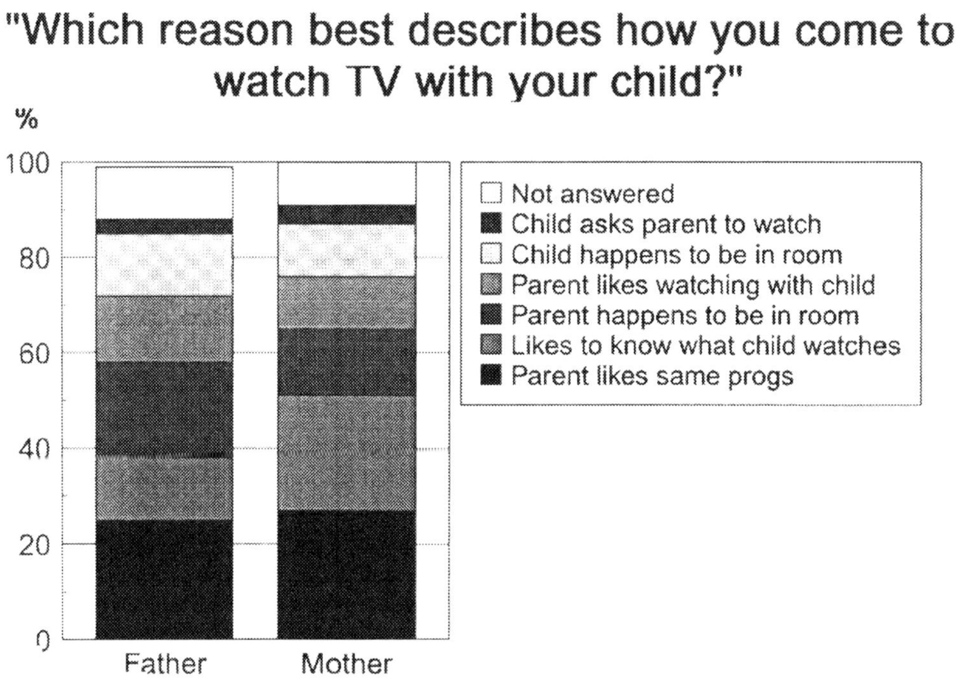

In Figure 9 we see that while viewing, parents say they often talk to their children about television, they talk about the good and bad things that the characters do and about the difference between the characters and real life. This is what one might call 'constructive' mediation. However, when we look at the other end of the chart at behaviours such as restricting the amount of viewing, forbidding the child to watch certain programmes and specifying particular programmes, we see that these are less common. This is of relevance to the debate on the V chip designed specifically to control the child's viewing. If we can believe what the parents are saying then it appears that they think that they are providing the necessary parental mediation through discussion; prohibition is not part of the mediation repertoire. However, in the context of over 50% of children having a television in their bedroom when they are watching alone or with their friends, then parents may well be mediating downstairs, though probably not in the child's unregulated bedroom environment.

Figure 9: Parental mediation of child's viewing

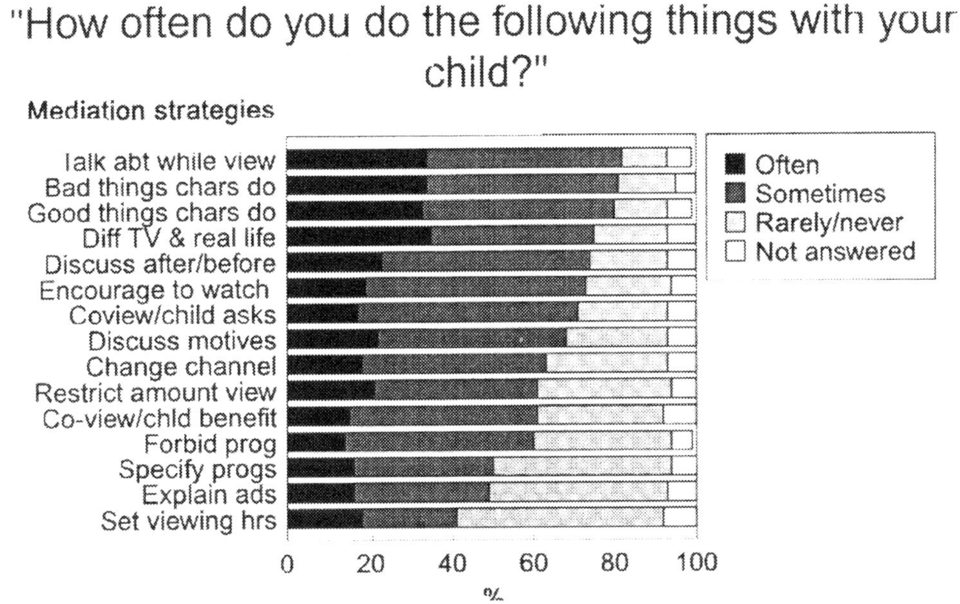

As a final comment, we suggest that while it is premature to draw conclusions when we are just starting our research project, our review of the literature together with initial pilot findings underline the clear need for integrative theorising supported by both qualitative and quantitative methodological approaches. Both the arrival in the home of new forms of media, particularly increasingly interactive media, together with the multiplicity of televisions, phones etc. in childrens' homes, raise new questions for research. Convergences across media, and relations between home, school, community and work further complicate matters, emphasising the importance of a broad-ranging empirical research design. Furthermore, children, young people and the new media are a considerable focus of interest for researchers across the European Community. It is of note that the 'concerns' raised by different national contexts differ somewhat, depending on cultural factors and technological/media systems issues. Hence our interest and commitment to a multi-national comparative study.

References

Drotner, K. (1992) 'Modernity and Media Panics' in M. Skovmand and K.C. Schroder (eds) *Media Cultures: Reappraising Transnational Media*, Routledge: London.

Durkin, K. (1995) *Computer Games - Their Effects on Young People: A Review*, Office of Film and Literature Classification: Sydney, NSW.

Fischer, C.S. (1994) 'Changes in Leisure Activities, 1890-1940', *Journal of Social History*, Spring, pp.453-475

Himmelweit, H.T., Oppenheim, A.N. and Vince, P. (1958) *Television and the Child: An Empirical Study of the Effect of Television on the Young*, Oxford University Press: London and New York

Independent Television Commission (1994) *Television: The Public's View*, ITC: London

Journal of Communication; issue: 'The Net', Winter 1996, volume 46, No.1.

Kinder, M. (1991) *Playing With Power in Movies, Television and Videogames: From Muppet Babies to Teenage Mutant Ninja Turtles*, University of California Press: Berkeley, Cal.

Livingstone, S.M. (1996) 'On the Continuing Problem of Media Effects' in J. Curran and M. Gurevitch *Mass Media and Society*, (2nd edition), Arnold: London.

Livingstone, S. (in press) *Children, Youth and New Media Culture*, Youth, Media and Modernity Series (ed.K. Drotner), Centre for Youth and Media: University of Copenhagen.

Lunt, P.K. and Livingstone, S.M. (1992) *Mass Consumption and Personal Identity*, Open University Press: Buckingham.

Media Research Group (1995) *Children, Young People and the Television Screen: A Selective Review of the Literature*, unpublished report.

Pearson, G. (1983) *Hooligan: A History of Respectable Fears*, Macmillan: London.

Ritzer, G. (1996) *The McDonaldization of Society*, Pine Forge Press: Thousand Oaks, California.

Schramm, W., Lyle, J. and Parker, E.B. (1961) *Television in the Lives of Our Children*, Stanford University Press: Stanford, CA.

The Future of Production

Chair: Helen Boaden
BBC Network News and Current Affairs

Roger Bolton
Roger Bolton Productions

Mike Spencer
Head of Special Projects, Granada Television

Michael Pilsworth
Chief Executive, Chrysalis

Helen Boaden: Welcome to this session, everybody. We're all delighted you've invited us and we're very pleased to see all of you. My name's Helen Boaden and I work down the road at the BBC in Network News and Current Affairs. In case you don't know the panel, they are, Roger Bolton of Roger Bolton Productions, Mick Pilsworth, who is Chief Executive of Chrysalis and in charge of planning, and Mike Spencer, who's just got a new job as Head of Special Projects at Granada Television (which is part of their satellite development). Mike has kindly agreed to step in for Charlie Tremayne, who's had to go to Morocco on urgent business. It's a tough life.

The title of this seminar is 'The Future of Production', which is an almost overwhelmingly broad subject for an hour and fifteen minutes. We've decided to tackle it in two stages. First, the panel members will talk about their company's plans for the immediate future over the next twelve, eighteen months, two years – the kinds of pressures they face and what strategies they have to counter those pressures. Then we'll try and fast forward to look at what the situation might be in five to ten years' time. What will broadcasting look like then? What kinds of programmes will we be watching? Who will be running and owning the networks? And, frankly, will any of us have jobs?

I thought that, although I'm the Chair, I'm also the only person on this panel from the BBC. So I thought I'd talk briefly and from my own experience – because I'm not elevated enough to have a strategic view about a lot of these things – about the next eighteen months at the BBC. And then we'll turn to the other members of the panel.

Obviously, we are in the uniquely privileged position of having a guaranteed income through the licence fee. However, I think, with the rising costs of performing rights, especially sports rights, the BBC is facing some fairly serious decision-making about how it spends its money. They talk about 'mind the gap'. Well, the funding gap for the BBC over five years could be as much as £600,000,000, certainly in the regional directorate, which is what I'm part of at BBC North. They anticipate a funding gap of £86,000,000 over the next five years.

So, only last week, all the staff got letters outlining what in our directorate is called 'step change'. It is basically about cutting jobs in the long run; trying to do the same amount and the same quality of programming, but doing it with less money. And over five years, there will be percentage cuts. Each of us will have a fixed target, each programme and each department. It's called 'process re-engineering'. The idea is, instead of bringing to your programme-making all the sets of assumptions that all of us have about what we do, you start with a blank sheet of paper and thereby question every single pound you spend, what you think is automatically necessary. And many large organisations, particularly public sector organisations, have gone through this procedure and the figures sadly show that 70% of them fail to achieve the efficiency savings they were aiming for. The BBC obviously wants to be in the 30% that succeeds, but, in the immortal words, time will tell.

That's a brief resume of the BBC's position in the next eighteen months. Roger, do you want to talk about your...

Roger Bolton: Yes. First of all, I would like to say I'd rather be here than in Morocco. Thanks very much for inviting me. It's been a long winter. I've seen the future of production and the publisher-broadcaster is not part of it. Indeed, when I asked Barrie Cox, the Director of ITVA, the ITV Network Centre, whether the publisher-broadcaster was dead, he gave a one word answer: 'Yes.' I don't want you to think because I was part of Thames Television and Carlton got the franchise as a publisher-broadcaster, it affects my judgement or my feelings... Of course it doesn't.

But it's not so difficult to see why the publisher-broadcaster model is dead. ITV companies want to control costs and, just as importantly, rights. They also want to launch cable stations and satellite channels and spend as little as possible on them. Hence the attempt to squeeze more production out of existing resources. What they don't want to do is let money go out of the company. They now have fresh outlets for production. Granada, for example, is still, I think, a shareholder in BSkyB, certainly has a relationship with them and is about to launch its own satellite services. MAI now owns Anglia as well as Meridian and is a powerful shareholder in Channel 5.

In a more loosely-regulated environment with increased competition, these companies increasingly have one central aim – increasing shareholder value; otherwise known as increasing profit margins and cutting costs. I don't know if it's true or not, but one of the most interesting things you may have picked up from this morning's *Independent* is that it looks as if your future boss, Mike, may be the former Mercury chief. And you can see why. It makes a hell of a lot of sense to take somebody who knows all about fibre optics and telephones into running a television company. It may be untrue, but there we are.

So, however, this renewed emphasis on in-house production, as opposed to the publisher-broadcaster, ought to give greater security for the few ITV production staff left inside, like Mike Spencer. Independents can look forward to having their quota respected, but only just. There is an up side, of course. It is that ITV's greatest hits have been the UK-produced original programming. The European quotas are a useful safeguard, but, at the moment, the UK audience is rooting for UK programmes.

Channel 4, meanwhile, is pursuing a twin-track policy. It's still trying to let a thousand – well, a few hundred – flowers bloom. Not a bad idea, since that keeps the indies on their toes, keeps costs down, and ensures that the indies always smile at the commissioning editors as they clean their shoes. It also guarantees casualisation. More of this later. The other track at Channel 4 is the Michael Grade 'I can beat any other broadcaster in the rating game'. Hence *The Girly Show, The Word, The Red Light Zone,* and other such outstanding contributions to our culture. The marketing team at Channel 4 have the late night lads-back-from-the-pub audience in their sights and they won't let go. But Michael is also buying up stars like Gaby Roslin before he has shows for them to present. This gives a new twist to the expression 'independent', as in, 'You can have the show if Gaby Roslin presents it,' or, as is allegedly the case with Frank Skinner and the BBC, 'If you want me, you have to take my production company, i.e. my agent and any show I tell you I want to make.'

But the BBC is, well, the BBC. The only reason there is a funding gap is because the BBC won't choose. This is extraordinary – that an organisation with the amount of guaranteed income they have is complaining – but it's a form of cowardice, of course. What do you do in a public expenditure round if you want to keep the Cabinet together and you want to avoid difficult situations? Everybody takes a 5% cut. The most difficult thing in the world is to decide that somebody takes a 25% cut and some people ought to stop being members of the Cabinet altogether. The BBC has consistently refused to take those very difficult decisions, but it will, of course, survive, because it's becoming increasingly clear that the free market can't deliver a wide enough range of programmes.

PACT (Producers Alliance for Cinema and Television), however – I'm a council member and so am totally biased on this issue – believe that the BBC should separate its commissioning and production functions. We suggested 50% of the programmes it broadcasts should be reserved for in-house production, thus ensuring the BBC remains the biggest programme factory, probably, in the world; that 25% be reserved for independents, as now, and that 25% be open to the best ideas from any sources. At the moment, Heads of Department are expected to deliver their own and their staff's ideas, and also the independents' series which will kibosh them. Unless we get that separation we will have a continuation of the present situation, whereby independents waste the majority of their time sending in ideas which never had a chance of being commissioned in the first place, and, where they do, have some ideas nicked by in-house BBC Heads of Department and transferred to their own staff. This only happens in a few cases, but enough to be a significant worry.

Meanwhile, Channel 5 will attempt to survive with a programme budget of less than half that of Channel 4, which again is half that of Channel 3. So expect some programmes to be made for £15,000 an hour. What does this mean for production outside the great programme warehouses of the BBC and ITV? It means multi-skilling with a vengeance. The cable news companies' practices will invade Channel 5. It means casualisation, with short term contracts and large gaps filled with yet more unpaid and pointless development. It means less training. It means independents without programmes ruthlessly cutting overheads, i.e. people and offices. And what it will also mean is more and more middle-aged people, particularly women, leaving the industry as they find it simply not possible to support and sustain family life in such circumstances.

There will be no shortage of young people ready to take their place. There are now around some 35,000 media students being misled into believing that they have a career in broadcasting ahead of them. Television has become like acting. The market doesn't work. The unfortunate thing is that it's still an awful lot of fun working in television a lot of the time. And the viewer, for the moment, is probably better served than ever before. More real choice, more bad, but more good.

The longer term concern is that quality, range and depth will diminish. We need now to consider whether we want most of our television made by young white males and most of our news drawn from the same narrow agenda with the same imported pictures, but with different graphics as the accountants become increasingly reluctant to let journalists leave their London offices, and those bi-media journalists are too busy to realise that they're all reading the same press release.

So. The one thing I haven't written is what my strategy is in these circumstances.

Helen Boaden: Suicide?

Roger Bolton: The truth is, I don't have one. You can't have one because, in a sense, all you can do is keep your overheads as low as possible, hope that fate smiles on you and you manage to select the right Channel 5 bid – which I did, fortunately. Try and work out how to introduce and train your staff in multi-skilling to produce programmes at £15,000 an hour. And then think of possibly an alternative career in about three years' time. As I have two daughters aged eight and six and need to work for the next fifteen years, I shall have to give that a lot of thought.

Helen Boaden: Thank you. Any questions for Roger? Or do you want to leave them till after the others? I think I'll just go home, actually. Mick, you wanted to take it up.

Michael Pilsworth: Our overhead is unfortunately rather larger than Roger's, I suspect, and we're stuck with it. Our overhead alone is about £5,000,000 a year, and we don't have the option of either trimming it or getting out, realistically.

I want to start with the image of independent producers and then give you some facts about the markets as we see them, and, coming back to the reality of the current situation, looking ahead to the year 2000.

The image we have with people who are our customers, i.e. broadcasters, is that we all drive round in big cars, make lots of money, spend far too much time in select London clubs like the Groucho getting the talent drunk and seducing them into long-term exclusive contracts, which is the only reason we get anything on air.

The reality is that we're operating in a business that gives us an average net profit margin of 5% on turnover, which, although it puts us about on a par with Barclay's Bank, is well short of what most businesses look for as a return on turnover. It's a low margin, a fairly high-risk business.

Now the facts. The independent market is worth, at the moment, in total, in broadcast production, about £500,000,000 a year. That's the total value, which is split more or less evenly between the various terrestrial channels; BBC1 about 32% of that by value, BBC2 also 32% by value, ITV 38% by value, and Channel 4 just under 30%.

All the commissioning is skewed towards entertainment, drama, and current affairs. Those are the areas that we tend to predominate in as independents. That's the current market. If you look at our customers' prospects, it's a rather dismal picture. BBC1 currently has 33% of the audience share, falling by the year 2000 to 29%. BBC2 has 10.6%, falling more slowly to 10.2%. But both channels inevitably, by the year 2000, will probably have a maximum share of 39%. BBC budgets currently total television about £545,000,000. Independents get about 27% of that – about £148,000,000.

Turning to ITV and Channel 4. Steady real growth in their income to the year 2000. But the total share is going to fall; ITV's share of the revenue from 71% currently to 57%, a 20% drop in overall commercial television share, and Channel 4 from 19% down to 15%, a drop of 4%. ITV audience share now 37.3. By the year 2000, 36.3. Not a huge drop, but a big drop in overall share of revenue. Channel 4 – in 1996, Channel 4's audience share is 11.3%, and that's going to drop to 9.7% in the year 2000. Their advertising share is currently 19.1%, dropping to 15.5%. At the moment, they've got 40% of the total market and 30% of the value.

600 independent producers, fighting over that declining cake. Even if you add cable and satellite, which is now in something like 18-20% of homes spending, they've got an ad share currently of 6% of the total revenue cake for commercial television. That will increase to 13% by the year 2000, which is about 460,000,000 a year, plus subscription. Even with that, you're looking at a declining cost per hour scenario.

So those are the facts that all independent producers have to face. That the budgets per hour are going to fall, and there will be more channels. The market over all in television will be larger, but unit costs will have to fall. We'll face over the next few years, to 2000, continuing buyer hostility – the broadcasters don't like independents. We compete with them because we're all trying to build up libraries of intellectual property rights. You'll see continuing concentration of ownership, both in broadcasting and independent production, an increasing penetration of all the new channels and existing channels by talent-based production companies.

Roger earlier on mentioned Frank Skinner, who has got his own production company, but, if you look at the list, it includes people like Lynda La Plante, Ian McShane, Jimmy Nail, Lenny Henry, French and Saunders, Clive James, Brian Connolly, Jack Dee, Chris Evans, and writers like Laurence Marks and Maurice Gran, Grant and Naylor, Jeff Dean – they've all set up their own production companies. So again, if you're a production company without talent attached, you face being squeezed, not just by the concentration of ownership on the buying side, but also by the fact that the talent at the other end of the economic equation is actually deciding to set up its own production businesses.

So, unfortunately, I can't cheer anyone up after Roger's prognostications of gloom. It still looks fairly gloomy to me.

Helen Boaden: Strategy?

Michael Pilsworth: The strategy is obviously to try and buy talent and set up your own channels.

Helen Boaden: You've got a channel, Mike.

Mike Spencer: It all sounds very depressing to me. It makes me think everyone wants to go back to the days when there was a comfortable monopoly of commercial television and Roger was doing very well at Thames and as long as you were white and Oxbridge educated you could get jobs in television.

Roger Bolton: Just, neither Mick Pilsworth nor myself went to Oxford or Cambridge.

Helen Boaden: You were quite rare.

Mike Spencer: But you did recruit those people.

Michael Pilsworth: Did you go, Mike?

Mike Spencer: I didn't. I just think we are in the very middle of the breaking-up of a monopoly, and whether it be public sector broadcasting in the shape of the BBC or ITV, Channel 4, satellite, or whatever, we are in the middle of a revolution and it can be very depressing, and it's certainly right to talk about pressure on budgets. It's right to talk about the insecurity that a lot of people now feel working within the industry.

Nevertheless, the figures that Mick was quoting about share markets and the rest of it – it remains an expanding market, and although individual channels' share of audience and, indeed, revenue, may in total go down, it's a huge industry and will be around for many years to come. And the trick for Granada is, how do we keep up the kind of production base we have in Manchester employing over a thousand people with six main studios, eight edit suites, and all the rest of it?

And at the moment, at least, ITV and Channel 4 and the BBC don't encompass the sum of our ambitions, and so, in the autumn, we are launching eight part-channels on Sky of which I am involved with two. And the kind of production deals involved in that, and the budget involved, and the whole way those channels are made, bear no resemblance to what the four of us have been used to in the past. And it will be interesting to see if it really works because the whole means of getting on air with really very small budgets requires a completely different mind-set to that which has applied in the past.

But, as to the future proliferation of channels, this arguably allows greater access for people coming into the industry, and the 35,000 media students Roger was talking about will have opportunities. It will be very different from what has gone before. But, nevertheless, some of it will be worthwhile and some of those people hopefully will prosper in this new era. So, yes, we're in the middle of a revolution and it's unpleasant and it's much easier for me in a staff job, as Roger points out, to comment on that than it is for people outside trying to get programmes commissioned or, indeed, get employed directly by one of the bigger broadcasters. But I think I'm not so pessimistic for the future, and I have a one year old son, so I need to keep in work a few years longer than Roger. And I feel it will be possible, but it will be very different and there's no point underestimating the problems that exist at the moment; but, in the future, I think we can have quite a vibrant broadcasting industry in this country. And there will be good things in it. There will be worthwhile, quality things that will be properly funded. There will be other stuff that you and I may never watch but may nevertheless establish some kind of niche. So I'm not quite so pessimistic as everyone else seems to be.

Helen Boaden: Thank goodness for that! Two rather gloomy views and a more optimistic view. Before we go on to the broader question of the future in ten years' time, anyone like to ask a question?

Questioner: Would you open your facilities to independent people to make programmes, at the BBC or Granada?

Helen Boaden: Well, there's the interesting situation where the BBC actually uses Granada's facilities because they're cheaper for programme makers than their own. So, yes, it does happen.

Questioner: So anyone could come along and say, we want so much time?

Helen Boaden: Well, a contract would have to be negotiated. It's a complex thing for the BBC, because the BBC isn't actually allowed to make a profit out of its resources. At the most, it can only break even. For Granada it's a business, isn't it?

Mike Spencer: We welcome it. We'd get into trouble if we advised or urged the independent companies to use our facilities, as they are supposed to be free to use whatever facilities they want. But, from our point of view, obviously any business that comes back into the building, whether it be in-house production or by an independent, is welcome, because it's all about maintaining that level of investment in new equipment.

Questioner: And that gives you the opportunity to see what's happening – to choose, or let them sell it elsewhere?

Helen Boaden, Mike Spencer: Yes.

Roger Bolton: Can I just pick up briefly. I'm gloomy about independent production. I also said that I think there's more good as well as more bad television. There are lots of very curious contrasts here. The optimistic side is that the most popular programming in the UK is, on the whole, made in the UK, which I think is a tremendously good thing. It's also true that far more people get the opportunity of working in television than before. I don't accept the Oxbridge thing, but it was true that a few people got in and then had quite a lot of security, and now we have vastly more people get in with vastly less security.

And I think there are particular dangers for journalism. We can all make programmes cheaper. But what gets cut, particularly in the journalistic field, is the research. And if, at the same time, for reasons of efficiency, you tend to put all your journalists together, be it in Millbank or be it in White City, and if they're all feeding off the same data – which I think they are – then what you begin to see is the same narrow agenda dominating.

Thus, when we have Europe coverage, it is almost entirely seen in terms of the problems within the Conservative party at Westminster, because a few backbenchers like Teresa Gorman walk round to BBC Millbank centre at nine o'clock in the morning, stand on the stairs, and wait to be interviewed by radio and television programmes. She says something outrageous. Someone says something in opposition to her. She comes back again and a totally artificial story is created.

Another thing that gets cut is the ability to travel. You tend to make programmes much closer to your base. You can't afford to pay for overnights for people to stay in hotels. That tends to mean you're drawing your experiences and doing your filming where your base is. Now, as long as we have companies like Granada operating out of Manchester, and as long as Helen can keep going where she is, at least we'll get those voices. But the vast metropolitan tendencies in broadcasting mean that it's increasingly difficult to get other experiences and outside voices... And that's where the danger lies.

And, finally... I'm an ageing hack with a great future behind me, but there is a real worry, if you believe that television is a cultural vehicle. You don't want, for example, all your programmes made by young people. You don't want all your programmes for children made by people who don't have children. Not because these people should be disqualified, but because you want a range of experience brought to bear on television, and I'm simply saying that this degree of casualisation that exists if you're not within a larger company, to some extent deliberately created by Channel 4 and others, and accidentally created in many ways by Parliament through the independent system, means that it is very difficult for people to sustain a career through television.

Helen Boaden: I think that's very true in an enormous number of work areas, and I think casualisation is the byword for many people in many different sectors. I totally agree with you about the damage of it, but I can't see that television is going to be totally exempt.

Jo Langham Brown (University College, Warrington, University of Manchester): I'd just like to quote here from Doug Henwood: 'If you strip away the high-tec gloss, the future for producers looks in many ways like the nineteenth century, or even the early days of the Industrial Revolution. Times of massive polarisation and displacement, exciting or even liberating if you were on the right side, frightful and eviscerating otherwise.' I think this issue of casualisation which is coming up so much should be seen not just in terms of the media industry but in terms of society. One wonders, in fact, in which ways the media is reflecting that effectively.

Helen Boaden: You mean in programmes on the subject? The BBC did some very interesting research recently that showed that, contrary to what they believed, people were totally uninterested in stocks and shares and profoundly interested in issues of the workplace and perhaps more surprisingly, in trade union rights.

Jo Langham Brown: Well, I'm quite shocked that a programme I watch quite regularly, the *Business Programme* in the morning, seems very rarely to examine the worker in the workplace.

Helen Boaden: That's because it's *Business Breakfast*, and that's its remit. I take your point entirely that the workplace is a critical area for all of us, whether or not we have work. I think the BBC has caught up with it rather late. We have done some excellent programmes, but I think this emphasis on business is a sort of hangover from the 1980s.

Roger Bolton: It's an inevitable consequence, if I may say so, of the centralisation of the BBC and the desire in the middle 1980s to get control of what was thought to be an organisation out of control. It wasn't. So one of the first things they did was to take the only networked current affairs programme outside London, *Brass Tacks*, and kill it. And to take the money and resources and create another programme, which has just been killed, *Public Eye*. The net result is that Helen does not have – as doughtily as she fights – a single network current affairs programme which she has any editorial control over in Manchester. Because you have this desire at the BBC not to offend.

Helen Boaden: I think that will get worse.

Freda Chapman (Broadcasting and Entertainment Trades and Cinematographic Theatre Union – BECTU): I wanted to pick up on one of Roger's comments when he said he foresaw increasing difficulty in sustaining a career in television. One of the things that I've been observing over the last two or three years is the immense difficulty a lot of our members have been having in sustaining a job. Not a career, just a job enough to have a normal adult lifestyle, do the things that people like to do – get settled in a house, bringing up kids and all the rest of it. I obviously have a particular perspective on this as I talk to people when they've been on the receiving end of some of the more draconian employment policies, particularly of the major employers. What I see at the moment is the change. An awful lot of people have left the industry over the last couple of years and, yes, there are the 35,000 students who are willing and eager, and at least at the beginning of their career are prepared to put a lot of themselves in and not receive a lot back for it in monetary terms. But that can't be sustained either.

Helen Boaden: They grow older, too. Their lives change.

Freda Chapman: What I wanted to ask the panel is whether you can actually see, with the kind of industry you are foreseeing, and I'm looking particularly at the major employers of the broadcasters, whether you can see it being able to sustain the number of people with the kinds of skills that will make those programmes? Can you actually keep them in continuing employment and provide enough incentives for the people who can make those programmes to stay in the industry and continue doing it?

Mike Spencer: Well, I hope so. I think it's vital that we do, because television will always be a talent-led business, and that's not just on-screen talent, it's all the talent behind the camera. But volume is a problem. We all know the reason for short-term contracts and casualisation. It's because there are no guarantees of output, and unless – looking at Granada – one is working on *World in Action*, *This Morning* or *Coronation Street*, they are the only series which are forty-seven to fifty weeks of the year. They can pretty much guarantee employment.

Freda Chapman: I think *This Morning* is in a different category because of the move. I accept the point about the others.

Mike Spencer: It would still employ people, though. That's my point. So I think all companies have got to wake up to the fact that if they're going to keep the talent and they truly believe the talent is important to keep, then they must do, ultimately. In the jargon, we are a software industry, and ultimately it comes down to grey matter how successful these companies are. To keep that talent you've got to pay them and give them the sort of terms and conditions that keep them in the industry. Because, over a period of time, if the industry is deflated and quite so Victorian as you describe, people will stop trying to get into it. I hope.

Roger Bolton: That didn't happen with acting. I do think there is a real parallel with acting. It's absolute nonsense that so many people want to become actors and will accept so little money for so long and so little security. But they do, and I think they will in television.

Helen Boaden: Mick – your thoughts on that?

Michael Pilsworth: Yes. Well. We are very much an employer of short-term freelance contract staff. Our ratio of permanent or long-term staff to short-term staff is about 5% to 95%, so we only have something like 200 permanent staff because we have to sell every single show we make. We don't have any guaranteed long-term output. So we can't offer long-term security. Having said that, the very talented people, the managing director of a production company or divisional level or highly talented writers, we are tying in on three year contracts because we need to keep that relationship with them.

So I think what I'd draw from that is that the people who are very talented will have security of employment on fairly long-term effectively staff contracts, or will have their own companies. As I was saying earlier about the actors and writers and comedians who have been, if you like, freelance, and gone from project to project, increasingly they have all set their own destinies and have their own production arm.

Helen Boaden: As for the BBC, I think it has some very good equal opportunities policies and some very sincerely held beliefs about equal opportunities. But the economics of it don't make sense, because you want your core workers, the people who work all year on programmes that last all year. But then you want the flexibility to put people on three or six month contracts so you don't have to pay for them when they're not actually making programmes. And you can see the strains within the organisations where, on the one hand, they have a genuine commitment to equal opportunities, and on the other hand the economics don't stack up.

Michael Pilsworth: It is true at the moment that managers and accountants have more stable jobs than the creative people.

Helen Boaden: That's not actually true at the BBC – they're actually sacking people all the time, because they're overheads-de-layering, as it's called.

Roger Bolton: We shouldn't minimise the fundamental. I'm intrigued by Mike talking about the end of monopolies when you see Granada take over LWT and about to have I don't know how many channels. I don't see you've got a monopoly but you've got these large groups forming. The good side of it is that you ought to be able to give more stable employment for those that are within. That's the good point. The down side is that in the end Gerry Robinson is interested, and has to be, in maximising shareholder value. That is the dominant. I don't blame him. That's what the Act of Parliament has delivered. I think an area worth looking at, the down side and the concerns, is news, and we need to look at continuing regulation in some form. You see, there's no real, fixed economic price at which you can deliver news. I don't think news will ever make money. You can always do it more cheaply. You can always force the price down and do it largely without the audience knowing, because what you are losing by cutting the price are largely intangible things. If you and I were to set up a news operation, we could set up a pretty good one very cheaply. Get a couple of attractive presenters, do a deal with international news agencies, predominantly American, to take their pictures. Rip and read. What you don't do is, you don't open your own view area, you don't send your own journalists, and the net result is that you're allowing someone else, usually Americans, to set the agenda. You're allowing them to point the cameras in one direction rather than the other. You're losing your ability to individually verify what is being said. But you can produce a very attractive news programme nonetheless, and much more cheaply. Unless you therefore have a degree of regulation, what you're going to see is the costs of news gradually coming right down.

ITN is a fascinating problem. It needed to become less dependent on Channel 3 and Channel 4, in case one day Reuters or whatever are brought in as news suppliers, so it is desperate to get the job of supplying news to Channel 5. So it put in a low price. It got the Channel 5 contract. Yippee! Immediately, Channel 3 says, hold on a second. You're giving Channel 5 news at that price. Channel 5 is in direct competition with us. You can only deliver news to Channel 5 at that price because we, Channel 3, are subsidising you. Right. We're going to cut the price to Channel 3. So they're damned if they do and damned if they don't.

What we're talking about is a degree of regulation, which is required. The other thing that can be done about working conditions, and which I feel very strongly about, is for younger people. I notice that Mirror Live, for example, is advertising the equivalent of an MBA for people 23–28 at Canary Wharf. You're very fortunate if you get it. You just don't get paid. What Channel 4 could do in the budgets, they could insist they pay researchers to be present in the editing of films so they can see how films are put together as opposed to only being involved in the research stage. Channel 4 could say there's a minimum price, for example, for runners, and for a number of grades. It is difficult for Channel 4 to do it in a competitive situation, but the broadcasters could attempt to build in some safeguards. They could allow holiday credits. They could do a range of things collectively. And I do believe, if Channel 4 were to try and do this, the BBC would probably be shamed into following suit. I do not want to know what would happen with ITV or Channel 5, but what is sad is that those organisations which call themselves public service are not prepared to take the lead in these areas. I think the benefits would be marginal but worth having.

Bob Houlton (University of Manchester): I was very interested in the way in which the industry is being defined. Because it seems to me that commercial television has an umbilical link with retailing. The most glamorous industry that young people want to go into is directly connected with the retail industry, which they don't want to go into. And it seems to me what we've had over the last forty years is the development of a retail market around national brands and the establishment of large supermarket chains, and things like that. That era is coming to an end and as it's coming to an end, the funding for a kind of advertising for television is also coming to an end. Procter and Gamble are reported to be cutting back on their advertising budget, reducing it from 25% of turnover to 20%. That's going to have a massive effect on the television industry. The most successful retailer in this country has never advertised on television. And it seems to me that the industry is getting all excited over digital and multiple channels, but the reality is that because the retailers are now controlling the brands and establishing their own brands, the amount of money that's available to television is going to go down, and that's going to be the real crisis over the next five or six years.

Mike Spencer: I don't think so. I don't know about Procter and Gamble. There are now different ways of using retailer funding on television rather than just on advertising. I don't know in that case whether they're moving out of advertising into programme sponsorship or whatever. But if one looks at America, where this kind of debate about new channels and the proliferation of channels was taking place twelve or fifteen years ago, and everyone thought the big three networks would be swamped in this plethora of new channels – in fact there are four channels now because there's Fox, which is networked in America – they still account for 65% of audience viewing, and attract a similarly high percentage of total advertising. And the cable companies and the other home entertainment media have done varying degrees OK. But it's still ABC, NBC. If you're an advertiser and you want to sell your product, you're still going to go to one of those big networks to advertise. And I think that will be true in Britain for decades to come.

Granville Williams (Campaign for Press and Broadcasting Freedom): I echo some of the points Roger was making about the pressures on independents. But you just mentioned sponsorship, and it's clear I think that the ITC is going to look at relaxing some of the sponsorship rules. I understand West Country TV in the news slots are actually going to have sponsorship for softer items. I would welcome some comments from the panel about what that might mean for independents, particularly if you remember recently when Heineken caused a slight problem by suggesting they were going to have a bit more control over the programme, and that meant less wine, more beer, and what about those black faces? We don't want those... And it seems to me there's an issue there. And the other issue I'd like the panel to respond on is, there is a pressure in independents when you are dealing with current affairs programmes where political pressure can be put via the company on to the independent. I'm thinking about what happened with 20-20 Vision when Mr Mellor wanted a little bit of a programme cut. It seems to me there was a fragile situation where the company should have been the heat shield that took the pressure. It was, in fact, the independent that had to stand up and, in a very principled way, decide they wouldn't make the cut.

Helen Boaden: Can we just talk about sponsorship, Mike? Because Granada has some, doesn't it? *This Morning* has items sponsored.

Mike Spencer: The whole programme is sponsored by British Telecom, and yesterday they announced sponsorship of *Coronation Street* – I think with Cadbury's. The use of sponsorship in and around programmes is regulated by the ITC. I was certainly of the belief that you couldn't sponsor anything within a news programme and I hope that's the case. I think that would be a bizarre step, if one was suddenly able to plug a product in the middle of a news programme, even if it was how to look after your pet. So in that sense, as in many things, I welcome ITC's regulation. I hope you know that sponsorship can offer opportunities for broadcasters and independents sometimes to get a programme off the ground which otherwise they wouldn't be able to do. There's nothing wrong with that. I don't think that's particularly heinous, but it needs to be watched very carefully.

Helen Boaden: What about the issue of the heat on independents when they're doing something that's politically contentious? I mean, you've felt the heat many times from agencies as a journalist.

Roger Bolton: I just want to say on sponsorship, I think it's very difficult to believe that someone's going to allow sponsorship directly for news and current affairs programmes. There is of course a long-term danger that the fact a programme attracts sponsorship, that a programme attaches sponsorship, may make programmes that don't attach sponsorship disproportionately more expensive. I don't think you see that at the moment, but it's a worry that would occur. As for the heat shield thing, I think it's absolutely true that independents on their own would find it very difficult to make programmes in contentious areas because you often need more research after transmission than before, and you'd need quite a lot of lawyers. Channel 4 has an absolutely exemplary record in this and in backing people. The BBC also and I think ITV has a pretty good record as well. I think what happened, Granville, in the case you dealt with, is that the person at Carlton made a mistake. And the network centre, the ITV publisher, tried to step in there and saw the issues at stake. Now, whether it was because Carlton was a new broadcaster, whether it was because the people within Carlton didn't have enough experience, I'm not sure. I don't think it's possibly as worrying as it seems.

Helen Boaden: Mick – what are your views on that relationship? When things get difficult?

Michael Pilsworth: Well, I should hold my hand up and admit we don't actually make any factual programmes. I could say the reason we don't is that we just can't make any money doing it.

Serving the Community

Chair: Rob McLoughlin

Granada Television

Colin Philpott

Acting Head of Local Programmes GMR

John Gray

President, University of Manchester Broadcasting Symposium

Simon Schroeder

Nynex Cable Communications

Rob McLoughlin: Welcome to this morning's session. I am Rob McLoughlin from Granada Television. I'm here in a completely impartial capacity to talk about this morning's first topic which is 'Serving the Community'. The fact that I'm presenting a programme on Granada Television tonight at 23:10 called *The Line* is completely irrelevant but if you could write it down – we need all the help we can get.

Granada Television has promoted an enormous amount of activity within its own region and, indeed, one of the projects that we are in the process of completing is called the *Granada Community Challenge* – some of you will have seen a pamphlet about it in your folders. It is a project that we regard as interactive television because it is not Granada that is making things happen, it is various businesses and individuals within the region who have come together to take part in a scheme which is delivering something in the region of £6.5 million worth of new youth and community facilities in the North West. One of the projects which opened last year is a brand new youth and community centre in Blacon in Chester. Would you believe it, this is the first-purpose built youth facility in Chester for twenty years?

The role of a regional television company is being studied at the moment by academics from Manchester Metropolitan University and there will be a report published at the end of the year. Many of you might be interested to see how a television company actively encouraged such an initiative to happen and how it encouraged the private sector to interface with public and community groups in the North West. The project will cost £6.5 million and is about to be replicated by other ITV stations, most notably London Weekend Television later this year. So that is the kind of context we are going to be looking at this morning. How can broadcasters, not only just in the present but in the future, serve their communities? How much commercial sense does it make to serve those communities and how effective can it be?

To discuss this this morning we are joined by John Gray, the President of the Scottish Association of Smallscale Broadcasters, Simon Schroeder who is head of Media Relations for Nynex Cable Communications and we are going to begin this morning by hearing from Colin Philpott who I've known for a long time as a broadcaster here in the North West. He recently took over GMR, the BBC's local radio station and is now the Acting Head of all Local Programming for the BBC in Manchester, both radio and television. Colin would you like to begin this morning?

Colin Philpott: I'd like to begin with this thought: 'It might be rubbish but at least it's local rubbish' said a BBC spokesman. Actually it was the Managing Editor of a BBC local radio station and he was referring, I'm pleased to say, not to his own output but to a newly established, local commercial rival. I mention this not to slag off the opposition but because of the question of 'localness'. How local is local and what is the precise role of local radio? This is a very live issue for many of us in broadcasting within and without the BBC. My current job is Head of Local Programmes in the North West which takes in radio and television: it takes an overall responsibility for the BBC's local radio station in Manchester – GMR. For two and a half years before taking up this job I was Manager of GMR itself and I would like to concentrate on that this morning. I want to tell you very briefly the story of one station during a period of considerable change and I hope that you may find it relevant to some of the wider questions that are facing broadcasting at the moment.

Many of you will be aware that, about five years ago, the BBC adopted a new policy for its network of local stations. The emphasis was to be on providing information-based services, predominantly speech with priority given to news, sport, travel and weather. The policy encouraged the reflection of local culture and provided a forum for local debate and community involvement. Of course, this wasn't a complete break with the past. Indeed many would argue that it was a return to the original raison d'être of BBC local radio. In the 1960s and 1970s when those first stations emerged from the primeval swamp they were very local. Recently, I have had the opportunity of listening to some of that original broadcasting from GMR and Radio Lancashire because both stations have recently celebrated their 25th anniversaries. The 'sounds' of those stations from the early 1970s were very different from today – few local accents, lots of local information, local references, down-your-street news and a very strong sense of the stations providing companionship and being part of the community.

But over the years, two very critical things happened to BBC local radio. First, our commercial competition, predominantly music-based, increased greatly – right across the country; and secondly, for commercial reasons, the BBC committed itself to establishing a network of county stations as opposed to local stations (Radio Blackburn became Radio Lancashire, Radio Brighton became Radio Sussex, and so on). The strategy we adopted, certainly here in Greater Manchester during the late 80s and beyond, was to compete, if not exactly head-on but certainly shoulder-to-shoulder with independent local radio. Indeed the adoption of the name GMR was partly motivated by the desire to acquire an ILR-sounding name and WM in Birmingham and the GLR in London were other examples of the same thing. So circa 1990 here in Greater Manchester, GMR – the BBC station, and Piccadilly – the commercial station, were a great deal closer in style and content than they had been before and what they have subsequently become. Essentially, we were trying to match up to a station like Piccadilly. I think my predecessor as Station Manager would confirm that the station was trying to ape the style and trendiness of an ILR station.

When I started as Manager in early 1993 I inherited a station which had begun a process of disengagement from the shoulder-to-shoulder competition. Ron Neill, Managing Director of Regional Broadcasting, had committed all stations across the country to news-based speech programmes at breakfast, at lunchtime and drivetime. Consequently, by the time I took over, GMR's Breakfast Show had gone all speech and the lunchtime and drivetime sequences had moved in that direction. The rest of station remained basically music entertainment. My belief was we really had a split personality and we needed to be either one thing or the other.

There was no doubt that BBC local radio in this area had a bit of an image problem which had prevented it appealing to a wider range of people, particularly people younger than its traditional older audiences. My aim was to try and create a talk station for Greater Manchester. I believed then, and I believe it even more passionately now, particularly in an area like this which is a very busy news area and which has a rich tradition in sport, in the arts and many other fields, that we need a local talk station. Indeed, our marketing slogan became 'Greater Manchester's Only Talk Radio Station'.

So I set out to try and make us a market leader in a number of specific fields: number one – news; number two – debate; number three – sports; number four – information (travel, weather, other subjects); number five – to offer a range of specialist programmes. We had already been doing specialist music programmes and ethnic minority broadcasting and these continued. We also tried to attract new groups of specific customers which of course is also good for one's weekly reach, apart from anything else. So we set up weekly programme about the Arts, about Travel and about Business. We were still playing music – only a small amount in the mid morning, a little bit more in the afternoons and actually quite a bit more at the weekends, particularly on weekend mornings. The plan was unveiled to the staff in June 1993 and immediately it provoked an outcry. The staff weren't that keen because it involved some redundancies and some transfer of resources from one type of staff to another. A vociferous campaign, undoubtedly fuelled by the local evening newspaper, was mounted in opposition. For three weeks GMR was never out of the Manchester Evening News; letter followed letter. Most of the opposition focused on the removal of two particular presenters. I went on air to explain and justify the changes and about two hundred people rang in – hardly any of them to congratulate me. I even had one threatening phone call and a number of abusive letters. Although it wasn't very pleasant at the time, it did at least reassure me that people cared very passionately about the radio station.

We made all these changes knowing that the environment was going to get tougher. GMR was about to lose its medium wave frequency as part of a pattern of what was happening to BBC stations all over the country; an estimated 29 per cent of our audience were listening on medium wave and we feared that quite a lot of those would not be able to get us on FM because of poor FM reception in parts of the Manchester area. Of course, a raft of new stations were waiting in the wings – Jazz FM, Fortune, Kiss, not to mention Manchester United Radio, Talk Radio UK and, indeed the BBC's own Radio 5 Live which we had to see as competition.

Well, what happened after the changes? At first glance, the rather dull news that the audience share of GMR stayed almost exactly the same. Indeed, it has done so over the last two and a half years. At certain times of the week we did particularly well – on Saturday afternoons when we took, and continue to take, our rivals to the cleaners in sport. After some thought we realised that this levelling off of the audience was actually something of an achievement in the face of the loss of medium wave. Despite the arrival of all the news stations, we had maintained our audience size and we suspect, from research information, that we have done this by losing some and gaining others. We lowered our age profile, not dramatically but significantly, acquiring more people in the forty to fifty age range and losing some of the people over sixty five. We believe that we had achieved the goals that I set out earlier. Undoubtedly, we are offering more range and depth than we had been before. We now regularly beat our competitors, including the *Manchester Evening News*, to stories. I've already mentioned our success in sport. Our own market research showed us that there was a greater awareness of the station than ever before, a greater awareness of what the role of a local station was, and an appreciation of our value as an information provider.

To sum up: since then, as those of you from Manchester may know, we have re-jigged the station again and we renamed it on 11th December 1995 – GMR Talk – which was a further move in the same direction. We were convinced that we had been moving in the right direction so we actually pushed a bit further. Two years after the earlier changes we have removed virtually all music from the schedule and made a number of other changes to strengthen the station. Of course, we won't know until the summer, when the next full set of audience figures come out, whether that has been a success. There are many questions which GMR Talk, and the rest of the BBC local radio network, will face in the coming months and years among them the growth of incrementalism – more localised ILR stations are opening all the time. The BBC's financial pressures are unlikely suddenly to become more favourable; and the impact of technology and the bi-media principle (of working between radio and television) are all likely to have an effect. Indeed, there is the debate about the whole concept of how we define what is local and what is community.

I don't claim that the GMR story which I have briefly outlined provides any simple answer to any of these questions. I do believe, however, that it demonstrates the demand for local talk radio which combines authority with accessibility, which provides really local information and entertainment and that this is a demand which I believe, and of course hope, will continue. Thank you.

Rob McLoughlin: Thank you Colin. We'll hear from everybody else on the panel before we throw it open to the floor but could I just ask you a very quick question. In total reach, what sort of audience is GMR now getting?

Colin Philpott: The weekly reach is about 280,000 which represents about 14 per cent.

Rob McLoughlin: In the past you have done experimental stations, have you not, in areas like Rochdale and Wigan – opt outs?

Colin Philpott: I think in about '83 or '84. Over a year there was a series of, from memory, I think Wigan, Rochdale, Stockport, Trafford and Bury. Each station was on the air for two or three months.

Rob McLoughlin: We'll talk about that later because it will be interesting to see what effect that had and whether it had a greater or lesser effect than Manchester United Radio on the listening public in the North West. Now let's turn to a man of the future or so he tells me. Simon Schroeder is the Media Relations Manager of Nynex Cable Communications and, of course, many people over the last ten years have been talking about all the possibilities when cable becomes the norm. It may be providing the very localised services we have all been talking about for ten to twenty years in cities and even in smaller communities. So, Simon, one of the things we are asking you to present us with this morning is that vision. Is it going to happen? If it does happen, are we going to want it?

Simon Schroeder: Thank you very much indeed. It's interesting that Colin should mention the *Manchester Evening News*. It is not a publication that I am unfamiliar with. It's something that Nynex has been profiled in quite lengthily. Indeed GMR itself is something we're not unfamiliar with either and one can appreciate the difference in the immediate nature of GMR and radio (and having to give verbal answers and picking up intonations) in contrast to the written copy on hard newspaper and the effect that has. That's been quite an interesting exercise for me as a Media relations Manager over the last two years – working for Nynex – to see the way in which the different media treat issues of mainline public concern.

Of course, I'm not here to talk about local pavements today. I'm here to talk about what now lies beneath them and what it can do for us. Do we have the slides, Dave, at all? Wheel in the slides. Let's get the quotes over first. Mike Tracey said in a paper called *Laughing on Sunrays* that, 'We live on the cusp of fundamental change'. Bit of a cliché I know but it is true and anyone in the industry of broadcasting, cable or otherwise will recognise that fact. An interesting quote I heard recently from Anthony H Wilson was that: 'The transport of the future will be the bit and not the atom'. I think that actually says a lot when you think about intellectual property rights. Tom Peters, the international business guru was in Manchester recently, and he said that 'Business is a creative activity involving inspired hunches and leaps of faith'.

That essentially is very much what Nynex is involved in. We've acquired some franchises. In fact we're the largest group of contiguous franchises in the UK. We've gathered together a bundle of optical fibre, a huge bundle, and we've begun the long, and sometimes painful, process of laying it past the doors of 1.7 million homes and over 100,000 business in the North West.

Then part way through that process, we began to sit back and think. Certainly we are serving the community with telephony and television services, but the sheer carrying capacity of this new broadband medium, means, of course, that we can do much more than that. We could have presented the world with a glittering prize, a short term PR win. Instead we chose a different route. We chose GEMISIS 2000, a project which brings us into partnership with a university – the University of Salford, a City Council – the City of Salford, to develop a template for a civic super highway. Just to make you familiar with the acronym: GEMISIS stands for Government, Education, Medicine, Industry, Social, Information Superhighway. It's nothing whatsoever to do with Phil Collins. GEMISIS brings together a range of expertise from a wide range of interests.

Essentially, we provide the fibre and some back-up. The City provides some funding leverage and the University provides research and development. Of course, if only life were that simple. In truth, the roles of each of the partners are fluid and complex and they reflect the organic nature of the project. GEMISIS has proved a magnet to those who recognised the value of broadband communications by providing room for expression and growth. Its ripple effect should reach far beyond Salford and it opens up the slip road to the super highway to a wide range of professionals helping them to make more effective and efficient use of their skills.

Over 120 experts are now working away in the fields of community, health, crime prevention, education, training and research and business development to develop practical applications for use on the super highway. Nick Ross said, when he officially launched GEMISIS projects in November of last year [1995],: 'If just one of these ideas can be made to fly, then the implications for the way in which we live could be truly profound'.

Let's just take a look at a couple of those projects. One of them is the virtual chamber of commerce. This is where you can appreciate the way in which broadband cable can work. We all know that global villages of commerce are now developing and it doesn't matter where the individual footloose members of the village are. The fact is that they can now do business together very efficiently due to improved communications. Clearly a virtual chamber of commerce has some appeal – e-mail, video conferencing, database sharing, remote consultations, disparate realtime think tanks. The possibilities are probably endless.

Another of our projects is the tele-dermatology health project. Here we can apply broadband technology to medicine. Clearly, the idea of keeping students out of hospitals via the medium of remote video conferencing and bringing them in when they've had some schooling allows hospitals to function more effectively with regard to the patients' immediate needs and has some value in improving the way our society operates. Through GEMISIS the civic superhighway can do much to serve a community's educational needs as well. The schools project we have developed has initially been one of our most successful. What we've done with the schools project is provide a link between local community schools, local high schools and the University College of Salford so that pupils from those schools can access things, such as the remote CD-ROM for libraries. They can go on to the Internet (we do provide a censorship package before they get on to it). They can also get involved in remote language teaching. Again there are profound implications for education. One Spanish teacher, shared between six schools, allows the pupils to be up to speed with their Spanish. This clearly has applications for the way in which our nation can develop and the way in which we can bind society together.

I think it is true that there are difficulties. It's not the glittering prize but a project to develop a working template to help serve the needs of a complex and a changing society. It's going to require patient determination and flexibility of mind. We're already seeing this as we work our way through and deal with the different bureaucracies involved in what is a very complex web binding society together. It is true that, as a social cement, the superhighway plays both devil and demi-god. It present us with choices about the way in which we live. Certainly, we see this every day within the cable communications company Nynex. We see the media both courting us and slagging us off. This is something we get used to. We have to keep a focus on the way in which we can bring something worthwhile to the communities in which we operate. We are very fortunate in the Manchester area. We've got a huge and comprehensive fibre optic web. How various organisations choose to use it is going to be up to the way in which society lobbies us and puts pressure on us as franchisees. We have a limited licence period and have to be accountable to the legislators in terms of putting our franchises in place. Of course, we must be accountable to local society in terms of putting our franchises in place and, of course, accountable to local society in the way in which we offer our services – if we're going to get any sort of commercial return as we develop the network forward. That is really all I have to say. Thank you.

Rob McLoughlin: Thank you Simon. When Nynex first came into Greater Manchester you were criticised quite a lot and your publicity seemed to be aimed simply at providing more options in terms of television channels. Is the development of all this because you have been sensitive to the fact that such an accusation has prevented a real take-up?

Simon Schroeder: No, I think what this is is clear evidence of what, historically, is a telephone company waking up to the commercial realities of the world around it – broadband optical fibre. Anyone who reads the broadsheet press will know that has a myriad of possibilities and clearly Nynex, which over in the United States was essentially a telephone network (which, in way, BT was, and still is) were quick to recognise that there are a whole raft of possibilities that will allow them to develop this communications conduit under the ground in a way they hadn't thought of previously.

Rob McLoughlin: But is this now part of the business as opposed to simply offering more channels?

Simon Schroeder: More channels. You actually will see a very great drive towards encouraging a higher, what we call, 'penetration' in television viewing this year. Dawn French will be leading a major campaign. This is evidence, for the first time, that all the multiple service operators have linked up – all the cable companies have got together. They've spent £12 million bringing an advertising campaign together to promote cable television. It is certainly true that there is a push on cable television but that's probably because telephony has stolen a march. It's really taken off. We were able to offer very competitive telephone services and that effectively surpassed the performance of cable television. So we've got some catching up to do there. There are three elements really; there's the telephony side, the television side and the superhighway side – the civic side.

Rob McLoughlin: All right, let's leave it there for the moment. We'll come back to whether you can provide more local services of the kind John Gray might recognise in the future. John Gray, as I said last night at Granada, has had a very distinguished career, predominantly with the BBC. He was a World War II correspondent for the BBC. He has produced programmes both for television and radio in London and indeed in Scotland. And he's now President of the Scottish Association of Smallscale Broadcasters. And that isn't a reference to your height is it John?

John Gray: I'm coming over here which is nothing to do with my height. I've got to use this machine so that's why I don't sit down with the others.

Broadcasting, I think we should remember, started as *smallscale* in America, in Europe and in Britain. The first station I ever heard was Aberdeen 2BD which was for Aberdeen and 12 miles around – it was very local. The music in the afternoon, I remember, was the trio from Watt and Grant's restaurant and, if anyone has ever seen *Brief Encounter*, they'll know exactly the kind of situation and set-up that was. In 1949 at the time of the Beveridge enquiry into broadcasting I pointed out in the evidence I was asked to give, that the alternative to a national network or a network is not necessarily another network but is local broadcasting.

In the 1960s I was much concerned – I was still with the BBC – with the BBC's experiment in local radio. Then, they and our commercial friends were taking very much the same attitude – that local radio should be really local, probably reaching around 100,000 to 250,000 people: it was on this basis that the thinking was drawn up. But it did not happen and, unfortunately to my mind, so-called local stations, as Colin has said, ceased to be Radio Blackburn and became Radio Lancashire, and so on. This has made a very big difference because, to my mind, community broadcasting should really be of the community, for the community. Even at its best, and however much the BBC and its local stations try to involve people, it is still part of the BBC and there is still a bit of from-above-to-below.

The kind of station with which I have become concerned is from the grass roots upwards and in Scotland we have done rather well – largely because of the rural situation. I must pay considerable tribute here to the Radio Authority and particularly David Vick, who have fallen over backwards, within the limits of the 1990 Act, to help us develop.

I think community radio which we call smallscale radio (and I'll say why) either exists for specialist interest groups in cities or it exists in rural areas where the community is a whole community which includes the business community, the landlords, the tenants. Everybody is part of the total community and that can work very well in rural areas. In England there is the Community Radio Association of which I was an early member, still am a personal member but it is a more ideological concept.

In Scotland we're highly pragmatic. We called ourselves the Scottish Association of Smallscale Broadcasters because that is what we are. We define it by the fact that the control should be within the target area. That is either geographical or, in the case of ethnic stations, within the community it is designed to serve, This means that, taking Scotland as an example, Moray Firth Radio covers a big area and has an audience of about 180,000 but it is a member of the Association, whereas Radio Broad, a much smaller station but wholly owned by Scottish Radio Holding, the Jimmy Gordon empire, cannot become a member because, by our definition, it is not controlled from within its area.

That is where we start from. Recently there was a White Paper in England for Rural Development in England and Wales yet it made only passing reference to broadcasting whereas we seem to do rather well in Scotland – I'll come back to Heartland FM in a minute. The fact is these days the government welcomes the development of community radio in Scotland and recognises the valuable contribution it makes toward developing community life in rural areas. Whether you like this government or not, it is useful to have that kind of seal of housekeeping approval. It certainly helps when one is going for funding from either public or private bodies.

Well, where are we? Already in Scotland we have seven on-air stations – you'll notice particularly in the North and the rural areas. SIBS (Shetland Island Broadcasting Service) is run by a pack of Vikings with whom we get on very well but I regret that they're not members of SASB.

Shetland Island Broadcasting Services is run by a wonderful madman and his wife. Ian Anderson was first Musical Director for Radio Forth in Scotland. He was a pirate in his day – it goes with being a Viking – and he has an immense knowledge of contemporary music. He is also a technical wizard. He has made his own computer-driven sustaining service system so two people and a cat can, in fact, keep a station on the air twenty four hours a day, and respond to local needs, and be recognised when they walk down Lewick Main Street.

The others are all on the mainland, they're all either on air or going on air. I'll deal in detail with two of them in a moment. But, of course, radio broadcasting is not just full-time licensing services. There's the immense range of RSLs – short terms licences. They include, of course in the cities Edinburgh and Glasgow, not only the kind of thing I have been talking about but also ones for ethnic groups. They celebrate certain of the Muslim celebrations and religious ceremonies. They have RSLs in connection with the Edinburgh Television Festival, the Mayfest, the Glasgow Arts Festival which involve the people, and not the people outside but the people themselves who are concerned with doing these things. The universities do their own RSLs very effectively. Sweet FM is the name that Glasgow took as its title which is a wonderful title. And there was Fresh Air which was the Edinburgh programme directed at the Freshers coming up at the beginning of the session. Informative? Involving? Absolutely.

This [Slide] shows the spread of programming that Heartland does. It's on air Monday to Thursday evening only and during the weekend with programmes not programming. Certainly still over 50 to 60 per cent music but the speech is all local and it is informative. Heartland does not do any news bulletins because it says 'we can't do news bulletins well so we'll leave that to other services. We do what we can do well.'

The stations I mentioned involve 800 trained volunteers, very intensively trained. We may be amateurs but we're as expert as any professional broadcaster and we can outdo some of them. The Heartland station which is the one I'm most closely concerned with, before it went on air, did a RSL of a big sporting event – the raft race down the Tay. During a two and a quarter hour programme we had seven OB points feeding in. Very few small scale stations in

ILR or BBC, and I think Colin would admit this, would happily take on seven filtration points coming in on OB. We had one cock up and that was due to learning difficulties.

Can I take Heartland as an example of what we are doing? As I say, radio has the best pictures and I will now show you some pictures of Heartland. That is an old ice rink. It's the old Pitlochry Theatre and in that building we have Heartland FM. That little bit behind those two windows is where the station is. There is our transmitter. Interesting we don't use any of the BBC or the National Telecom facilities, we work with Hydro Electric which, for its own communication needs, has something like 120 transmitters, dotted through the Highlands. Again, in this slide, the police – we use their transmitters. We keep away from the big broadcasting organisations. We think we do it much better ourselves. [Slide] That is a scene from the transmitter. Heartland has a target audience of 5,500 human beings and 15,000 sheep. In four years not one sheep has ever complained about the programmes.

[Slides] That is the person you meet going in. Again all volunteers; a great bunch of ladies volunteer to staff the reception desk every morning. So that is our reception area and our office. That is the preparation area. Up on the left you have your logging recorders, the office computer, and that is the corner where all preparation is done. Radio Authority people will enjoy this. The warning is get your logging tape otherwise your're going to get fined £3000 by the delightful people on the Radio Authority – everything there is lined up to warn you that you must keep your logging tapes.

[Slides] That is the actual studio and you'll notice the cardboard covers over part of the control desks, the mixers. That's because we don't want to inflict 'techno-fear' on most of our trainees so all the knobs that the average person doesn't need to use are covered up. It keeps away the fear quotient. You only really need the bits below the cardboard which, for those who are technical, are the pre-fade, the remote control, and the fader. That's all people need to bother about for most of the time. That's another view of the little studio. People at work in the studio, it gives you some idea of the size and what's available there.

[Slide] Activity of Heartland, we finance the stations by selling chutney and jam. This shows you that not only do we broadcast but we do a lot of working with local groups, putting on concerts and ceiladhs. They make money for the station but they also involve the station in the community. In stations like Heartland we do very intensive training and we work with colleges of education who offer courses so people who work with us can have their training validated with courses. If you take the RSLs in to account as well, probably within the last three years, something like 2000 people have been trained to a fairly high standard of expertise. Very few of them want to go into professional broadcasting permanently. They want to serve their community and do so. Every aspect is done. On Heartland one of the most successful programmes is done by 16 to 17 years olds, *Teen Scene*. Now they're given help in training but they devise their own programmes, their own music. This applies right across the range.

I hope I have shown you there is something alive, vibrant and developing – good rural radio which involves its community and is made by its community. The last thing I would say is this. There was the age of the dinosaurs and then those huge animals were wiped out. What was left behind? Little animals which developed. I think the future of broadcasting lies with the little animals who are going to grow and develop.

Rob McLoughlin: Little animals selling chutney at 85p I imagine. Lots of issues there. Great enthusiasm. It brings back memories of lots of little radio stations I've seen over the years. But you're not seriously suggesting that the dinosaurs of the BBC should be going that localised are you?

John Gray: Yes. The other thing is that stations like that will never get more than 50 per cent of their money from normal commercial revenue. It's chutney and concerts and abseiling down church steeples and everything like that which gets you the other 50 per cent.

Rob McLoughlin: Now you're an enthusiast. There are no lessons here for the BBC in developing its network or for Nynex?

John Gray: No: but the lesson is there are great rural areas of England and Wales that should be doing the same thing.

Rob McLoughlin: How local do we want to go? Should we be having community broadcasts? Should we be insisting that Nynex should be developing very small community networks, either in terms of information or in terms of television, or in terms of radio services? Should we be putting pressure on the BBC to do the same. Who'd like to open the debate?

Colin Philpott: Can I just disagree with what John said? I think there is a lesson for the BBC in some of the stations that you have described. Indeed, the BBC is looking at that at the moment. A very interesting area to look at for this whole debate is Yorkshire where there have been three pretty localised ILR stations set up in the last couple of years -- Stray in Harrogate, East Coast in Scarborough and Minster in York. There's another one - Dales FM - which has either started, or is about to start, in Yorkshire. These stations have done extremely well very quickly, getting 30 to 40 per cent weekly reaches in their areas. They have been providing a service which is predominantly music, a pretty minimal news service but lots of local references. The stations are quite clever at sounding very local. BBC Radio York's audience dipped in response to them. However, it is interesting that, through a combination of pushing its resources out to local areas and publicity, Radio York's audiences have substantially recovered. So I think the BBC is very aware of the 'localness' argument. Indeed, we are due to publish a strategy for the next ten years about all of this but it has been delayed. Some wag is now calling it the nine and a half year strategy as opposed to the ten year strategy. This will address head-on the question of local networks serving more localised audiences.

John Gray: I think what I am saying is that there is an area of broadcasting that is neither conventional commercial radio nor BBC radio and which to my mind is the nub of community radio.

Rob McLoughlin: Are there any lessons Simon, for Nynex in any of this?

Simon Schroeder: I think clearly there are. I think it's fascinating that we have rediscovered singing round the living room piano and selling chutney to pay for it. I think that's wonderful and it's going to bind the communities together. People are really finding a community spirit and there is a lesson for all of us there. The route that Nynex chooses to develop its local services is unfolding day by day and it is unfolding in response to lobby groups. Clearly, we are talking to local news providers at all sorts of different levels to develop our programming. Clearly we have also got the interactive nature of our network. We can set boxes on top of our television sets which will, as time progresses, probably converge into kind of PC/TVs. It's a two way flow of traffic. Voice communication paints some of the most evocative pictures of all. I think it's one of the most entertaining. There is an area in which data transmission, printed news matter, simple e-mail interchange – be it local television of some sort – has an arena in which it could operate.

Rob McLoughlin: Would you throw open free space to the community enthusiasts John has been talking about?

Simon Schroeder: We're looking at doing exactly that in our local programming and targeting the sort of groups working in local communities that have previously found it difficult to find a platform. I think that we are anxious to avoid the rather clichéd Americanised local television which can develop on the hoof, without any sort of control and without any sort of sense of direction, clearly trying to appeal to the lowest common denominator. I think we've woken up to the fact that there is some sort of value to be added to society by a good local service. What we are now trying to do is stack up the commercial case for developing it and talk to the partners with whom we are operating.

Rob McLoughlin: I know you're sceptical about digital audio broadcasting but do you think, Colin, that DAB, when it arrives, will actually be the vehicle that is able to provide more opportunities for local stations like GMR or Radio Merseyside to opt out and offer alternatives (maybe small alternatives) to your normal main service?

Colin Philpott: It may well be – with the big money question mark before it. You know probably in an area like Greater Manchester we would have six or seven options, six or seven different ways for sport, six or seven different ways geographically. However, the BBC Local Radio network already has that possibility in many areas because we have more than one transmitter. Radio Lancashire is a good example of that. We have three FM transmitters, broadly speaking firing at East Lancashire, Central Lancashire and North Lancashire. So that possibility already exists in traditional technology.

Rob McLoughlin: Your people selling chutney in Scotland, are they also likely to be the people (or their sons, daughters or whatever) who in the future will be picking up camcorders and doing the television version of local radio?

John Gray: Yes, unlike the Community Radio Association, we are smallscale broadcasting. Dave Rushton is here – he is our leading enthusiast on the television side. We do envisage community television but, of course, it is much easier to acquire a radio expertise at a fairly high level than a television one and it is a more expensive operation in every way.

Rob McLoughlin: Some of you may remember when Granada did the Waddington television experiment, I think it was in the early 80s or mid-80s, it was certainly the local channels that proved the most popular for the first week or so. It had the 'oh look there's the butcher on television' factor. But, after a week or so, people actually got tired of exhibitionism in front of the camera and actually that channel withered. That's the potential, isn't it?

John Gray: That is a problem. I think much less so in radio. I think even with stations like Heartland and Nevis, and some others, you have a lot of music but the music is very different. It is again your local music which is presented which is very acceptable. As I said *Teen Scene Heartland* has its own top 20 which is compiled from two major dealers in Perthshire. We have, to my mind, an extraordinary late-night club scene programme . Again this is the choice. It is not from a selector computerised source, you are playing what matters in the area concerned.

Rob McLoughlin: These local stations also potentially provide another market. I remember going through Warrington recently and hearing one of the restricted services. I looked at my display on my radio and it came up and said the name of the station which was Radio Something or Another; a moment later it changed to give the number of the Ad Sales Department. Then it changed again and put an advertisement into my car which I actually thought was an infringement of my privacy as a driver. Nevertheless this is opening up new possibilities which could actually help to finance some of this – may it not in the future John?

John Gray: Yes, but chiefly in the more urban areas. You can provide services for the tourists – that's a big one. Nevis, in fact, gives its local traffic information not only in English but in French, German and Italian as well.

Rob McLoughlin: For the sheep presumably.

John Gray: Yes, the sheep very much like Italian.

Rob McLoughlin: Would anyone like to come in? There must be a question from the floor.

Bernard Lasevsky (John Moores University, Liverpool): With regard to Nynex, one of the statements you made was about combining society together and also referred to the debate about the Internet and the information superhighway. There's a lot of terminology and jargon. What I want to do is scratch below the surface. Basically the debate is about freedom and empowerment. On the one hand, it's going to lead to this democratic idealism, presumably in local areas as well. On the other hand, there's this kind of techno-apartheid idea that certain people will be excluded. Now, as far as I'm concerned, there is an opportunity for accessibility to information but how is the local community going to be guaranteed access to information other than paying you a £300 fee?

Simon Schroeder: I think it's not insignificant that the pavements we are ripping up do fall within local authority areas and clearly we have to talk to local authorities to carry out the obligation to meet certain milestones. We are, for example, investing in learning centres, five learning centres every year, where we're working with Business in the Community which is developing information technology centres in secondary schools that can actually become community centres to serve a wider area of the population, not just the pupils in the schools. That's one example. We've got environmental schemes we're working on to demonstrate a commitment to the community, plus we're looking at the idea of putting information booths in local libraries. We are conscious that there is the danger of a have-and-have-not society developing and that is always on one's mind. I think when you're looking at a system like this, which is dependent on high technology, the local environment exerts pressure on the company to call it to account. One would hope that local people, such as myself, who are now working for the company and who were involved in regeneration above the ground before they got involved in regeneration below the ground, would take that sort of pressure seriously and would make it a platform on which the company could operate.

Rob McLoughlin: Do you think competition from the likes of BT would help?

Bernard Lasevsky: What concerns me is the Government's policy of laying down an infrastructure which basically allows American-based companies within the region to lay down the infrastructure. So far as I am concerned their prime objective will have to be to fund that infrastructure through commercial means.

Simon Schroeder: Clearly there has to be a commercial return on the network to make it viable. I think it's encouraging that we're working on a ten year return plan in Nynex which, incidentally, is a locally floated company, one third floated on the Stock Exchange. Two thirds is still owned by the Nynex Corporation in the States, but clearly there is a local interest and a local financial interest now. There are also just under 3000 people, of whom only twenty five are Americans, who are employed locally, plus the thousands of contractors to whom the company brings work and, of course, there are the end users on either end of the cable who will be developing systems. It's simplistic to suggest that we're an American company which simply comes over and takes money back across the Big Pond. It's far more complex than that; we make a commitment to the community and to the people involved in developing the network which means that the proportion of return across the Big Pond is relatively small.

Rob McLoughlin: I know you want to come back but is there a final question from the floor

Judie Collins (ADCOMM): When I was working for a major broadcast monitoring company, when Radio Manchester (as was) did their pilot scheme for making the station more local, it failed because there were huge technical difficulties. You could get Radio Bury – the Icelandic fishermen were getting it off the banks of Iceland – but they couldn't actually get it in Bury. I think a local station like GMR does fail badly because it isn't a local radio station. It covers too big an area. There's no connection between North Manchester and South Manchester. I think this is something the regional television companies experience as a problem as well. Cumbria has always been a problem; it has been shifted from area to area.

Rob McLoughlin: Do you really believe that people in North Manchester aren't interested in South Manchester, even when you're talking about the Commonwealth Games or employment figures?

Judie Collins: I think Manchester has become much more of a community. Ten years ago, it didn't have the city feeling that, say, Liverpool had. Radio Merseyside has always been very successful. I've worked all over the country and I know where local radio works and where it doesn't.

Rob McLoughlin: So your message to Colin is 'go more local'.

Judie Collins: Yes.

Rob McLoughlin: We'll take a response to that and then we'll take a final question.

Colin Philpott: I do remember the experiment in the 80s although I wasn't directly involved. I think you are right that there were some technical problems. I think it's also true that it did very well in audience terms. I can't remember which was the most successful.

Judie Collins: Wigan.

Colin Philpott: They were getting enormous weekly reaches over a short period of time so there clearly is a demand but, as you've implied Rob, I think there is community of interest called Greater Manchester. The airport, Manchester United, Manchester City, do actually bind people together. I think there's also hostility to the whole concept of Greater Manchester which I think is a particular problem here. I think Radio Merseyside's success to a large extent (and we would admit this) is down to its concentrating very much on Liverpool and therefore, in a sense, being a more localised station.

Rob McLoughlin: Okay let me take a final question here.

Granville Williams (Campaign for Press and Broadcasting Freedom): It's a point really about the cable and the global and local business. It's clear that many of the decisions to invest in cable in the UK were because there was a very favourable regulatory, or rather lack of regulatory, framework. Recently you've got the US Telecoms Bill. That's really opened up the market again in the States. I know that some US-based cable companies are now retrenching and going back – or at least they're looking at scaling down their operations here. How does that affect Nynex?

Simon Schroeder: I think scaling down the operation is challengeable in terms of Nynex. We certainly reduced our 'build' programmes this year, but that's in response to pressure from local authorities. It's in deference to other utilities-type work taking place and it's in response to controlling the pace at which we manage the 'build' as we go forward. There's no question of saying, 'Oh we're going to pull out'. It's always been recognised that the cable industry started off with a hundred odd multiple service operators, now there are sixteen multiple service operators – the big ones – and there's only going to be three or four in a couple of years time. So we're seeing a period of convergence. If you look at the initial returns, one in five homes that we pass is now taking the services, and 90 per cent are taking the dual services – they're taking telephony and cable television. We haven't even started, apart from Frank Bruno's small affair with pay-per-view. It's coming in. There will be more of that later this year. Then, of course, we have GEMISIS where we're talking added value on the network and interaction with the society in which we operate. I don't think the cable industry is going to evaporate because I think the returns it's seeing and the potential it can see from some of the new technology is at last catching up with the cable that is actually under the ground.

Rob McLoughlin: You're saying there are going to be fewer operators?

Simon Schroeder: I think we'll see it go down to a very small handful of fairly powerful cable operators but we're not going to have a monopoly situation. There's always going to be at least a duopoly. Obviously, once the playing fields are levelled past the year 2000, BT will be doing a full remit so there's still going to be competition which will benefit the customer – but we're going to see convergence. I suppose the Dawn French campaign I spoke about earlier is the first evidence of the power of combining together. I suppose, depending on the success of that campaign at the end of this year, that will either accelerate or decelerate the process of convergence.

Rob McLoughlin: I'm delighted to say you're going to spend a lot of money on ITV to advertise it. I'm delighted to hear that, Simon. Thank you very much indeed. Thank you Colin. Thank you John for that illuminating talk. I'm going to leave you with this thought this morning. There is small radio station in Morecambe called the Bay and the bunch of people who run it decided to get some publicity a few months ago so they decided to send a Bay FM mug to Judge Ito (made famous by the O J Simpson trial). They were astonished – this is a true story – when they got a fax back from Judge Ito saying how delighted he was to receive this mug and he would treasure it. In fact, from that day to the end of the trial, if you looked at the O J Simpson trial and looked at his desk, there was a Bay FM mug with rulers and pens in it. You should tell that to your people who are selling chutney.

The Audience of the Future

Chair: Brook Sinclair
Director of ADCOMM Ltd

Alison Lyon
Counterpoint Research

John Eldridge
University of Glasgow

Brook Sinclair: We will now discuss the future of audiences. Audiences are not often central to symposia such as this because audiences are assigned to fringe halls. People know that audiences are there in vast numbers, consumers are there in vast numbers but somehow they are not often discussed and not always researched. If the research is done, it is not always presented. We're very fortunate today to have two people to discuss this issue and present it to you. One of them is Alison Lyon who comes from Counterpoint Research. She is a commercial researcher in the sense that she works for most of the major television companies and I am sure she guards some of their secrets: she will be explaining something about the work she is doing. May I say that I think it's fair to say that knowledge of the audiences of the future can only really be derived from the audiences of the present. I think Alison's research will be about present audiences but her thoughts will be about future ones.

The other speaker this morning is John Eldridge. John Eldridge is a very distinguished man, part of a very essential group in the history of research which attempts to change television – the Glasgow Media Group. For 20 years John Eldridge has been Professor of Sociology at Glasgow University. There is no higher chair in no greater town although I've got to say, John, its only the second best university. I would like to ask Alison Lyon to start and John Eldridge to speak afterwards. Thank you. Alison.

Alison Lyon: I think this particular title is the broadest and certainly the most complex I've ever been given to talk about. I hope you won't mind if I only look at one particular element of the audiences of the future. Many other speakers have explored the opportunities and possibilities afforded by new communications technologies. I'd like to look at the context in which they'll be consumed, i.e. the typical household viewing context.

No matter what technologies become available, and the limitless scope provided by the new carriers, there are two constraints – the audience and the viewing context. The developers and marketers of these new technologies, and those who wish to exploit them must acknowledge that context or it is difficult to see how their product will achieve the revolution in viewing that they hope to see.

The new technologies are being approached from two very different angles with current cable and satellite multi-channel packages in the middle. In the world of video-on-demand, which I see again BT was trailing in London last night, individual choice and individual action are everything. As someone said to me in a group discussion we were holding, 'No one should tell me what I have to watch and when you want me to watch it.' BT's promotional material on a video-on-demand experiment focuses very much on just how much choice is gives the television consumer and how it will mean the end of schedulers and the beginning of true consumer choice: 'Within 30 seconds the viewer can view and review their choice'. I'll argue that 30 seconds is far too much to ask of the viewer.

In between video-on-demand and the new digital multiplexes and the offers they might come up with, we have the multi-channel offerings of cable and satellite – tens of channels available parallel to each other, and also parallel to the mainstream terrestrial channels. Some structure is afforded by channel identity and personality. However, again the viewer is the one who is asked to research and choose. Currently, scheduling does seem to be more of an issue for the individual channels rather than for the Sky packages. As one very satisfied subscriber said: 'Television is things they choose to give me. Cable is the things I choose.'

At the other end of the scale we have what some may call, the tyranny of the four main terrestrial channels. Whilst extremely limited in choice, when compared with both satellite and cable packages and particularly when compared with something like video-on-demand, the scheduling and editing of the programmes carried by the four main channels provide a useability and simplicity that non-terrestrial and new technology broadcasters lack.

Branding, trailing and, in particular, a sense of structure, are even more fundamental in a multi-channel digital context. The technology can advance to provide hundreds of channels, some interactive, some specialist, some general interest. It can advance to the extent that the viewer simply has to press a button and their heart's desire appears. However, unless we find some means of guiding the viewers to their heart's desire, helping them negotiate their choice along with the rest of the viewing household, and some means of empowering them to use these facilities to the full – through intuitive user interface – unless this is provided, we may as well stick with what we have now.

At one extreme, the audience values simplicity and ease of use over choice. Someone summed it up as follows: 'When I come home at night I switch on that button and I don't want to have to think about which button.' Or: 'If it's not easy to find what's on, you bother even less. You stick with what you watched last week. You don't have to think about that.'

It seems to me that many of the noisy headlines, heavy with the promise of the new age in television and heralding the potential of new services such as video-on-demand and/or digital television, make two assumptions. One, that there is a single decision made about what is going to be watched, when, and on which television in a household. Two, that viewers are prepared to research, consider, source and order individual programmes, channels or brands on an hourly, or even half hourly basis, matching their moods, their needs, their interests, everything in this DIY schedule. Admittedly, if you are a shift worker the awe-inspiring choice at 2 in the morning of *The Learning Zone*, a documentary on prostitution in California or a stream of black and while films, then perhaps you will be prepared to put the effort into finding your ideal programme. However, this effort is surely put in from a baseline of very low expectations.

In reality, particularly during mainstream peak viewing times, the viewing context is very different. How do you feel when you sit down at the end of a hard day's work? In reality a complex series of negotiations is made, even in single person households. Few viewers, particularly families, enjoy watching programmes in different rooms on different sets. As someone said: 'It makes you feel really sad'. And they're unsure if multiple television actually solves the problem. One mother moaned to us that the problem with having more than one television is that you just have the same arguments because everyone wants to watch the one in the living room.

Thus accommodations and compromises are made. One correspondent reported that, in the early part of the evening, he was subject to the wishes and whims of his children and then his wife. He was allowed to choose when he could watch only after they'd exercised their prerogatives. He said: 'I usually get to watch *The Bill* because she's finished with her soaps. When the kids are up they have their monopoly for a while.' Someone else commented: 'Well that's the kids' time for the big television. They like cartoons and I can go on making his dinner'. A female respondent explained another constraint on programme choice: 'Well. I wouldn't watch that because I know my husband wouldn't like it anyway so there's no point'.

On the other hand, there might be a chance to snatch back control after he's watched *The Bill*. Another housewife commented: 'By that time I'm past thinking and he's fast asleep so I like a bit of light drama, something nice like that Catherine Cookson that's been on.' Even viewers in single person households claim that their guesses about who else might watching a programme could make a difference to what they watch. Someone commented: 'I wasn't really very sure about watching that. I thought it might be a bit of a nerd's delight. But actually it was excellent.'

What this means is that, unless a family has identical interests and tastes, there might be around half the audience watching a programme at any time who are not currently exercising their own choice. How many men complain it's their wives who make them watch *EastEnders* and *Coronation Street*? It's their fault that they've become hooked on those soaps. Interestingly, this has been one of the main justifications for regulation in this country. So long as television is not a matter of active and informed choice for each individual watching, there will be a requirement for the great feelings of the greater audience to be taken into consideration.

One father illustrated this by describing his surprise when, in the middle of a programme he was watching with his teenage son, something unexpected happened. He commented: 'It's when you're all sitting there, thinking you're safe and suddenly something like that hits you.' What had hit him was Mel Smith and Griff Rhys Jones kissing deeply for around five seconds: 'I don't think its embarrassing in itself but it's when you're watching with them it starts to get uncomfortable.'

The second point concerns the effort that the audience is prepared to put into watching television. Someone summed it up as follows: 'If I knew what I wanted then the chances are I'd have gone to the cinema. The great thing about television is that you're not sure what's in store.' That's what I found interesting about a programme they'd watched, a documentary about female circumcision: 'I'd never have voluntarily switched that on.' Someone else more brutal in their summing up said: 'I don't want to interact with my television. I want to switch it on and have it work for me.'

So perhaps a pre-packaged tyrannical schedule has a number of advantages. It provides a scheduling service in the audience's eyes as well as trying to hijack you for the evening. For instance, this is a comment someone in the audience made: 'They always put on soaps to cheer you up, take you out of yourself before the stuff you can concentrate on later.' TV challenges the viewer in unexpected ways. It can actually challenge stereotypes and provide a focus for raising otherwise avoided topics. One young man said he'd happened to sit down one night to watch *EastEnders* with his mother. It was when *EastEnders* had the daughter who ran away. 'My mother said to me (he's actually run away from home himself): Is that what it was like for you?' That provided a focus for them to talk about problems within the family.

So perhaps there is an argument that less – well presented – can be more. One individual put it as follows, and I must apologise to the Nynex man here: 'I must admit having just had cable for about six months, if anyone was trying sell me more channels, I would say please take back half of the ones I've got.' It is, put simply, more effort than most of us want to spend to analyse our moods and identify which programme suits that mood, find that programme and then route into a screen which, with video-on-demand, may be a far from straightforward exercise.

If we look at the example provided by video. That was supposed to be a way we could get more in control of our viewing. Whilst nearly all of us have had at least one video, their use is depressingly limited. Someone noted: 'I've had a video for six years now. I've managed to pre-record something once.' Then, in recognition of the difficulties in programming our videos, or perhaps in recognition of our reluctance to bother to learn how to programme our videos, user-friendly options such as Video Plus were introduced. However, all is still not well in the garden. Someone wailed: 'I've got a video with that Video Plus, which is good, but I can never find the newspaper with the numbers in it and it's more trouble than it's worth.' Even if we can work it out successfully, there's the issue of the discipline to label and store videos. Another frustrated respondent said: 'I've got a stock of around 25 videos with no labels or the wrong labels on them. So I keep buying new videos in case there's something I don't want to record over.' Heaven help the father who records over something that someone else in the household has recorded before they've had a chance to watch it.

So the future may not be all that straightforward. However, one thing is certain – television, as we know it, is going to change. Our children are going to make sure of that. Probably their children are going to push them even further: 'Our children tend to be much more technology literate,' someone commented in the groups. A child said: 'I've got a computer at home so I can show my dad how to get on to the Internet.' They're also used to handling a fast influx of information and images. Another commented: 'I don't know what's on when. I just zap. If my mum comes into the room she shouts at me.'

Many of them are growing up in a multi-channel environment where, for instance, BBC1 and ITV are simply another number on the cable box. They're much more used to interacting with the screen. But, at the end of the day, are they really going to want something different from television? Is their viewing context going to be truly different? I would argue probably not. As one wee boy, wise beyond his years, reported: 'I like watching the cartoons before my dinner. You forget about your day at school.'

It's interesting to note the impact that the proliferation of choice has had on day-to-day decision making. Before satellite and cable most of us had an idea what was on when. We could fill in the gaps with Teletext or the occasional look in the papers and listing magazines. Since the advent of multi-channel viewing we've all become much more reliant on the listings, reviews and recommendations. One wonders how we will make sense of the true video-on-demand or digital offers.

Perhaps the schedulers of today will simply become the programme librarians of the future. What used to be their decisions in the past will become our decisions – or will they? Perhaps the schedulers' new role will be programme reviewers and 'recommenders'. Or perhaps, rather than scheduling programmes for us, they will write software which will schedule for us. Certainly, some means of structuring access to hundreds of channels and tens of hundreds of programmes will be required by those of us who simply want a television to entertain, educate and inform us.

Perhaps, one day in the future, we'll buy our new television and television packages and part of the in-store service will be a household personality and character profile. All our tastes, preferences, and dislikes will be programmed in, as well probably as our comforts, stretch and panic zones – just to make sure we're still educated by our television. Each member of the household will take their turn and their responses will be programmed in. We'll take the new beast home and, as we turn it on, it will suggest a programme choice, suited to our tastes for that particular evening. At the end of the day, will this really be a new age or will it be the case that the appearance of a pre-structured, suggested schedule will, like now, lead on to exactly the same arguments, rank pulling, compromises and negotiations most of us engage in every day and night when we decide to watch a bit of telly? I'd be very surprised if it didn't.

Brook Sinclair: Now John Eldridge. We'll take questions after John has talked. Thank you.

John Eldridge: We've heard from time to time about dinosaurs and I guess when I've finished you might think I'm in the company of dinosaurs as well. I'll remind you that they did actually last quite a long time. I also aim to point out that there are a few predators around that we might want to take some notice of. I should also say I'm not a futurologist so that talking about audiences of the future has its own deep problems for me. But I certainly think there are some things or questions that we could ask one another and, perhaps more generally, talk about.

I mean, who wants to know about the audience of the future and why? Did previous generations ask about readers of the future? Well, I think sometimes they did. There was an interest in what could be produced for a population that became increasingly literate. Of course, particularly in the wake of the Industrial Revolution, the coming of the book, and the technology that made its production and distribution viable, did indeed create new possibilities for writers, book publishers, book sellers and, of course, for new readers and the growth of literacy.

As we know the products could vary from political and religious tracts to fiction ranging from Shakespeare to penny dreadfuls and Mills and Boon-style romances, from comics to technical and educational books on a wide range of subjects. There we could find a diversity of purpose. Information, entertainment as well, of course, as explicit ideological and value concerns about the kind of society that existed and how it could and should be transformed – the 'value' questions which are now at the centre of so much debate in literate societies. Some products exist to persuade us of a point of view and encourage us to action, others for enjoyment, even if enjoyment for some included horror stories and tales of terror.

Among our rulers and the circles of the élite there could be found those who recognised that literacy could be used as an instrument for social control, inculcating habits of obedience, defence and respect. Others also recognised that it was a gateway of access to ideas that were subversive in relation to the existing social order. Even the same book could become problematical from that standpoint for those in power. You'll find a lovely example of that in Christopher Hill's book on the role of the Bible in 17th century England.

This, of course, is an inherent problem for would-be censors. The same book that encouraged obedience to those in authority also permitted other questions. When Adam delved and Eve span who was then a gentleman? It was not just books like Paine's *Rights of Man* – you see that one coming as it were, it was signalled. There were other books that had this problematical status. The same book could manufacture consent but it could also manufacture dissent. That problem remains with us today. It's a problem around censorship. It's a problem about effects. It's a problem which one imagines will remain with us in the future.

If we think of the future we need the cautionary word of someone like Popper who made it very clear that it was very dangerous, politically dangerous, to talk about some kind of historical inevitability – that things were bound to work out in this kind of way because there were social underlying laws which determined it, that there was some kind of deterministic imperative. I mention Popper for another reason because he is often regarded as on the right of politics and, I suspect, was seen by Margaret Thatcher as one of hers. However, we should remember that for him the principle of liberty was central to his thought and he argued that social freedom was not to be equated with the free market. It will not be equated with the free market. He refers to a parade of freedom whereby unlimited freedom means that the strong are able to bully the weak and rob them of their freedom. Just as this can happen in terms of physical violence, so danger can be inflicted by those with economic power on those who are powerless.

For Popper this suggests a political remedy whereby social institutions, enforced by the power of the state, can serve as a check against unbridled economic power. For democratic reasons, the principle of non-intervention in economic matters has to be given up. It is the issue of democratic control which is central to Popper's concept of the open society. Will the future be an open society? Only in that way can we begin to make judgements or make possible considerations about what this future audience may be like. Will it operate within a democratic society?

I think it's important to say what somebody said this morning in one of the groups that the teaching of history now is not what it might be. There is no sense of historical depth or change, of where we come from. It's one of the plagues of certain forms of post-modernism that it's just ahistorical. Let's remember that the press was described as the fourth estate in relation to the Lords, spiritual and temporal, and the Commons. It had, that is to say, the democratic potential to be a weapon for freedom, challenging old aristocratic orders and new tyrannies. It's fascinating to see, almost 150 years ago, *The Times* offering its editorial view on the duties of the press, and you might be surprised to hear from a place that is seen as so Establishment that:

> The first duty of the press is to obtain the earliest and most correct intelligence of events of the time and instantly, by disclosing them, to make them the common property of the nation. The statesman collects his information secretly and by secret means. He keeps back the intelligence of the day with ludicrous precautions until diplomacy is beaten in the race with publicity. The press lives by disclosure. Whatever passes into its keeping becomes part of the knowledge and history of our times. It is daily and for ever appealing to the enlightened forces of public opinion. You may say educated forces of public opinion anticipating if possible the march of events, standing upon the breach between the present and the future and extending its survey to the horizon of the world.

The duty of the journalist we are told is the same as that of the historian:

> to seek out the truth above all things and to present to his readers not such as statecraft would wish them to know, but the truth as near as he can attain it.

It is a bit like a dinosaur, isn't it, to make a call for truth in our day? But this is for me as good a definition of the democratic potential of the press as one could wish to find.

However, this is the point I really want to emphasise: none of this can ever be taken for granted. It couldn't then, and it cannot be now. There is a pivotal question. Which way do the media face? Towards the powerful which we can recognise in the practice of corporate journalism, or towards the public? It is a question about the extent to which the media sustain a significant independence from ruling groups and economic interests such that they are able to perform a critical role in contributing to the health of a democratic society of publics.

There is no predetermined future of our society, including the extent and nature of its democratic character, nor about the future of our media structures and activities. History is on no one's side. It's very comforting to think it's on your side. It's very disturbing to think that it is not. But it's on nobody's side. What we've got to come to terms with is the fact that there is a cultural struggle to do with competing images of the kind of society we want and the values to be espoused.

This struggle has political and economic dimensions and the media are one important area in which such struggles take place. Media space is contested space. When we've gone through the question of changing technology, organisation, structures, strategies, questions of ownership and regulation, and so on, we have to recognise we are not dealing with neutral value matters – as though they are just a question of applying techniques to solve problems. We are dealing with questions about who is occupying space and for what purposes. Any concept of democratic space in the media and elsewhere has to be contextualised in the presence of powerful, anti-democratic forces.

These forces ironically can parade in the clothes of freedom, notably the notion of the free market. It should be a source of astonishment to us that the language of the free market is invoked so routinely by large corporations and multinational conglomerates who not only operate in rigged markets but help to do the rigging. Unless societies like ours, through political choice, seek to make them accountable our future audiences will be delivered to them with their choices pre-structured.

Let me give an example here of a well-known figure whose name hasn't passed many lips in the last couple of days but is about to pass mine – Rupert Murdoch. Not so long ago he gave a lecture to the Edinburgh Television Festival and he said: 'I've never heard a convincing definition of what public service television really is and I am suspicious of élites, including the British broadcasting élites, which argue for special privileges and favours because they are supposed to be in the public interest as a whole. My own view is that anybody who, within the law of the land, provides a service which the public wants, at a price it can afford, is providing a public service.'

So then, he tells us, it is competition in place of monopoly or duopoly that should be the driving force. Matters of quality are simply judged because they are in the eye of the beholder. Towards the end of his lecture, Murdoch describes Sky Television as a 'destroyer of monopoly power and creator of choice'. Then he complains about the legislation that has been called into being to prevent newspaper companies from participating in the opening up of broadcasting markets. This, as you know, is a continuing struggle and argument. 'The fact of the matter is,' he said, 'in Britain, cross ownership of the media is a force for diversity. Were it not for the strength of our newspaper group and our human capital resources, we surely could not have afforded to double the number of television channels available in Britain from February 5th.'

Now we might, I suppose, say on hearing such things that monopoly is also in the eye of the beholder. All this from the man who a year later effectively hijacked his rival BSB from under the embarrassed eyes of the IBA.

The competition we are witnessing is not free competition but the competition of multi-national conglomerates. It is not open to anybody to provide a service which the public wants. The choice that flows from this is not consumer choice but that which is performed by those with the capital to play the game. In place of the comfortable duopoly we have the world of take-overs and mergers. In other words, a drift and a thrust toward monopoly capitalism. Public service broadcasting in such a world is simply what comes out of these new formations. The democratic character is camouflaged by a populist rhetoric. The individual consumer, who may or may not wish to pay for access, is not to be equated with the social beings who, as citizens, discover that life is about co-operation as well as about competition, and that virtue and quality are not the natural outcome of the free market.

So we have here the whole notion that future audiences are, in some sense, at the mercy of predators. Now, of course, sometimes when the predator attacks, you can fight back. But let's remember, and it's explicit, that audiences are delivered to others as consumers, that is to say to advertisers, and they are also delivered potentially to politicians as voting fodder. I just want to make two points about the kind of future this suggests.

The whole question of advertising has a considerable history. I would draw your attention to the classic essay that Raymond Williams wrote, now quite a long time ago, on what he called 'Advertising, the Magic System'. The point I want to make is the way in which even conventional borders can be broken down between advertising and what is taking place. 'The border line,' says Williams, and this is a few years ago now, 'between the items or photographs picked up in the ordinary course of journalism and broadcasting and the similar item or photograph that has been arranged and paid for, either directly or through special hospitality through a publicity agent, is obviously difficult to draw.' Enough stories get through, and are even boasted about, to indicate that the paid practice is extensive though payment, except to the agent, is usually in 'hospitality' – if that word can be used in that context.

Certainly, readers of newspapers should be aware that the 'personality' items presented as ordinary news stories or gossip will often have been paid for one way or another in a system which makes ordinary advertising by comparison look respectable. Nor is this confined to show business. It has certainly entered into literature and it has probably entered politics. The extension is natural in a society in which selling by any effective means has become the primary ethic.

Today, the blurring of lines is a much more developed phenomenon and, unless it is challenged, it will, of course continue. We should notice, in particular, the role of public relations agencies in relation to the preparation of video news releases. These are pre-packaged news stories prepared on behalf of business or other interest groups which are then sent to newsrooms or transmitted by satellite to television stations throughout the world. These can come in two versions: fully developed videos in an already edited story which can even include voice-overs and a script indicating where the local news reader should read the appropriate lines. The second version is raw footage from which the edited version came. This can then be edited locally and interspersed with other material. It is in such ways that advertising, public relations and propaganda are interrelated in contemporary social practice.

If Williams' central theme is about the sensuality of selling in late capitalist society and the implications this has for our culture and our way of life, we can recognise that this touches on power as manipulation. Yet I want to emphasise there can be sales resistance and we can see this because advertising agencies themselves can face credibility problems and even go out of business. It is not all one-way traffic. If it were all one-way traffic, what we would be identifying would be a mass society. We're moving more and more towards one in which opinions are manipulated by the few over the many.

We are not so far from the cultural pessimism of the Frankfurt school who, after all, had reason to know about the ways in which Nazi political propaganda could penetrate German society. But even that power was not total.

Now I want to take just one example here, just on the advertising front, and refer you to Robert Goldman's *Reading Ads Socially*[1] which is a lovely book. He sees modern advertising as emerging out of a transition from competitive to corporate capitalism. He argues that we are living with the consequence of the attempt to transform the sphere of culture and desire via corporate advertising into a sphere of capitalist economy. Clearly advertisements are intended to connect with potential buyers. Typically this entails a process of framing. We, as audience or reader, have to recognise it is an advertisement we are looking at. There will be differentiated factors which is why so much attention is given to the logo – messages are encoded in a way which we can interpret. By now advertisers can assume we have a general understanding of the advertising code.

What I want to point out is the growing sense of reflexivity and knowingness which seems to be developing. We know that when an advertiser is confident that the advert is recognised and significantly approved, as perfected in market sales, then a long running campaign, sometimes over years, can be established.

We can see this in the history of the Guinness adverts in Britain. The first slogan, 'Guinness is good for you', appeared in 1928 with distinctively stylised posters and was so established that the slogan could eventually be assumed to be known by the reader to the extent that it could be playfully left out – even the slogan itself. 'My Goodness, My Guinness', 'Pure Genius' – they've entered the vocabulary of our culture. Recently, Guinness has shifted an underlying macho image in an advertisement featuring a gay couple. There are market researchers who consider advertising strategies and there are advertising analysts who offer comment on such innovations. So take this from Virginia Valentine of Semiotic Solutions. I have trouble believing in both these names but here we go: 'The question you have to answer is this: Is Guinness exploiting its own code of eccentricity or is it breaking beer codes, trying to place Guinness outside beer culture? The gay couple are right on line with the Guinness code of playfulness.'

Now it's no accident that advertising analyst companies have titles like Semiotic Solutions. We need to recognise that those involved in such practices are very likely to have read the likes of Barthes and Eco and to speak confidently about signs, codes, signifiers and symbols. They may indeed have degrees in media studies, cultural studies or public relations, and see themselves and their practices as part of the post- modern world.

What I want to say, and time is running out, I'll draw to a conclusion soon, is that the reflexivity of the advertiser addresses the reflexivity and scepticism of the consumers. We know that you know that we are trying to tell you something and we know that you know how to resist things. We also know that you can identify the bogus world of adland, its models, its actors and its media distortions of reality. You want to see some connection with reality – life as it is with evidence of real people, far removed, we may note, from those 'real' people in detergent ads who have learned to say why they prefer one cleaner to another, even when tempted with an alternative.

I want to make one special point here. What is usually bracketed out from all this knowingness, sophisticated reference systems and the ability to deploy cultural quotations through music, art and photography is any understanding of the division of labour and the organisation of production which make these commodities available to all.

Hence questions of low wages, unemployment, poor working conditions, long hours of work, non-recognition or de-recognition of unions are, we might say, out of frame. The urban young people who feature in Levis advertisements are not dissimilar from those who work for low wages in fast food establishments. The clothes we buy may come from low wage economies which may even use child labour. Those who make garments for the fashion industry, that produce the highly visible products for fashion advertisements, often work on very low wages in uncongenial conditions without union protection. This we do not see and Goldman does well to remind us of such things by commenting on the way in which post-modernism as an ethos has failed to approach and to deal with this.

There is then this kind of reflexivity, where advertising is a continuing element in the whole game in the search for the captive audience, but the captive audience becomes more elusive. There is a kind of knowingness but, underneath it, there is a failure to address the question of the kind of world we live in.

I would like to say something about the way in which that kind of public relations stuff is also fed through by various processes to the whole business of political packaging. Political packages also make their impact, not just in party political broadcasts, but also in the way propaganda is offered us as news. I'm thinking of the way in which privatisation took place and became a central news item – it's important to say that.

One last thing: if we want to ask questions about future audiences, we do have to ask questions about the kind of society that might be possible, that we want, and that we are going to have to struggle for. Now there is one analysis of the future which we should take notice of which is Ulric Beck's work on the 'Risk Society'. The central point is that the Risk Society has brought into being a whole lot of contingencies and problems around pollution, radiation – issues around the environment as a result of the process of industrialisation.

What I want to say is that kind of reality will come breaking through whatever the future mediascape has in store for us. That kind of reality will come breaking through and we'll have to address that as people and as publics. The media may focus on it from time to time. We remember the Milford Haven oil tanker and all the media interest. Ask yourself one question: Are the oil tankers still going in and out of Milford Haven? Where is the democratic control? These are the things that can be challenged and we can articulate these challenges. One of the challenges we also have to make theoretically is to the kind of stuff that goes under the name of post-modernism – endless descriptions and celebrations – which does not put into focus real problems faced by real people in a very uncertain world. Thank you.

Brook Sinclair: Would anyone like to talk optimistically about the future? If there's a question, or you'd like to talk about it, fine.

Questioner: It was a comment for Alison Lyon really. Broadcasters are particularly preoccupied at the moment with the development of electronic programme guides and, given your scenario about the fact that people aren't really using Video Plus effectively, what about PDC technologies. I gather Channel Four is going for the full developed version of PDC in the New Year and other stations are too. What do you think the prognosis is for the future in terms of electronic programme guides? Are the audience going to be as manipulated as we think they might be?

Alison Lyon: I'd say probably, 'Yes', given the mastery of remote control that an electronic programme guide is probably going to require. The sort of user-friendliness of being able to open a magazine or go into a video store and see the person's face who is recommending something to you – it has to be a very extraordinary EPG to provide that kind of service and recommendation, the user-friendliness and usability that are available in other media at the moment. I just can't see another moment in the viewing day being dedicated to finding out how you work the dratted EPG. It's yet another, on top of a lot of things the viewers are being asked to sort out for themselves.

John Mundy (University College, Warrington): An intriguing analysis from John there. What worries me is that while my heart agrees with the sort of analysis you're making, what I'm crying out for is some strategic overview of how this resistance, through the process of cultural contestation, actually materialises itself. You know what I was trying to say earlier in the small groups. What I think is happening is that we are being re-positioned as audiences in much the same way that youth was re-positioned in the 1950s. It was necessary for competitive capitalism, particularly in the States, to re-position youth so that they became buyers of all the commodity products. That clashed enormously with the infrastructural values, for example, of American high schools which were deeply anti-materialist and into organisation, discipline, and so forth. The re-positioning of 50s youth culture was a process of re-positioning consumers to take advantage of the new technological goods that were on offer. I see the same thing happening to us now. It's not something that I entirely agree with but I don't know what the strategy is to resist. What I said in the paper was that you get outbreaks. You get the outbreak over the Bruno-Tyson thing. You recognise the cultural inertia of pay-per-view. Interesting that the man from Nynex said: 'Well, there's more of it coming folks.' I'm sure there will be. There is resistance but there is no strategy and I just wondered if you'd got more to actually say about saving our souls.

John Eldridge: Well that's not a bad list for a start. Was there somebody else who wanted to add to that.

Granville Williams (Campaign for Press and Broadcasting Freedom): I agree with what John is saying. Certainly, I'd attest to the resonance of your analysis and it's quite clear that I've been involved with the campaign since '79 and, if I were to draw up a balance sheet, I'd be in deep debt because on many of the issues that we've been concerned about we've seen major retreats. If one looks for example at the Broadcasting Bill. There's a very interesting case study there. I'm sure you're aware of the way that a group of media organisation sets up Market Access International to do the lobbying to get a political agenda changed. We are seeing the results of it now. It seems to me there is a major inequality between the kind of democratic dissenting voices which are very widespread. If I could give you a quick anecdote. I wanted to go to America to San Francisco to a Media Democracy conference and I got the money to go – very difficult but I got it. I phoned up and said can I have a place and they said: 'No, Sorry we're oversubscribed. You're number 251 on the waiting list.' Now that's at the heart, if you want, of a major media concentration. There is dissent. There are concerns but how can they be expressed, especially after yesterday with Jack Cunningham and the articulation of New Labour's 'vision', that seems to me a real problem.

John Eldridge: Thank you very much. If I had a strategy I would have told you. But I did make the point about futurology. What I'm reminding ourselves of is that there always is a struggle and it is a struggle over values, over the way in which they are incorporated. That is not a Luddite thing to say because we can fully recognise that all kinds of new technology, whether we are talking about the book in the first place or the latest kind of technology available – that can be used in all kinds of ways and they all carry with them democratic potential.

Questions of ownership and control and power must stay on the agenda. What happens is such questions are subordinated or neglected because we speak in technical terms. We see it as a language of certain problem-solving things and we make all kinds of assumptions about it. There are significant absences in our discussions about these things. Now we are talking about the possibilities of struggle and, you know, battles are won and lost. That's the reality of it. That's the message I got from Thompson's major review of the working class. There were battles lost. It didn't mean they were wrong or at least you might have agreed with them but they were real struggles. So the question of agency comes in. When I hear about research reports on active audiences – big deal. They can kind of have a little 'think' about whether they're going to do this or that. What I want are audiences who become activists.This can happen in unexpected ways. It can happen when reality breaks through as a result of some of the consequences of the risk society. We see it now with BSE. These things happen and sometimes they are unexpected and even unanticipated by many people.

The last thing I'd say on the question of strategy is, what was the Thatcher strategy? Well, maybe there was one there. Many of us around at the time wouldn't have thought possible that it could be the way it has become. How many people would have predicted in 1978 how it was going to be in 1989 – or now? You know I defy anybody to say they could do that. Now the lesson I get from that is an optimistic one, believe it or not, which is things can be utterly different. Can you imagine? But they have to be struggled for and they have to worked for. Therefore, if they go by default, it is then left to the powerful and, at that point, the audience has just become passive whatever kind of research label you want to give it. There are ways in which the public can be re-activated. That is the hope that I put before you.

Brook Sinclair: I think Bryan Luckham wants a few words.

Bryan Luckham: In posing my question, I'd like to link up with what was said in the first paper yesterday which was very impressive. But one recognised straight away that, although it was international and considerable in scope, and so on, it was partial. We really don't know what is the totality of the pattern of communication. I mean one has to ask – has gossip diminished, old wives' tales, informal social communication, social interaction? We often don't know and we perceive those threats, those possibilities as much greater realities than they often are. I recall Francis Williams – the historian of the press – talking about the 1945 General Election which, as you know, was an overwhelming Labour majority win that the *Daily Mirror* which supported the Labour Party, devoted 10 per cent of its space to coverage of the election and, on average, readers spent 10 minutes reading the *Daily Mirror*.

What I think this says is the media often reflect and follow public opinion rather that determining it. If one wants a strategy, one thing I would say is, 'Don't panic'.

Brook Sinclair: I just want to make one observation about that. It's always true in research that the opposite of a statistic is true. If 27 per cent of people are hotly in favour of something, it's possible that 73 per cent are against. It's also true about watching television; 50 per cent of the nation might be switched to television in the course of one night but it's also true that 50 per cent of the audience goes out. So you also need to research the audience that goes out and ask what it is doing and, maybe it is having a gossip, doing something else, being politically activist.

Jo Langham Brown (University College, Warrington): George Bernard Shaw said, 'all reasonable men support the status quo, therefore, all progress is the result of unreasonable men.' I'm sorry about the sexism – unreasonable 'persons'! The trouble with the media is that it does marginalise the 'unreasonable' – the dissenters. We have the classic case over BSE. Lacey was called a neurotic. I think those of us who see ourselves dissenters find it very difficult to be optimistic, spaces of dissent are not really there in the mainstream media because of the tendency to homogenisation. It does not leave much room for the 'unreasonable' people on whom progress might depend.

John Eldridge: You see I think BSE is a question of the breakdown of trust. This is a very good example of something coming out of a situation which has got terrible dimensions to it. Of course, one thing we learn from this is that those who live by public relations can also die by public relations. No one will ever say John Gummer's name again without remembering the hamburger. That is very important because it means attempts to manipulate do not always work. It reminds us that there are important ways in which critical judgements should be offered. In that instance the Minister knew perfectly well that the scientific work was not completed. Yet the public relations discourse intruded and, if I could use the word, 'contaminated' democratic activity. But I take hope from that.

Student Questioner: What I'd like to say is this. When you talk about optimism you talk about political theory. What comes to my mind, as an American, is the concept of original sin and religion which is inherent. The potential of man can go either way. The media can go either way regardless but the potential exists. There is good potential and bad potential. That's, like you say, based on values. It is a value judgement.

If you're going to be optimistic it is only possible if you put faith into something. You have to put faith in the individual or into the collective. You talk about market forces in this negative connotation because there is this distrust of a concentration of power – which is justified. We have seen manipulation. We have seen exploitation which is a concentration of power. But in the same sense when you talk about putting the choice into the individual there is this lack of faith in the individual in your society. You say this person cannot make choices. What I'm saying is, if you want be an optimist, you have to choose. You cannot say you don't trust the individual, you must trust individuals in society as a whole. You trust only a few people making decisions. How can you be optimistic? You have created a system where there is no potential for hope. I personally put faith in the individual and I'd like to say let individuals do it. That is what the market is about. If they don't know they can go to the right sources. I don't know anything about health so I go to a doctor. I don't make any decisions on health. I'm rational enough to know that. What I'd like to say is that if you're going to want to be optimistic put your faith somewhere. That is all I have to say. Thank you.

Alison Lyon: Can I just say, I would never say the audience is not capable of making choices. All I was saying was that, in that context, they are unlikely to bother. They want a scheduler like you want a doctor. It's how you get to those schedulers and how you get to the programme developers and those who own the media. Give the audience a say at the point that we talked about. There is a whole programme of audience research alongside political activity. It is a very different thing but it is important that media companies realise it.

Brook Sinclair: We end on a very interesting note. Thank you very much indeed.

Reference

1. Robert Goldman (1992), *Reading Ads Socially*, London: Routledge

The Broadcasting Bill and Digital Programming:

Working in a Changing World

Chair: Martin Wainwright
Northern Editor, The Guardian

Tony Lennon
President of BECTU (Broadcasting, Entertainment, Cinematograph and Theatre Union)

Michael Morris
Director of Personnel, Royal Opera House

Martin Wainwright: Yesterday, when I realised this event was going to be today, I rang a friend at the BBC at Oxford Road and said, 'Could you just tell me very quickly what digital programming is?' So I fall into the *Private Eye* category of 'newspaper hack baffled by new technology'. But I've done what we journalists call research. I've printed out a quick bit of data from the computer base and I have discovered that Virginia Bottomley thinks digital broadcasting could transform our viewing and listening habits. But another commentator says Mrs Bottomley's revolution means not enough money to provide the channels that most people don't want, through a technology which is about to be superseded. So I'm hoping to learn from our two speakers here. Tony Lennon is the President of BECTU, and he's very much in the front line of this matter, both as an engineer at the BBC and, of course, in his Union capacity, with all his members facing the uncertainties and opportunities brought about by the new technology. Michael Morris stands to be a beneficiary of digital broadcasting, in that those of you who saw that wonderful fly on the wall programme about the Royal Opera House, had it been digital television, would have seen him in even more clear and graphic detail as he wrestled with the negotiations over how many thousands of pounds the staff should get for moving scenery and so forth. He's not really here in that capacity, but because he's had 29 years with ITN and is therefore thoroughly versed in broadcasting. So I'm going to ask Tony to start off and Michael to follow.

Tony Lennon: Thanks very much, Martin. I was faced with two killer questions when I came in today. One of which was, 'Well, since it's a digital discussion, you'll obviously have a multi-media presentation, won't you?' Which I haven't. The other question was more searching: 'Why is it that a trade union person and a human resources wallah from the employer side are doing possibly the main discussion of this event about digital broadcasting?' Well, Martin's given me an excuse, which is that I'm an engineer. I'll leave Mike to think his up while I'm talking.

But let me just quickly describe what I'd like to explain to you. I'd like to cover the concept of digital technology in the broadcasting and multi-media sense. Because, actually, when we talk about digital in the industry and in the Union, we increasingly are talking about a seamless continuum which really spreads from publishing via CD-roms and other forms of information dissemination, right through to the other end, which is mass broadcasting of entertainment product of one sort or another. And it actually embraces, along the continuum, more or less any intellectual product you can think of at the moment – and as I always say, there's probably plenty that haven't yet been invented.

So, in a sense, that's what we mean by digital. Though I also must touch on the question of the development of digital broadcasting as outlined in the Broadcasting Bill which is currently going through Parliament. It may have profound effects on the future of public service broadcasting in Britain. It may not change it at all, or it may completely kill it off. And lastly, I'd like to talk about some of the pitfalls from an audience and democratic point of view that lie ahead on the great digital platform that is gradually unfolding before us into the next century. And it's not all going to be good news, by any means. But I'll come to that in a second.

Let me begin by just going back to that continuum, and doing the thing I really ought to, which is mentioning the workers – coming from a Union, as I do. Without any question, we are witnessing now an almost uncontrollable concentration of ownership. Not just of the traditional boring old things like radio and TV stations and newspapers, but a concentration of ownership of every kind of published intellectual material in the hands of fewer and fewer companies on a global level. Democratically, this poses the problem of how do you grapple with these people? Who do you ring up to sort things out?

But the effect of this on workers is that we are probably on the verge of the media or multi-media or entertainment industry becoming one of the worst Klondyke free markets for labour that we've ever seen. It's going to be impossibly difficult to apply regulation in any shape or form to the way that people are employed, certainly in this country. Companies are multi-national in their nature, which makes it very difficult for ordinary unions, ordinary governments, to get hold of them; and it is increasingly becoming an industry where the cutting-edge skills are found in younger and younger people who are burnt out very quickly indeed, partly because their skills just become irrelevant, partly because they're happily allowed to work themselves into an early grave in the knowledge that there'll be another crop coming out of universities – or, as happens in game companies, another crop coming out of the fifth form – next week.

So, from a worker's point of view, the future is quite horrifying, although the changes do imply an increase in the amount of entertainment and media product that is made, and, possibly, a broadening in the scope of material that is produced, which will allow people to explore themes and ideas which at the moment don't get much of a look-in.

Let me move on to the multi-media and the digital thing. I've said already that multi-media spans this great continuum of products. The thing that knits them all together is actually a technical development where anything you can name can now be converted into digital form. I won't bore you with the technicalities of why digits are attractive, but amongst other things, they're easily portable, they don't suffer degradation, they can be chopped about quite easily. Many of the techniques for manipulating products in a digital form can be learned by anybody, and many of you will have kids at school at the moment who are already doing precisely this kind of manipulation on their own PCs in the classroom or at home. And above all, digital products are a highly saleable, flexible, sexy way of marketing information.

Now, the name of the game in the media industry round the world at the moment seems to be 'buy up any intellectual property that you can'. That means programmes, but it also means a whole load of other things. It means sheet music, it means books, it means drawings, it means architectural, industrial designs – anything that might easily be re-saleable when it can be passed from point to point, inexpensively, is being bought up by the big global media interests.

Their lesser interest, actually, is the means of getting this to people. Strangely, that is perhaps the less developed part of the great change that we're seeing. In this country, alright, a tiny, tiny fraction of this exploitation of intellectual products will be the showing of TV programmes via digital means. Where, at the moment, we've got British Telecom under a legislative straightjacket where they're not really allowed to carry live TV, they're running experiments in Ipswich and Colchester, and have just started one on Westminster Cable; and we've got the prospective Government plans for digital TV in this country, but they're not even passed through Parliament... And thirdly, we have Rupert Murdoch, waiting in the wings, but quietly developing his own digital satellite system which will not involve the old public service broadcasting chain of transmitters. It will be digital satellite TV, straight into the dish on your roof.

So, strangely, the means of delivery is probably lagging behind the strategic thinking of the big companies, who have made sure they get in there first and buy all the product up. And actually, that's one of the reasons that the deals which have been reached with the film libraries and national libraries and institutions in many countries of the world, that's why they've been happening over the last five to ten years. So, the ease with which this digital stuff can be moved around is absolutely crucial, and that's why we can't really talk about digital TV in Britain or anywhere else without being mindful that this now seamlessly interlocks with a whole multi-media industry which is still in its infancy, but which I think inevitably, given the amount of money being pumped into it, is going to become an increasingly serious factor over the next five to ten years.

So that is where I start talking about multi-media. Very quickly to bring people up to speed on what's happening in this country – and, although I'm talking to an informed audience, it's always worth spelling out the bare bones of it – the Government's proposal is that frequencies will be made available for the broadcasting of digital TV. It's basically pictures. Some of them will be 4x3, as they are now, others may be higher aspect ratio, a more cinemascope-type format, and that will really be up to the operators of the channels to decide how they do it. There will be six people – organisations – actually operating channels. Not all channels will cover the whole country. It ranges from about 98% coverage down to something like 70–80%, depending on who you ask about it, and, on each of those channels, it will be possible to carry something like six TV programmes. Now, depending how you use the space, you may want to put high definition television on, in which case you get fewer TV programmes on each channel. You may wish to degrade the quality, in which case you can probably squeeze on a lot more than six.

That, essentially, is what is being proposed. It's going to run on the existing network of terrestrial transmitters and aerials, so there will be no addition on the roof for people. And at the moment, the starting date mooted by Government is some time in the next two to three years. That's what's being said. There is a major drawback, however, to the Government's proposals. The immediate increase in the number of channels isn't really going to be all that dramatic. There doesn't seem to be a lot of interest from operators, especially when you consider the investment costs, not just for the operator building a new transmitter, but investment costs for the audience buying a new box to put on top of their TV.

So there's a great uncertainty about that. Secondly, there is this threat of Murdoch in the background, who has the hardware infrastructure there already, has deeper pockets than many of the people who existed in the public sector broadcasting system in Britain, and therefore may have a lot more money to plough into getting the thing started up his way. Now, if Murdoch gets started with satellite digital television, I think it's an absolute dead cert that the Government version will not get off the ground. But, make no mistake: the Government's version is far preferable to anything that Murdoch is going to offer us. It will be publicly regulated. It will not be owned by just one person. It will allow a space for the existing public service broadcasters to continue selling their wares and, particularly when you look at the existing broadcasters, it offers them a solution to the future pressure on airspace costs, which is going to rise over the next 20 years or so. There are lots of demands for radio spectrum, particularly for mobile communications and applications like that, and the people who want it are prepared to pay money – which, at the moment, the broadcasters don't really do for the spectrum they occupy.

If this pressure grows, and the public service broadcasters who operate in this country face increasing bills for the airspace that they use, they will have missed a great opportunity if they have not already made provision for switching to digital TV, which occupies a lot less expensive space but enables you to squeeze the same number of programmes into it.

Now, that's the technical and home-baked economics lecture finished. That, basically, is what is happening on digital TV at the moment.

There are others closer to the debate in Westminster than I am, but my reading is that, unless a white knight, like the BBC and a couple of big manufacturers and one or two of the commercial operators, unless they step in soon, there is no guarantee that the official UK digital service, publicly regulated, will get off the ground. When people say, 'Don't be so gloomy,' I remind them about the official high-tech UK satellite broadcasting system on Marco Polo, which, in 1988–89 was in the hands of British Satellite Broadcasting, which went broke, or, to put it another way, merged with Murdoch.

So history has already given us one instance already of the brave new technology in pseudo-public hands not actually delivering. And I think, if you believe in public service broadcasting, there is a real threat there.

I've covered the technology of digital TV. Let me just mention digital radio. I think the prospects for digital radio getting off the ground are, at the moment, even slimmer than the Government's digital TV.

So far, the investment in the technology has been confined really to one or two of the big broadcasters, and one manufacturer. I'm told the number of receivers capable of receiving digital broadcasting in this country at the moment is just over a dozen, and even Viva in London would regard a dozen as being a relatively small audience. That's not a recipe for mass broadcasting to take off. The problem for radio is that, although the immediate pressure on spectrum for radio users is less because, believe me, the last bit of spectrum that mobile communications will want is that bit of medium wave down there – although FM is, I suspect, slightly under threat – the immediate pressure is less, and I suspect the great digital age won't offer a significant improvement in radio reception that would encourage people to buy the new kit to do it. Even if it were available.

In other words, there will probably always be a demand for mobile radio. The existing quality is probably going to be acceptable for mobile use for a long time to come and I think, therefore, we can be more sanguine about what happens to radio in the future. But don't expect a massive explosion of choice because of digital broadcasting on radio. It is not going to happen in the near future.

I said I was going to raise a few political and economic issues about digital broadcasting and where it's going. The first is this – and as a techie, I will always go back to this thing – the first is, isn't it strange that the Government should be legislating now on digital broadcasting at a time when we're all waking up to the fantastic possibilities and the immense importance of the whole multi-media world that may lie ahead of us? Isn't it funny that the Government has legislated on broadcasting without actually dragging in the telecoms industry at the same time? In the same way we look back on reports of the BBC of ten years ago, and think, isn't it funny how much of it came true, we might well look back on the current legislation in ten years' time and say, isn't it funny how little of it happened, because they missed out telecommunications in their thinking. Wouldn't it have been better if the British Government had actually stood back and looked at what it was presented with, which is a mix of not just existing broadcasters, but telecom operators, various institutions, other providers of information, all of whom may soon be sharing the same high technology and the same kind of platform to move their product around. Why didn't the Government do that when it would have made sense? And I worry that in ten years, the casualty might well prove to be the kind of public service broadcasting that we take for granted in this country, because there is very little space for that on the real Klondyke hillsides of the multi-media world which we're beginning to witness.

So, having left out telecoms, my second question is: where is the public space being created in the new digital multi-media era? To explain what I mean by that, radio started, and before very long we had the British Broadcasting Company, followed by the British Broadcasting Corporation, and then a host of other radio broadcasters in this country who were under public regulation. They occupied a space carved out specifically for broadcasting which had public social objectives. I listen to some programmes and wonder if it achieves them, but that was the intention.

Television came along. We had the BBC, and then the Independent Television Authority with its contractors, again occupying a space in the technology carved out specifically for the execution of public service aims. And, yes, we've probably said it before, because it's that kind of conference, but, by and large, British television still does it better than anybody else in the world.

We now see the next step-change, the next increment in technology for the mass dissemination of audio-visual and intellectual product. It is a change which actually brings quite new potentials, because it's two-way. It can be. The other important aspect about digits is the way that they are joined together is interactive and you can talk back. Now, with that step-change, I ask the question, where is the public space this time, in this new technology, where those same social aims and goals will be expressed – which becomes crucially important if you watch the old technologies withering away behind them, because where the hell are your social values in audio news product then? I think the frightening answer is, apart from the library, galleries and institutions which are at the moment experimenting of getting into commercial contracts with the purveyors and shippers of information, apart from that, and Government setting up sites on the worldwide web – sorry I had to drag the internet into this one, it's inescapable – apart from that, there's actually very little coherence in any government's approach to the crucial question, how you regulate the effects of this new technology and what came before it in terms of the public sector provision of information and entertainment, and what my lie ahead of it, which are profound economic implications, or point to point communication on a scale we've never known. So I just don't think that question's been answered, and I don't have an easy answer myself, though I've got a panacea at the end which might help.

The third important question I pose, since this is a broadcasting meeting, is the question: on this new platform, where really you've coded everything up in a way that can be easily manipulated, switched through various forms of viewing and access media, what is broadcasting? OK? Now, it sounds a question that might cause a few frowns, because it should be so easy to answer. It is the mass dissemination from one point of intellectual product intended for many, consumed by many, simultaneously in many cases.

But, if you actually look at where the multi-media platform is taking us, you can't really answer the question in that simple way. For example, are British Telecom really broadcasting at the moment, with near video on demand? Or is this a simple, one-to-one exchange between consumer and supplier? Is somebody who uses the Internet to operate Internet relay chat, which is a way of talking to any who care to listen by choice across the Internet, is that person broadcasting or is that person engaged in a parallel series of one-to-one relationships with people who have selected to tune in and share that interactive communication?

If you start to ask that question, how do we define broadcasting, you realise how inadequate the current legislation and some of our current definitions are. For example, the thing that differentiates British Telecom from the broadcasters at the moment is about one and a half lines in the European Directive, *Broadcasting Without Frontiers*, which defines what separates broadcasting from everything else. Now broadcasting, as we know, not just in the UK but in Europe, is an area of our economy where we have social values. The other bit, non-broadcasting, is an area where we may have taste and decency, but not really much else, and, if you look at the way British Telecom are being so light-touch regulated, it would be wrong to expect an immediate raft of obligations to be placed on them if they ever go live with their video-on-demand system.

Now, in that environment, again I ask the question, are we going to see that definition of broadcasting blurred so much that the area our social values live inside is compressed further and further. while a vast, probably commercialised sector opens up on the other side, relatively free from the kinds of obligations we expect our broadcasters to observe?

Finally, let me spell out once again from a union point of view where we think the employers are coming from. Some of them are very pleasant employers, but, ultimately, the commercial objectives are the same. On the hardware side – and this applies to digital broadcasting as it does to telephones, as it does to cable companies and everyone else – vast networks of wire and glass have been built up and the companies that own those networks have a sole interest in shipping digital information along those cables. To a large extent, they are not the slightest bit bothered what that information is. So, whether it's exclusive Stock Exchange information being shared by a few brokers in the City of London or it's a useful socially-orientated TV programme intended for millions, they are not bothered. All they want to do is ship digits. And that's very different from the hardware attitudes that underpinned broadcasting, where we have long had the view that the equipment exists to serve the broadcaster – there must be a 100% coverage liability, etc., etc.

So that's where the hardcore people are coming from. The software people are aiming to exploit their intellectual property rights – by the way, earning money off the backs of people who got paid very poorly for what they created many years ago and never imagined would be re-used time and time again for somebody else's profit, but that clearly is where the software people, as I suppose I ought to call them, are coming from. And you can just sense in broadcasting the beginning of the change, where many operators are now looking at TV by the yard. How do we fill eight hours a day? Can we buy it off the shelf? Great, we've got a channel. So that, from our point of view, is actually where they're coming from.

I'll finish with my panacea, and that is that all the horrible things I've implied may happen may not happen, and one of the things that will guarantee they don't happen is if, in this country, we commit ourselves to proper regulation. And we'll have to be very imaginative about how it is applied. Regulation must be one of our watchwords, and proper funding. And the funding needs to be ploughed primarily into creating that public space in whatever the new media are that retain a foothold for our public values.

So that's a kind of panacea. And I'll finish on a worker's note which should leave all of us feeling slightly more optimistic than you might be, listening to what I've said. There's a fascinating piece in the *New Scientist* this week about the making of the latest Disney digital movie, *Toy Story*. Now, digital technology, from the worker's point of view, and actually from anybody else's point of view, poses all kinds of threats to employment. And make no mistake, kids are already on their kitchen tables with PCs doing all the functions of editing, manipulating and re-packaging multi-media product that, ten years ago, would have been so specialist, hardly anyone could do it. Anyway, for workers, you automatically assume that digital TV, digital techniques, are going to put you out of work. I was very pleased to hear that the 110,000 frames of video which had to be cobbled together to create *Toy Story* each took between two and fifteen hours to be rendered on a super-computer, and to do it Disney had to hire in 117 super-computers plus operators to spend months and months doing it. So, you know, as one employment door closes, another one perhaps is just beginning to yawn open, and maybe it's time we got some of our members to start retraining on computer programming.

Martin Wainwright: Thanks for a very lively and stimulating talk which certainly emphasised the size of this subject, and the enormity of what's facing us. The discussion will now be taken up by Mike Morris, who draws on almost thirty years with ITN in broadcasting, and also on his more recent experience at the Royal Opera House, which so many of you have seen on television. Mike, I think you emerged as a goody in some rather hair-raising company. He wasn't that really horrible man who sacked the box office there. Over to you, Mike.

Mike Morris: Thanks very much. I'm going to begin by trying to answer the question Tony posed, which is, why am I here? And I'm not entirely sure. Maybe I was invited to give you a chance to look at someone who, after 29 years working for a television news company, was then daft enough to allow the BBC to come and film him for a year. But maybe that's not it.

Perhaps it's that someone who's been filmed by the BBC for a year might like the chance to get his own back, and speak up for the broadcasted, rather than the broadcaster. And, before I get to talk about the subject, I know you're all dying to know: what do the people at the Royal Opera House think about the programme? I think the general view is, it's a bit like the French Revolution. It's a bit too soon to tell whether it's done the Opera House good or bad. All one can say is, it's had a very good effect on the box office and a lot of people have come along to see if they can get the latest edition of *La Traviata* and the row in the crush bar as well. I think that, more seriously, one or two reputations have been damaged, maybe irretrievably. But the organisation as a whole, in the long run, will benefit. I suppose as someone who is, by profession, a journalist, I would say that, wouldn't I? But I do believe that openness does pay – though I bumped into Andrew Bethell, the producer of the series, in Channel 4 yesterday, and he's having a hard time trying to sell the idea of fly-on-the-wall television to anyone else.

I'd like to begin with a bit of history, and I'm sure all of you are familiar with it. When I started in the television industry in the 1960s, and indeed, for twenty years thereafter, the television industry was a very highly regulated one.

There were really only two major players, the BBC and the ITV companies, who acted together and were a single producer and employer, really.

Employment within that system was very stable. It was unusual for people to move from the BBC to ITV and back again. Job security was good and earnings were high and I remember when I first became Director of Personnel at ITN, a figure which has stuck in my memory is that, in 1988, the average earnings of television news cameramen was £55,000 a year. That's 1988. Well, they're nothing like that now, as you can probably guess.

Then along came the Broadcasting Act in 1990, creating a new framework, which at that time we thought was going to be the future. Now, of course, we know that it was only a step towards a future which is going to be even more different to the past than the current regime is. What we've got now is a semi-regulated industry. There is now an openness and a competition in the industry which was lacking before 1990, and the effect that this has had on employment has been devastating. If you take the commercial companies alone, they have halved and probably more than halved the numbers employed.

When I first became Personnel Director at ITN in 1988, there were 1,200 employees. There are now less than 600 and ITN produces more programming than it did then, including news for radio. There has been a shrinking in the BBC, but nothing like on the same scale, and the BBC remains protected, because it has a protected source of income. And of course, there is regulation of the right to broadcast and the right to appear on certain frequencies. Even now, over 60% of the workforce in broadcasting is self-employed or freelance, and so I can only agree with what Tony said about the Klondyke nature of the industry.

So, what is the future going to bring for employment in the broadcasting industry? I share Tony's doubts about how quickly this future is coming. But it's not just a question of the regulation or the laws which are enacted by government. The changes are coming through technology anyway. And what you're seeing is a convergence of technologies, where broadcasting, television, information technology computers and telecommunications are all converging to produce one great new industry. It is the new industry of the 21st century.

What is going to happen to broadcasting in that environment? And to the people who work in it? I think the answer is obviously one which we don't know, but in order to try and catch up on what has been happening in the industry since I left it two years ago, I decided to buy the latest edition of Broadcast, just to see what's happening on the cutting edge of broadcasting, employment and industry. And as I used to do, I turned first of all to the ratings, which I always find is a good indication. And in the week ending 25th February, first in the ratings was *Coronation Street*, second in the ratings was *Coronation Street*, third in the ratings was – you've guessed it – *Coronation Street*. In fact, if you look at the top ten programmes, there's only one that wasn't on the air when I left, two years ago, and that's *The National Lottery Live*.

Now, there's a serious point here. It's not so much only about the hardware and the means of delivery; and Tony, as an engineer, tended to concentrate on that. I think what you're seeing more is that programmes are being defined by their brand. And there is some comfort to be found from the power and the stability of the brands that exist in broadcasting. And the reason why *Coronation*

Street is where it is because it's such a strong brand. When I joined the television industry in 1965, I think that *Coronation Street* was number one then, too. So, people who work in television and work in organisations with only strong and well-established brands can take some comfort from the more established areas of the consumer industry, if you like, the confectionary or consumer products where, however low the cost of entry on a material or production basis may appear to be, actually the power of the brands does protect the existing products.

I then turned to the letters page. I quote from a letter written by someone who signs himself 'Media Graduate'. It could be someone in this room. 'As a media graduate, I'm frequently offered work for short periods of time and without pay. This situation is endemic throughout the industry, but seems an inevitable fact of life in an overcrowded market.' And I thought, that's certainly something that wouldn't have happened under the old regime, and where's it going to take us in the future? And again, I haven't got the answer to this. But perhaps what I'm saying is that broadcasting and people who work in it may find themselves in what is quite a small niche in a vast new industry, and that people who work in the making of programmes for broadcast may find themselves doing this almost as a hobby, and that the real business of – I don't know what to call this industry, information broadcast telecommunications – whatever it is, will be somewhere else. Which leads me, I suppose, to my final point, which is, what's going to happen to Personnel Directors and Heads of Industrial Relations in this new world, and, even more seriously, what's going to happen to trade unions?

I think that the future for a general trade union like BECTU is as unclear as it is for the industry as a whole. My sources deep within the BBC tell me that, even within recognised grades at the BBC, membership of BECTU has fallen below 50%. What it is in commercial television, I dread to think. Even less do I dare contemplate what it is in the freelance world. So, there is a problem where you've got no employer to get hold of: what does the union do? And what is the relevance of unions in that environment? It's a very difficult question, and I haven't got the answer to it. All I will say is that, as a personnel director in broadcasting, I always worked closely with the unions, particularly BECTU, and always found them very realistic people to deal with, and one common factor, and one welcome factor, between what I did then and what I do now is that I still find BECTU sitting across the table in the theatre.

And I'm happy to end on a slightly optimistic note in that, unlike broadcasting, in the theatre there appears to be a growth in the recognition of trade unions, rather than the other way round. And I've just agreed to recognise BECTU as representing a large number of administrative staff in the Opera House. And again, ending on what I hope is an optimistic note, the Opera House has just received the promise of a large amount of money from the National Lottery to rebuild the theatre. And one of the conditions which the Arts Council have put on the Opera House is that it should reach agreements with the unions, particularly the talent or performing unions, to enable the product of the Opera House to be freely and widely available through broadcasting.

So this is just another example, if only a small one, of how, as Tony said, as one door appears to close, another is opening, and the scope and access to broadcasting is going to grow. And there will be opportunities in the theatre and all sorts of other areas for the television cameras to get in. We must be optimistic, and see this as the great industry of the future.

Martin Wainwright: Mike, thanks for some really interesting insights. I thought the point about the brand names in an industry which is really obsessed with novelties is something very much to ponder. And now, it's over to you. Any questions?

Questioner: It's not a question, it's a comment. Looking at the spectrum and the use of available spectrum, something that no-one's actually mentioned is the use of the spectrum for things like Teletext and for electronic programme guides. You mentioned mobile phones, but I think we're obviously concentrating on broadcasting and digital and so on, but there's another range of predators out there who are looking for that. I just wondered if you felt we will lose the momentum and they will come in as well, if we're not careful.

Tony Lennon: I can't make specific predictions, but what I can say is, the general thrust is greater and greater pressure on spectrum for a whole variety of uses. It's interesting that you mentioned Teletext, because remember what I said about the hardware people who are just wanting to shift digits. If you look at the Broadcasting Bill, you'll discover that, among the range of uses that the so-called digital TV space can be put to is precisely the carriage of that kind of data services. So it's not just in other bits of the spectrum. It might well be that there's pressure on spectrum licence ostensibly for entertainment to start carrying data services. But I don't think this general pressure is going to abate. And yes, I make the gloomy prediction that if public service broadcasters don't take heed of that and find other platforms for their socially-useful product then they could well get caught out in ten or fifteen years' time when the operators of whatever it is, Teletext, data services, switching off and on remote electricity sub-stations – you name it – really start snapping at the heels of broadcasting.

Helen Read (The Guardian): If I was to save up and buy that thirteenth digital radio set, would that mean I could timer-record The Archers?

Tony Lennon: Actually, I don't think it would, because the ones that exist are all engineering prototypes and timers are things that marketing people put on devices, not engineers. I'm still looking for a radio that will do that.

Questioner: You've used the word 'regulation' quite a lot, both in terms of the historical development of broadcasting and the recipe for the future. What are your thoughts about the kind of regulatory body? How could it deal with it both nationally and internationally?

Tony Lennon: That's a question almost as big as the whole subject of where digits and broadcasting might be going. If you look at the basic principles of this, what our governments have taken as their right is the right to license the bit of technology which is the key to delivering the product, whether it's radio or TV, and controlling who actually runs that delivery system. And they've taken it as a right to specify to some degree what kind of product is carried on that delivery system, and they've taken it as a right, and actually a legal obligation not to carry certain types of material. Now, in a terribly broad sense, that's what our regulatory authority framework has been based on.

Now, let's look at the problems before I try to give you any answers. Firstly, regulating the delivery system. Well, funnily enough, the one system bit of this multi-media tapestry that could probably be regulated is actually the Government's version of digital TV, because that starts and finishes within the UK. It's based at a fixed address, the Daventry transmitter, Headington Road. It can be visited by Her Majesty's Government, and is likely to be operated by UK-based companies or companies that would fall under UK company law. So that one's good. The more seamless stuff – the 'what comes down your telephone line from whom' – if it's a telecomms operator based in this country, fine. But if your telephone band is broad enough to bring in stuff from elsewhere, who knows? And the famous Internet, and any form of open standard platform that leaks over the edges of the country is so difficult to regulate that I suspect most people would give up trying. Although, having said that, the US Government have just banned discussion of a number of things, certain forms of violence, pornography, discussion of abortion amongst other things from its Internet modes and is attempting to police it. So I await to see what happens there. Anyway, the delivery system: the only one that can be fully regulated is the Government's proposed system for digital broadcasting, in terms of regulating who does the operating, actually specifying the content, licensing people. But again, much satellite is out of reach, unless Europe is prepared to take really decisive steps in regulating what goes on. The possible winner of the great UK battle for digital TV at least, Rupert Murdoch, is already out of the country, operating from a satellite that is not licensed in the UK. And you then go on to what can be banned and you end up with another problem, which is the Red Hot Dutch problem, which is, if there can be open delivery to the UK, via a number of means, of things that are not deemed socially acceptable or worthwhile, how do you stop them?

Now, the Red Hot Dutch case simply involved banning the decoding equipment. In a world of open standards, which I think is where digital technology is probably taking us, where the integrity of the product can be maintained, some form of encryption might be used, but the basic technology all locks together and is used by everybody; I think it's difficult to imagine visiting every home to make sure the open standard universal decoder box – it will probably be a mixture of a TV and computer by then – isn't being used to decode things it shouldn't be decoding.

So I think on regulation there's a real problem, except for the traditional model we know. My view is that the equally effective route to this is to use whatever regulation you've got against a background where you are actually willing to do the unthinkable in Britain at the moment, which is actually to spend money, public money, ensuring that there is this public space I talked about. Now create the public space, make it good enough, and you may find that you buck the trend of this appalling free market out there, attracting all the audience away.

And I would hate to end up, for example, in the situation national public radio is in the United States, where brave and dedicated attempts in a country of 280 million people to run just one, one tiny broadcasting chain with social values at the front, depend on regular appeals and subscriptions and people becoming members. If we don't spend public money on the public space in the new medium, then, in a sense, our discussion of regulation is probably irrelevant because there are very few points at which regulation can be applied for social benefit. That's why, more than ever before, I believe the model we have established in this country of public funding and then locking as much of the commercial sector into the publicly funded bit as you can is probably our best chance.

Mike Morris: I'm fascinated to hear Tony taking on the Reithian mantle, talking about the need for the public space and the appalling free market. I actually don't think the free market is necessarily appalling, and I think that, whether we like it or not, it's here, and I think that Tony will secretly agree that, in the future, technology won't admit of regulation, and the best that we can hope for is that we can police standards of style and decency in the material that comes. But as to licensing suppliers to provide programmes which we think are suitable and desirable, I just don't think that's going to happen in the future.

Tony Lennon: Can I just come back on that?

Martin Wainwright: These union leaders!

Tony Lennon: I was probably dismissive in ruling out the private sector when I talked about the public space. It's a more complex argument. I'm not saying that the private sector is all bad. That would be folly. And actually, the private sector to a large extent forms part of this great public space of broadcasting that I keep talking about. What concerns me are two things. The private sector on its own does not deliver the same things we are used to getting in the public space that has been created for broadcasting. Left on its own, it won't deliver some of the things we want. Now, maybe the economics will change that. If the public space no longer exists, where does the demand go? That's from the economists. The second thing is that new things are going to start happening on this medium. Many of us actually don't know what they are. What I'm advocating is, those new things, as well as the old things, should be subject to the same kind of values as the things we are used to getting and enjoying. And my concern is that if that is left to the private sector, then we actually won't see the growth of those values in whatever the new services and products are.

Martin Wainwright: Thanks very much to you both, and can I just end with a plea to each of you. One is, Mike, I'm really pleased on the conservative *Coronation Street* front to see you're a Director of Personnel, and I hope you never become a Director of Human Resources. And Tony, I hope that, being a huge expanding industry, it won't be BECTU, it will be BECTI, O, A, God knows whatever these things begin with…

Tony Lennon: Twenty-six letters may not be enough.

A View of the Future

Chair: John Gray

President, University of Manchester Broadcasting Symposium

Tony Stoller

Chief Executive, Radio Authority

Interviewed by Nick Higham

BBC TV News, Social Affairs Unit

John Gray: To my mind, having served the Radio Authority a long time, I won't say it's perfect but I think it's the best regulatory authority we've had in the field of broadcasting. And speaking for it, we have Tony Stoller. And at the other end of this long table, we have Nick Higham, who has been asking searching questions about broadcasting, both outside the BBC and the industry, and within it. Gentlemen, you have time for about six rounds. Will you start the fight.

Nick Higham: John, thanks very much indeed. This is billed as a conversation about the future. It's also billed as a conversation between Tony and me. I first met Tony about fifteen years ago when he was Secretary of the Commercial Radio Trade Association, with the Association of Independent Radio Contractors (AIRC), which then occupied a rather elegant Georgian house in Bloomsbury. Since then the Trade Association has moved, first to a rather utilitarian office block just off the Edgware Road, and then to extremely nondescript premises in a very nondescript part of London, somewhere between Paddington Station and Notting Hill, while the radio industry, despite some vicissitudes, has gone from strength to strength – and I think that proves Higham's First Law of Trade Associations, which is, the more insignificant the industry, the grander the trade association.

Tony – and I mean this with no disrespect – has been associated with the commercial radio industry since it was very insignificant indeed. I think he joined the Independent Broadcasting Authority as a regulator in 1974, which was about a year after the first station went on the air. He has seen it from all sides. He was, after a time, Head of Radio Programming at the IBA. Then he went to the Trade Association. Then he went to run a radio station, Radio 210 in Reading. Then, rather surprisingly for those of us in the radio industry, he left and went to join the John Lewis Partnership, and ended up as Managing Director for many years of the John Lewis department store in Southampton.

Imagine the broadcasters' surprise when he came back last year. We thought we'd seen the last of him, but no, far from it. He returned to the radio industry as the Chief Executive of the Radio Authority, and I think when everyone had got over their surprise they thoroughly welcomed it. So the first question is, Tony: why did you come back?

Tony Stoller: I suppose the glib answer to that is, I sometimes wonder myself. But I have to say, that's not true. I came back because the job that I was offered is the job I always wanted, and that was the opportunity to come back to what I always think – and John, your words are very kind, thank you – is a small but almost perfectly formed regulator. And also to an industry which is increasingly fascinating. I never really expected to come back and I spent ten years as a shopkeeper saying I hadn't missed radio, hadn't missed broadcasting. And I spent two days back at Holbrook House with the Radio Authority and realised I had missed it dreadfully and it's very good to be back. It's an interesting and stimulating industry at a stimulating and difficult time.

Nick Higham: Now that you are back, what do you make of it? It's stimulating and interesting. Beyond that, what would you say?

Tony Stoller: I think the line I have tended to use is that radio has grown up. Saving your presence, the BBC has been grown up for a very long time. Maybe even for slightly too long. Commercial radio has suddenly found itself as a fashionable medium, to everybody's great surprise. Nobody's more surprised about it than I am. It's found itself moving from when I left it – 30 licences, pretty uncertain future – to 180, getting on for 200 licences, the medium that all advertising agencies suddenly want to put money into, which is the exact opposite to where I left it ten years ago; a medium which now attracts more listening to commercial radio than to BBC radio, a medium which has grown up, and one, therefore, which is having to come to terms with the problem of being grown up, just as before it was trying to come to terms – I thought rather unsuccessfully – with the problems of a difficult adolescence.

Nick Higham: And what about the Radio Authority itself? It had the reputation when you joined it of being a somewhat wayward organisation. It had made a number of very controversial decisions. It deprived LBC of its radio licence in London, it had granted an FM licence in London to Virgin. It was not without controversy. There was a job to do restoring its credibility.

Tony Stoller: I don't think so, and I would say that even if a member of the Authority wasn't in the audience. No, I don't think that's true at all. I think that any regulator, especially in such a fluid industry, is bound from time to time to make decisions which, from an outsider's point of view, look a little out of tune. I mean, I wasn't there for the decisions you refer to, the reasons why they were arrived at. But I'm quite clear that there will continue to be situations where the Radio Authority is looking from its own perspective, and that will not be the perspective that's most obviously perceived from outside. One thing I have learned in my six months back, which I had forgotten, but which was impressed on me very quickly, is never to believe what you are told. Because, on any particular issue, you will be offered three or four absolutely authoritative views which are, unfortunately, always totally contradictory. It's like Douglas Adams, one of the great users of the radio medium, and the notion that the answer to the ultimate question and the ultimate question itself cannot co-exist in the same universe. They are mutually exclusive. And that, clearly, is what happens regarding views about broadcasting regulatory decisions and a range of other decisions about broadcasting. Never believe the authoritative answer because there's another authoritative answer being given at the same time, and it's different.

Nick Higham: Well, give me the Authority's authoritative answer to the question: what do you think of the Broadcasting Bill? That must be exercising a lot of your time at the moment. What do you think of it as a piece of potential legislation?

Tony Stoller: I think the Radio Authority is broadly content with the Bill, or what the Bill is trying to do. I mean, there are lots of points of detail, and we might come on to those in a little while, but the Bill seems to be setting out from a radio perspective to achieve two things; and the Authority shares those aims. The first is to tidy up the ownership regime. Now, it's not for the Authority to say whether it should be tidied up to be more liberal or less liberal, but at least there is an opportunity to get some of the untidinesses of the 1990 Act sorted out and tidied up, and the Authority welcomes that. Equally, the Authority welcomes the Government's attempt to make possible digital audio broadcasting – DAB. And clearly, by extension, digital television, as well. And so from both those points of view, we broadly welcome the Bill.

There are some points of detail that we still think need tidying up. That's unsurprising. I understand that the 1990 Act began as a bill with 60 clauses and ended up as an act with 200 clauses. The Broadcasting Bill 1996 starts off with around 100 clauses. On that basis, by the time we get through the Commons Committee stage and the Report stage, we can expect to have 250 to 300 clauses. There's still a lot of detail to be gone through. But the broad aims of the Bill are those which the Authority would hope the Government would be addressing at this particular time.

Nick Higham: That's a very bureaucratic form of words, but I think we know what you mean. Let me ask you about a couple of those points in detail. On ownership, particularly. There are a lot of detailed rules now in the schedule to the Bill on the extent to which local newspapers may have an interest in local radio stations. At one point, there is a reference made to the Radio Authority assessing whether it is in the public interest or not for a newspaper to have a stake in a local radio station, and indeed whether it's in the interest of the workings of the respective markets – the newspaper and radio markets. Now, I imagine you know a fair amount about the radio market. What the hell do you know about the newspaper market?

Tony Stoller: Oh dear. My past is going to be exposed. I began in newspapers. In fact, I began in a city I'm not sure I'm allowed to mention in Manchester. But it's further left. I began working with the Thomson Organisation and I worked for the *Liverpool Daily Post and Echo*.

Nick Higham: You personally may have had some experience, but what does the Radio Authority know, and what justification is there for asking the Radio Authority to pass judgement on the newspaper market when it's assessing who should and should not own a radio station?

Tony Stoller: It's an interesting point. If I can be non-bureaucratic, one of the things which surprised the Authority when it saw the actual Bill was the extent to which the cross-media ownership between newspapers and radio had been liberalised. We've had a concern which we've expressed for a while that it somehow seems to us to be against plurality and diversity – the current phrase is; but, if you prefer, anti-democratic – that the major local newspaper and the major local radio station in any area should be in the same ownership. That seemed to us to be a fairly obvious principle.

We were surprised to find that the Government has actually, in its Bill, departed from that principle fairly early on. We're even more surprised to find the Newspaper Society is heavily lobbying to say how much they are being discriminated against. We understand, if the Government is going to have this amount of liberalisation, it wants to have some checks in place and the public interest test is the test the Government has decided it wants to put in place to ensure the joint ownership can't be abused.

Nick Higham: But, by the sound of it, you would rather you were not put in what is potentially a slightly difficult position. You'd prefer there were clearer rules banning newspapers, rather than you at the Radio Authority having to make difficult decisions.

Tony Stoller: I think I will come back and give you a bureaucratic answer. The Authority's job is to do that which Government charges it with, and I think if there is going to be an assessment of four factors to determine the public interest – diversity, plurality, the operation of the markets, and competition – that, inevitably, you will find both halves of the regulatory process getting involved in that, and the Radio Authority will necessarily be making judgements on diversity and plurality. The competition authority is going to be making judgements about competition – that's what they're there for. And, somewhere in the middle, sits this difficult question of making a judgement on markets. Would we like to do it? We accept that, if the Government wants a reservation, it's going to have to be done. And anybody approaching this particular topic is going to approach it from a place of partial experience. If it is a newspaper regulator, they'd need to acquire knowledge about radio, if there were a newspaper regulator. If it is the competition authorities, they'd need to be able to interpret diversity and plurality, which are not obvious commercial competition points.

We will have to learn. We will have to acquire some experience. I think anybody would. John Gray has been gracious enough to say the Radio Authority hasn't done too badly in the past – some of your decisions not withstanding, Nick. We'll do our best to learn the new areas we have to learn.

Nick Higham: You mention the lobbying over newspaper ownership. But there has also been a lot of lobbying over the question of whether or not one company should be allowed to control two FM licences or two licences on the same waveband in the same geographical area. At the moment, the Act doesn't permit that. There are those who say, in fact, if you give two licences to one company, you're more likely to serve the public by getting a diverse set of programmes than you are if you license separate operators, because, of course, one company won't want to compete with itself.

Tony Stoller: It's a much more complicated argument than it's been addressed as. You're right, as you say, at present, the rule is, a company may own one AM and one FM licence in a particular area. The Radio Authority has taken the view for a while and has advised Government accordingly that that actually is a good principle. It doesn't stand awfully well in small areas, because in smaller areas, the chances of a second commercial local radio company operating effectively are reasonably reduced. That means if you are going to, say, use the example of Aberdeen, it's relatively unlikely that a second substantial company can thrive in an area of that size. Therefore, if you're going to get more than two commercial services into that area, the Authority thinks there's probably a case for liberalising the rule in that instance, in smaller areas. Where we feel a great concern is the extent to which our own remit for broadening choice, increasing diversity, gets compromised in the larger areas.

What we've done – and again, let me stay in Scotland – what we've done in central Scotland, where there is quite a dominant radio group, Scottish Radio Holdings, is to introduce both Small FM and Regional FM licences. These provide competition. If, however, you liberalise the rules on one licence per waveband, you would allow the dominant group, Scottish Radio Holdings, to buy its main competitor, Scot FM, or to buy its smaller competitors, people like Q96. We think that works against the remit we've been given, and from that point of view, we've advised Government that a complete relaxation without proper safeguards is simply not a good idea.

Nick Higham: Doesn't it work in the interests of the listener, though, if you have a powerful, professionally-managed, well-financed company, which is operating a number of different services which it will take care are different, and therefore give different groups of listeners something different to listen to?

Tony Stoller: It depends what you regard as the most important thing for listeners. If you regard the most important thing being that all possible music formats shall be available, notwithstanding any other element, then I think you could make that case. The Radio Authority takes the view, and I rather think Government and commentators would take the view, that actually, commercial media which do more than just produce music, which in some way will carry news or dictate a news agenda, will carry advertising, are not at their best when they are in a monopolistic situation.

It worries us that if you have four licences in a single ownership, that you would only have one opportunity to set the news agenda. You would have only one opportunity to select which stories you carry and which stories you don't carry. You will give advertisers only one place to go to. And if, indeed, you get to a situation which the Bill envisages where the local newspaper may also own or have a sizeable holding in that local radio group, you run the risk of a single large commercial monopoly which is also a news agenda monopoly in a local area... And that troubles us.

Nick Higham: You mentioned that the Broadcasting Bill also talks about the digital future, and it proposes a system for you to license new digital audio broadcasting. Last year, in a speech, you were talking about digital radio, and you said: 'It is the Radio Authority's view that digital will need to reduplicate and extend existing services. That's preferable to introducing a whole raft of new channels and leaving existing services to cope with the vagaries of analogue transmission.' A rather downbeat approach to the whole business of digital. And, indeed, you went on to be really rather negative about digital audio broadcasting. Why?

Tony Stoller: I hope I went on to be very cautious about digital audio broadcasting. The Authority is certainly not negative. DAB offers, if it's going to happen, a really significant move forward for radio. But there are a number of difficulties in making it happen. The first has already been referred to. Tony Lennon in the previous session, 'The Broadcasting Bill and Digital Programming,' observed that there aren't many digital radio sets available. The Radio Authority does not have a digital receiver, even though my Head of Finance eventually persuaded me that we would part with the mere £2,000 required to buy one. Philips are out of stock. And the first difficulty which you have is, at the moment, there is nothing to trigger the receiver market and receiver manufacturers. Remember that we do not manufacture radio sets in the UK, with the exception of Morphy Richards and Roberts. And, indeed, I speak now as a shopkeeper, or having recently been a shopkeeper, there is no capacity to manufacture mass market radio sets in the western hemisphere.

Nick Higham: How is licensing digital services which merely replicate and extend existing system services going to stimulate a market?

Tony Stoller: Come on. Allow me a longish answer!

You have a difficulty with the lack of radio receivers. You equally have a difficulty therefore with a perceived lack of consumer demand. You can't demand something if you can't listen to it. You therefore have a problem as to what entrants you will get into the programme-provider pattern. Who's going to want to provide programmes when there aren't enough receivers, when there isn't a market among the consumer? And it seems to us that, initially, it is going to be those companies which have an established track record, which have established facilities, and who are going to want to, if only for a defensive reason, plant themselves firmly in the digital field. And for that reason, we think it is necessary to encourage the existing operators and to give them a reason to get involved with digital. But really, you do need to replicate existing services to begin with. And one of the good things that we have seen in the Broadcasting Bill is something we have pushed the Government for very hard, and that is incentives for existing commercial operators to get involved with DAB.

Nick Higham: Well, they've agreed. The Government have agreed to extend the existing analogue licences by eight years if a company gets into digital broadcasting. Even so, the investment in digital transmission, the investment in marketing a digital service, scarcely seems worthwhile. It doesn't seem a sufficient quid pro quo. What's in it for a commercial radio company?

Tony Stoller: What's in it for a commercial radio company will be what's in it for the listening public. What's in it for the listening public will be whether either quality in itself will be enough to drive the sales of sets.

Nick Higham: You mean sound quality?

Tony Stoller: Sound quality. Because digital does produce. The engineers tell me I can't say 'CD quality sound'. I have to say 'near CD quality sound'. Anyway, digital does produce good near CD quality sound. Digital does get over the fading in and out of AM and the pops and crackles of FM and the losing of it when you're driving by high buildings. Will that be enough for the listener? Will the addition of some new services? Not that many. Audio is not going to have the sort of explosion of services which video is going to have.

Or will somebody come in, as Murdoch did with satellite dishes, and see a commercial opportunity to drive it forward? Somebody like Sony, maybe, who manufacture sets, are used to running radio stations. Somebody who owns what Tony said we now have to call 'software products' – a music library. If there is enough in it for the listener, there will be enough in it for the commercial radio station broadcaster. Conversely, if there isn't for the one, there won't be for the other. And I think it's admirable that the BBC has taken a step forward, has tried to break this particular closed loop. This is exactly what public-funded broadcasting should be doing with its own experimental broadcasts. We've managed to nudge a little experimental broadcasting on the commercial side, as well, initially in Birmingham, and now in London.

But, in the end, it is going to be decided by whether the consumer is interested in going and buying a radio set. Again, back to being a shopkeeper. I wouldn't have been able to sell digital audio sets except to a few hi-fi people unless the price comes down to £49.95, approximately. Maybe £59.95. But you won't spend more than that on Granny for Christmas, even if she will be able to listen to her favourite programme in better quality. And that's a nut we have to crack, and that explains my caution.

Nick Higham: And I imagine that you would agree, therefore, that digital broadcasting at best is something that is going to take off in the medium future, not in the near future. Can I ask you about the near future? The Radio Authority is busily licensing new stations at the rate of about two a month, and you say that you intend to go on doing that more or less indefinitely for the forseeable future. Quite a high proportion of the stations you've licensed latterly could be classed among commercial radio's walking wounded. The latest RAJAR (Radio Joint Audience Research Ltd) figures aren't very encouraging. Talk Radio has a 4% reach, 1.5% share of listening. There's Jazz FM in the North West, 4% reach, 0.9 share of listening. Premiere in London, 2% reach, 0.4% share. Viva, 1% reach, 0.1% share of listening in its area. Even Radio 3 gets a 1% share, for God's sake, and GLR gets 0.4%. You can't even license stations in London that get a bigger audience than GLR. Hasn't something gone wrong in the Authority's desire to encourage minority interest, specialist interest radio stations?

Tony Stoller: I think that's most unkind. No, I really won't have you saying rude things like that about Radio 3. I'm a great supporter of Radio 3 and I wish it well, genuinely. I wish it well.

I think the Authority takes the view that it is not our job, nor would we want it to be our job, to prescribe formats for radio stations. Our job is to identify where (a) frequency opportunities exist, and (b) where demand exists for those who wish to run radio stations, and to provide that opportunity. It would be most surprising if all of the stations we license succeed.

What is remarkable to me is how few failures there are. If this is a grown up and mature industry, which is highly competitive, you would expect, if anything, more failures – not as a mark of the problems of the system, but as a mark of the robust health of what is still a very new industry. I think a number of the stations you have mentioned have a variety of difficulties. I could very easily quote other stations working in the same market, like, for example, Heart in London, or Jazz, also in London, which are doing very well. Kiss in Manchester, a splendid example of breaking new ground. But if you're going to have stations like Kiss breaking new ground, you're also going to have stations like Jazz FM North West breaking new ground. And both are not going to succeed in the same way, even if both succeed at all.

We will go on offering the opportunity to those who want to try out a new format which will broaden local choice for as long as the frequencies hold out. They won't hold out indefinitely. They will hold out forseeably for the next three or four years. Beyond that, the band gets pretty full. You have to be cautious. There was a famous statement by the Government in 1920 that the ether was full, when there was a suggestion that you start to use radio waves for something as nasty as entertainment. But we really do believe we're getting to the point where the ether is very nearly full. We will go on finding opportunities. A lot of those will be small stations.

One of the attractions of the use we're able to make of the new spectrum between 105 and 108 megaherz is the ability to introduce a large number of small stations and see if they're going to survive. A lot of the experience so far is that they will, but that again is a new challenge for the Authority, as well as for the operators.

Nick Higham: You have to license those on the basis of the rules, though – the same rules that apply to their larger commercial competitors, and large commercial companies in big cities. Is there not a case for licensing something rather different? Not simply on a smaller scale, but with a different set of rules, and a different set of regulations which one might perhaps conveniently term 'community radio'?

Tony Stoller: I don't think there's an argument for a separate tier of community radio, because I think that, to a very large extent, the ILR station is able to cope with that great variety of small or large stations for different models. Community radio exists and thrives within the ILR system, and John Gray is standing proof of that. The Authority has just licenced OBAN, a very significant and enthusiastic group of amateurs who wish to run what many of us would consider to be a community radio service and can do that within the present system. There are lots of different models that have been tried out – some haven't worked – for running a community radio station within the commercial radio system.

What I think you get, however, with some of the community radio lobby, is a belief that there is actually the need to quarantine some aspect of frequencies away from the pollution of commercial radio. That therefore requires a review of public funding. I don't think this government is likely to be driven down that particular road. If another government were to go down that road, you then run into the practical problems of operating a third tier; the most obvious of which is, how do you separate that off from the main commercial band? Because, if you give a licence to a community operator and that does not succeed, are you then going to withdraw the licence, or are you going to allow the commercial side to come into it? Where are you going to find the funding? How are you going to find the definition? How are you going to explain to all those people who run jolly good community stations within the existing system but pay their own way, that here is another group of stations which are being given an inside track?

So, no, I don't think there is any need for a separate tier. But I do think there is a need for the Authority to be able to find flexible ways of introducing new models. And – final point – the Authority has recently agreed to invite applications for less than the full eight year term on two licences coming up where we know there is strong community interest, because we know some community groups can get funding for less than eight years. And I'm sure that sort of flexibility can continue.

Nick Higham: Let me ask you, finally, generally about the future. My lords and masters at the BBC are very alarmed by what they see as the rise of commercial radio. They see a doubling of commercial radio stations in the next few years. They think these new small scale stations that you are licensing will have enormous impact on ratings overall. Individually, they will have small numbers of listeners. But in their areas, they will have a large share of listening. And if you gross that up, it could play havoc with the BBC's share of listening. What future do you see for radio as a whole? Do you think that picture of the future for the BBC is an accurate one? And I would ask you, subsequently, what do you think the future for your own organisation is, if it comes under a Labour government, which has, after all, said it might abolish the Radio Authority?

Tony Stoller: Let me start with the BBC, to give me a chance to think of the answer to the second part of the question. My own view is that the BBC has a very clear role to play within the duopol that is UK broadcasting. And, as far as radio is concerned, the BBC in many ways does things which it's most unlikely a commercial operator would ever do. And I think that, in many ways, the BBC needs to be defended and supported, I think it comes under quite often unfair attack. And certainly, the notion that you could replace the BBC with entirely commercially funded services seems to me to be daft.

However, I do think the BBC needs to define its role more clearly. I think, in particular, it needs to understand that the type of broadcasting which it is offering will have a clear and solid place within the market. But it will gain clarity and it will gain solidity if it doesn't try and ape the successes and the activities of the commercial side. We talked about Radio 3, and I am conscious that the BBC has particularly strong brands and, in marketing terms, if it seeks to dilute those brands too far, it will get itself into trouble.

I also feel that the BBC for many years has pursued a policy regarding frequency use which can only be described as dog-in-the-manger. The BBC sits upon a substantial number of really good FM frequencies. It merges radio stations together. Oxford is up in arms. Dorset, where I live, down on the south coast – Radio Dorset is being effectively abolished. But the frequency is being retained. I think the BBC has actually to work out that it has a very important role. It has one which, actually, I think the commercial side should be supporting and endorsing. But it won't achieve that, and it certainly won't get that support and endorsement, unless it realises that it shouldn't really be playing in the commercial field.

Nick Higham: What about your organisation, if there's a Labour government?And, indeed, in the digital future, in which there is clearly a question mark over traditional Radio Authority-style legislation?

Tony Stoller: I think, in the very long term, if digital ends up by freeing enough spectrum space, then the basis of all current regulation is going to fade, because much of the regulation is based on frequency scarcity. I think, as I've already indicated, on digital from a radio point of view, that's quite a long time away. I do feel, though, that in some ways the Radio Authority offers a model for the way in which regulation may well work in the future. We're not a BBC-style organisation. We're not like the IBA. We're not even like the ITC. There are 32 people working at the Radio Authority. We find ways of licensing and regulating almost 200 stations. That is the type of challenge, maybe writ very much larger, which regulators are going to face in five or ten years' time.

I know there is a statement from Louis Mooney, caught a bit off-guard, saying, 'Don't bother with the Radio Authority, we'll put it all into OFCOM.' Put it all into one large super-regulator. Well – maybe. Maybe one day there will be a need, because spectrum use will converge and to a degree taste and decency regulations will converge, to get better coordination between the different regulators. That might begin with better coordination between the Department of National Heritage and the Department of Trade and Industry. If they can do it, we can do it. The jury is still out.

Summation

Colin Shaw, C.B.E.
Director, Broadcasting Standards Council

When I was a small child and looked at the atlas, much of the atlas was coloured in red. When my children were growing up, rather less was coloured in red. Now that my grandchildren are growing up, hardly anything shows red any more. Indeed, the Empire looks more like fly marks scattered over the Atlantic Ocean than anything more reputable.

And I suppose, in radio and television terms, much the same thing has happened, because the BBC was the red part of the map – certainly when I was young – and, over the years, it has diminished to the present condition, in which the BBC is a part, though a very important part, of a system which is quite clearly expanding and expanding.

When we've been planning this Symposium in recent years, we've had something of a dilemma because I think we certainly started off, at least at the time I came in, thinking about broadcasting very much in public service terms. And we realised, in concentrating on that, that perhaps the emphasis on the BBC was no longer quite as relevant as it had been. And in trying to sum up the conversations of the last two days, it seems to me as a recurrent theme, we're beginning to talk much more about the social responsibilities of broadcasting in general as the main concern of the Symposium.

The last time that broadcasting was looked at globally in this country was when Lord Annan's committee sat between 1974 and 1977. Mrs Thatcher didn't believe – well, she didn't believe in a number of good things – she didn't believe in the occasional reappraisal of the value of broadcasting, and so there hasn't been one, apart from the Peacock Committee, which was a sort of one-off enquiry of a rather different kind, and certainly with different motives.

I believe that one of the things that should happen is that, from time to time, and particularly in times of social, economic and technological change, broadcasting needs that kind of overview to be taken. And I think it is useful, year after year in this Symposium, to bring back some of the issues which would be relevant to that kind of enquiry. So I think, rather than look at the individual sessions we've had, what's emerged to me as a theme, the message which I would like to give to my successor as Chair of the Symposium, is to think of this at least as one of the prime concerns for the Symposium in the future.

I will now turn to a duty which falls upon the Chair at this time to express thanks on behalf of all of you. To the Allen Hall staff, who have fed and watered us; to the technical staff, who have helped us and made us audible in some cases and inaudible in others; to my colleagues on the Steering Committee, to Tim Lees, and particularly to Marjorie Burton, who has played a leading part in making the Symposium happen; and to Sue Ralph, who I'm sure everybody will agree has made a triumphant debut as the Director of the Symposium this year. I think it's an onerous and nerve-racking task to take on the organisation of this. You have a Steering Committee which is a bit like the Cheshire Cat, sometimes there and sometimes not there. But somehow, she has held us all together and made it happen with the success I think we've all felt in the last forty-eight hours. And to anyone I've forgotten, my apologies, and warmest thanks.

I'm stepping down, leaving the active business of the industry, and I leave it with great regret. I've had a whale of a time. It's rather shameful, I think sometimes, to confess how much one's enjoyed one's career. But I've been in broadcasting since... I wrote radio plays in 1948–49. I joined the BBC in 1953, long before some of you were born. And I really had enormous fun. I was in at the birth of BBC2 and was one of the principal people at the IBA concerned in the construction of the constitution of Channel 4 – and that was one of the most exciting periods of my life.

And, in the last six or seven years, I've had the task of trying to make a body which was universally reviled, the Broadcasting Standards Council, rather less universally reviled, and even at odd moments earning a moment or two of respect from people.

And it's all been tremendous fun, and I'm going to miss it quite a lot but I hope still to haunt places like this where those things that have concerned me so much are brought into debate year by year.

Thank you.

Presented Papers
(in alphabetical order)

Inside the New Recruits

Jo Langham Brown
University College, Warrington

The argument of this paper, which is a report on work in progress, is that the real challenge of production is the education of the new broadcast, multi-media professionals of the future. This symposium, in focusing attention on the world of multi-media and broadcasting in terms of production and audiences, is failing to pay attention to the most fundamental issue of all for the new society of the second millennium – the 'cultural' formation and value systems of the future producers of the software whose mind-casts will fuel the info-tainment industries of the next century. In the market economy of today all our eyes are on the audiences and their needs because the dominant model of broadcasting is no longer one of public service but that of consumer sovereignty. But without the programmes there can be no consumption and without producers there are no programmes. My research is beginning to examine the questions: Who are they – the new programme and multi-media suppliers of the future? What are their values? How are they being trained? What assumptions do they have? What are their motivations and their understanding of the world around them?

One of the greatest problems today for those of us who educate and train some of the new practitioners is the future shape of the industry and the sudden increase in the pace of change, not only in terms of the technology but also in terms of the world economy, globalisation, issues of national identity, and intellectual and moral values. These all have vast implications in terms of education and training yet few in the industry, or in the political and academic establishment, seem to have grasped what we, involved in more practical based courses, are increasingly aware of – that there is a huge gap opening up between the young people about to enter the industry and the professional groups involved in their teaching and training (whether this 'training' takes place in academia or more traditionally in the workplace).[1]

The educational reforms which have brought so many young people into higher education, and which are blurring the lines between the old divisions of vocational and academic education, are modifying the nature and thrust of university teaching. Media/television studies are in the vanguard of the change – perhaps because of the sheer numbers of those attracted to the discipline and because media studies courses in Higher Education increasingly include a substantial practice-oriented element.

The students registering for media degrees are, in some ways, a new breed at the portals of academia. We believe they deserve attention and analysis. Media studies is the fastest growing university course in the country[2] Why, scream the tabloids, do students want to study soap operas? Yet, leaving aside the fact that media studies students today don't just study soap operas, in all the pejorative speculation there is very little solid information about the real reasons for the media studies phenomenon. We need to discover why students are studying the media. Why does the term 'media' hold such resonance for today's students?

As higher education responds to the market-place, and to the impact of high technology on employment, all of us have to accept that young people want knowledge and jobs in what they instinctively see as a rapidly expanding area. Anthony Smith has pointed out that during the twentieth century the concept of entertainment has changed from that of a group of activities at the edge of a working day to that of a group of industries which see their role as providing for the totality of leisure time available in society.[3] In such a situation it appears inevitable that media courses of all sorts will be over-subscribed and flooded with applicants.

The first graduates of these courses are just beginning to enter the industry in sizeable numbers where they will form a new generation of professionals whose notions of professionalism (which should be formed during their education and training) will be further shaped by their experiences in the increasingly freelance world of television, film, radio and video. In education, outlook and values, the new recruits are different from who have gone before.[4] If academia has begun to change in response to the first wave so too, in its turn, will the industry. How will the new recruits perceive the working practices they encounter? How will they view the structures and the culture which has come down from a period of extensive regulation which is now drawing to its close? What notion of professionalism will they bring in with them and how will they adapt to the situation they find there?

Educators and practitioners together need to grasp the nettle which the new educational systems and procedures present and take stock of the impact of the reforms, not only in terms of their own institutions, but also more importantly on the young people themselves. Industry practitioners need to ask themselves questions about the values they would like to see communicated to young people in the workplace.

It is important for academics and the industry to reflect at this crucial point of time on whether the government's approach to education and training is really preparing these young people for working in the industry in the 21st century. We have to ask ourselves some difficult questions, for example, is it academics, established practitioners, or the newcomers who really have a realistic grasp of how to respond to the technological earthquake which may be at hand? The turnover in careers and the pace of change in broadcasting are speeding up. One of the few certainties of modern life is that working lives are getting shorter (and with the two year degree in prospect so is the time spent in higher education). The entrenched hierarchies and bureaucracies which used to govern broadcasting no longer have the luxury of many years to spend on moulding their new recruits. In some ways the initiative is swinging towards the new blood who, proportionally, will have a much greater impact on the industry's culture as the grim reaper of redundancy and early retirement moves to remove the higher-paid and the over-forties from the broadcasting landscape at an ever faster rate.

The disappearance of the career-for-life is not a shock for the young but, even if they are not shocked they are affected by it. They live in the shadow of a revolution in technology which is increasingly discussed. The young people I teach and place in the industry today are willing and enthusiastic and prepared to work extremely hard, but they are perplexed by job uncertainty and the diminished expectations in terms of salary and perks.[5] Some of the more intelligent of them show signs of anxiety, bewilderment and cynicism as they come up against the fact that a degree which was supposed to be an open sesame to secure employment no longer guarantees job security.

Of course, as we all know, with a few exceptions such as medicine or law, a degree was never supposed to be about professionalisation: it is supposed to be about education in a broader sense. Yet this is not what young people themselves imbibed from all the emphasis on staying on after school. Many of them don't know what academics mean when they talk about education in terms not linked to making money or finding jobs. Over the past few years a gap has opened between what academics usually mean when they talk about education and what the government, the general public and the majority of the new entrants to higher education understand by the term especially when it incorporates a dimension of training. The gap has widened and persisted because, as the educational 'reforms' have bitten deep, academics on the whole have not offered a particularly vigorous or robust defence of educational values. I think those of us whose courses involve an element of training are particularly aware of some of the pitfalls in the emphasis on training. The NVQs have been criticised for leaving insufficient room for theory or developing 'a reserve of understanding to give the necessary adaptability and flexibility for a rapidly changing working world'.[6] In my own research into NVQs I found similar criticism.[7] Standards which are purely industry-initiated tend to lose sight of any notion of broad educational values. Inevitably employers take a utilitarian and somewhat mechanistic approach to their workforce where skills are emphasised to the exclusion of everything else. The government, in stressing that employers know best, is neutralising the impact of educators who have traditionally taught students to question everything. In short, the accusation is that students are being trained as fodder for the global economy of the future and any knowledge and appreciation of the arts, the sciences and languages is missing. In other words too much training and too little education.

In terms of the NVQs there is criticism that an approach to training, which consists of working backwards from an industry's perceived need, is inevitably flawed and, as far as vocational qualifications are concerned, young people do appear to be being directed into fixed areas too early. Other criticisms focus on the innately right-wing values of most employers who have a very narrow concept of training. Employers tend to shy away from critical thinkers and problem solvers and prefer a notion of training which imposes something of a mental straitjacket. Conformist automatons may not be what the future needs and the new British training system could be seriously flawed, storing up some very negative consequences from its very inception. However, I should say at this point that such criticism is not so current in the film broadcast and video industry where Skillset seems to have fostered a less rigid approach among employers. In any case, employers and managers in the British broadcasting industry tend, we hope, to be more sympathetic to the values of creativity and imagination (otherwise they would be cutting an industry with a very rich tradition down at the knees). One is less sanguine about some of the media moguls presently commanding the slopes of the new global entertainment industry.

For media academics the present climate of change presents serious challenges. Over the last decade larger classes and tired teachers have been one of the less happy consequences of the reforms in Higher Education. In addition, the collapse in their social and economic status may have affected their students' attitudes towards them. Thatcher's children have been brought up to a world view of the entrepreneur as the hero of the times. This may have led them to undervalue and misread the university experience and to equate the whole HE experience with a ritualistic rather meaningless rite-of-passage.

However, a sense of alienation between students and staff may not be simply the result of outside factors. In some ways the popularity of post-modernist theory in media studies has scored something of an educational own goal. In asserting that all images and views are of equal value, post-modernist have undermined old-fashioned notions that education is about the creation and sustaining of values. However, we will take heart from a riposte quoted in Anthony Smith's recent TS Eliot Memorial lectures: 'To realise the relative validity of one's convictions and yet stand by them unflinchingly is what distinguishes the civilised man from a barbarian'.[8]

One of the most striking characteristics of today's undergraduates and graduates is their apoliticism and their ahistoricism. Perhaps, under the influence of post-modernism and post-structuralism everything appears to have dissolved into a series of relativities, of clever deconstructions which look neither backwards or forwards. Has the media studies discipline adequately prepared our students for a media environment where economics and politics are increasingly intertwined? The primacy of text over context in academic fashion has left many young people to face a globalised workplace with no mental hinterland which might help them to assess issues of power. This is a tremendous handicap in a world which, as they are beginning to sense, is increasingly divided between the powerful and the weak.

However, the industry should take note that something may be stirring in the groves of academe which may be about to make an important impact on the media studies canon. An article by Colin MacCabe in *The Times Educational Supplement* talks about the need for a 'grammar of value'. MacCabe goes on to say: 'The analysis of contemporary capitalist forms of culture is almost always divorced from the analysis of traditional forms to the detriment of both ... we will not begin to fully appreciate contemporary forms of cultural production until they are situated in a long-term historical perspective.' He goes on to call for a more serious engagement with established disciplines and for more engagement of cultural (and by implication, media) studies with a wider range of audiences. 'Students concerned with pursuing cultural theory and analysis (should be) constantly confronted and engaged with the artists, architects film makers, musicians, writers who are currently involved in creating new cultural forms.'[9] The same applies to media students who, as part of the their courses, should engage with working media practitioners.

The brave new world of the future

One of the main motivations for pursuing this project is to understand the impact of new technology and the new practitioners.[10] Never has there been a time when there has been so much crystal ball-gazing going on. One can hardly open an industry journal without reading some speculation about the future of television and the changes which the technological revolution will bring in its wake. We have heard ad nauseam that the future is digital, that broadcasting which, for seventy years has functioned with one technology – analogue – is about 'to go digital'. According to the experts digital technology, however, is not just another technology. It could for all sorts of reasons change our conceptions and perceptions of the world around us and alter our mental landscapes.

In addition, our traditional visual media – the complex technological industries of cinema and television – are converging at the present time into global entertainment conglomerates and fortunes will be made or lost on backing the right or wrong technological options. The industry has tended to concentrate on the nuts and bolts: how much will it all cost? But the broader question of the impact on the imagination has also attracted much attention and 'the future' which is, after all, always unknowable, has suddenly become a central focus of debate, much discussed, written about and researched (if we can call speculation about the future research!).

Digital technology, which used to be associated entirely with the very distinctive computing industry has now become a central issue of concern for the broadcast/film/video/entertainment industry. Suddenly, in what really seems to be a space of two or three years, sound, music, video, sophisticated graphics, as well as text and data, can also all be expressed in binary digits and re-assembled for computer speakers and screens. For the entertainment industry the changes which flow from this are extraordinary and throw up a multitude of problems for those planning to earn their living in the entertainment sector.

One key factor is the shift in the notion of 'information'. The term now encapsulates everything pumped out by all the various forms of the communication media, all of which can now be expressed in binary code (that is digitised) – a development usually referred to as multi-media. The computer screen, which once displayed facts and figures, can now also produce voices, music and moving pictures. Not surprisingly, this development has profound implications for the entertainment industry which has diverted and amused everyone throughout the century. It is not so much the case that these older forms of media, such as film and television, will disappear but that the essential interchangeability which digitisation provides will alter our perceptions, attitudes and expectations. As McCluhan suggested so many years ago there are subtle effects of the medium which influence what we can know. Or to put it another way, digitised media could change how we know what we know.

For today's media students the digital revolution has enormous implications in all sorts of areas. Today multi-media is associated with the computer screen but there is no reason why the television set, which provides one-way broadcast entertainment into the home, could not in the future carry much more information. However, it would seem that when computers can play moving pictures and television sets can carry out computing functions, the distinction between them dissolves. This has important consequences because, when computer and television screens converge, notions about the 'separateness' of entertainment and knowledge/information could disappear also.

In the light of this we believe a key question to explore with undergraduates and young practitioners is whether they see news as essentially distinctive from information and entertainment. Our hunch is that already some of them do not. Traditional news 'values', which emerged from a period when broadcasting was heavily regulated, may be disappearing with the arrival not only of the multi-channel environment but also of a generation which have imbibed the values of the tabloids with their mother's milk. As they move into the industry they could overthrow many of the old assumptions. If we believe that some of the old public service values are worth hanging onto then we had better start defining, justifying and defending them robustly and 'unflinchingly' and laying out clearly the consequences if they disappear for ever.

In a stimulating series of lectures Anthony Smith explores the implications of digitisation, interactivity and virtual reality in terms of the 'sensorium' we all possess.[11] In a brief reference to the history of moving pictures Smith discusses the search for exactitude in representation. It must have seemed with the invention of the cinema (based on the phenomenon known as 'persistence of vision') that the final culmination of representational illusion had been achieved. However, the sensorium adjusts to an improvement in illusion and then feels deceived when a better mode turns up. This has happened throughout the twentieth century with various advances in cinematic and television technology.

The degree of adjustments to which audiences (and practitioners) have been accustomed in the past, however, will pale once digitised technology truly arrives. Smith suggests that digitised technology is a much greater break with the past than ever before because the mind has been trained to respond to representational technologies which are analogue and the illusion of a digital medium is essentially different. An analogue recording traces an actual event, a digital recoding is the transcription of a series of symbols; analogue is an imprint of reality; digital is a transmutation of modes. One question Smith raises is whether this will ultimately alter our evaluation of forms and objects and craftsmanship.[12]

Smith shows how our culture has in the past celebrated a world of 'objects' and 'originals'. Progressive degradation of the original was an inevitable consequence of taking copies, but digital technology is completely free of such corruption. The original is merely a series of numbers which can be replayed without limit – re-expressed and re-interpreted. Digitised images can be made to perform actions absent in reality, conjure up people from the dead. They are indistinguishable from what is thought of as objective reality; 'they pass every test of verisimilitude'. Smith suggest the significance of this has not really hit us. We are far from having achieved the assimilation of the digital mode into our imaginations.

An investigation of the psychological and perceptual impact of the introduction of digital technology on students and young media practitioners at the present time would be immensely valuable. There is a generational gap opening up between those who have grown up in an analogue environment and those for whom the digital mode is the norm. Phil Tippett, a traditional animator who now works on a daily basis with digital technology, is of this opinion. He admits that he doesn't really understand the appeal of the virtual world but his younger colleagues are different, they are 'absolutely at one with it. Maybe its a generational thing'.[13]

Tippett may display a somewhat reserved approach but the same can not be said of the two best-selling, up-beat prophets of the new technology, both American, both academics with strong business links: Nicholas Negroponte, director of the Media Laboratory of the Massachusetts Institute of Technology, founder and writer of Wired magazine and George Gilder, director of the High Technology Public Policy Project of the Discovery Institute in Seattle. Negroponte who, according to Douglas Adams writes about the future with the authority of someone 'who has spent a great deal of time there' (!) is an enthusiast for the new technology. The digital age, he says, has four very powerful qualities which will result in its ultimate triumph; decentralising, globalising, harmonising and empowerment. Decentralising will mean the collapse of management hierarchies and the traditional centralist view of life in the workplace. Globalisation will mean great changes for the nation state and Negroponte hints at world unification while admitting that resurgent nationalism suggests a certain cynicism about this. Harmonisation means that 'while politicians struggle with the baggage of history, a new generation is emerging from the digital landscape free of many of the old prejudices'. (He should talk to the Euro-sceptics among my students.) For Negroponte the digital age means that young people today 'are released from the limitations of geographic proximity as the sole basis of friendship, collaboration, play and neighbourhood'. Digital technology can be a natural force drawing people into greater world harmony. In his final point Negroponte focuses on empowerment: 'The access, mobility and the ability to effect change are what will make the future so different from the present. Being digital is different. We are not waiting on any invention. It is here. It is now. It is almost genetic in its nature. The control bits of the digital future are more than ever before in the hands of the young.'[14]

We want to explore these themes in our research. Do the young feel empowered by the technology? Do they indeed see themselves as world citizens? Are they democratic and non hierarchical in approach? My impression is that some of them feel weak, enfeebled and stranded in a world where the corporate mentality dominates. How many feel 'free, happy and equal' as apologists for the new age assert? Are they feeling threatened by reports of the continuous 'restructuring' of industries, the laying off of workers and managers because of the computerisation of jobs? How aware are the new recruits of heavy employee workloads?[15]

It seems to be the case that all eyes, including those of this symposium, seem to be on audiences, consumer choice, technology, media concentration and media moguls but very little attention is paid to what it could all mean for the workforce. The new technology is likely to de-skill and de-professionalise. Doug Henwood speaks of the way production is increasingly played down by postmodernists and publicists of the information age. They prefer, he says, to revel in the sphere of consumption but:

'If you strip away the high tech gloss the future for producers looks in many ways like the nineteenth century or even the early days of the Industrial Revolution, times of massive polarisation and displacement, exciting and even liberating if you were on the right side but frightful and immiserating otherwise.'[16]

In the epilogue to his book *Being Digital* Negroponte for a brief moment strikes a more sombre note in a passage which refers to intellectual property abuse and invasion of privacy which multi-media will bring in its wake over the next decade.[17] He does make a reference to the loss of jobs and the way lifetime employment is in the process of disappearing but he lightly skims over the dark side of what another commentator has called 'wired savagery of the future'.[18]

The dark side of the new technological future is beginning to attract the attention of other soothsayers. Robert Reich, the former Harvard Professor who moved to head Clinton's Labour Department, in a speech delivered in honour of the 100th Labour day spoke of a future society divided into three groups, 'an underclass largely trapped in centre cities, increasingly isolated from the core economy; an overclass of those in a position to ride the waves of change; and in between the largest group, an anxious class, most of whom hold jobs but are justifiably uneasy about their own standing and fearful for their children's futures'.[19] The idea of the 'anxious' class has now entered the collective consciousness. In this research project we want to investigate if the new workforce is really anxious or if it is only the older generation which has been rendered impotent by the scale of change.

The rapid pace of change does raise questions about the evolution of the media studies curriculum. The future requires critical rigorous minds capable of examining the intellectual and technical assumptions of the powerful. As I indicated earlier, one of the areas which the academy and the industry needs to examine is contemporary nostrums about training, especially the blinkered concentration on very short term, utilitarian goals. Behind all the rhetoric of a high-skilled learning society, might the real agenda be a form of de-professionalisation?

Global capitalism driven by technological advance appears to be unleashing a world, not of upward mobility for the undeveloped world, but of social splitting for the developed world, in which the gap between the highest and the lowest incomes is increasing rapidly.[20] In addition, people who have jobs, as all of us know, are working harder than ever before.

Those employed in the broadcast, film and video sector in Britain are not large in numbers at the present time. The BFI Handbook lists them as around 209,500 of which 32% are employed in broadcasting, 14% in the independent sector and 54% are employed as freelancers across all sectors – but the numbers will grow. Increasingly, there is a necessity to develop courses where young people can acquire a broad and interdisciplinary knowledge of the theory and practice of broadcasting and where they can be equipped to understand and negotiate all the different currents and undercurrents that are flowing towards the future.

Broadcasting requires a new breed of producers and leaders capable of grasping fully the multifaceted image of the evolving digital media. We, the older generation, have to ask ourselves if we are serving our young people well. Sometimes I think that Higher Education is suffering from artero sclerosis and the broadcasting industry is busy burying its head in the sand. Neither attitude will be very helpful for the future. It is for this reason that John Mundy and myself have embarked on a project which we believe will assist ourselves and our students in understanding and facing the problems and possibilities posed by the Brave New World.

Notes and References

1. Bridging the generational gap in terms of outlook and values is still hampered by, on the one hand, the continuing suspicion and hostility of the industry towards media education and on the other of media academia towards anything which smacks of practice or vocational training. Of course, matters have improved – the two solitudes are beginning to break down, as industry practitioners move into academia and media graduates move into the industry. However, the rapid increase of young people with media degrees who seem to assume that this provides them with a professional qualification (similar to that of engineering or medicine) is straining the relationship once again. Media courses are churning out hundreds of graduates a year and this is in danger of creating a backlash in an industry already swamped with too many freelancers trying to find work. See *Spectrum*, Autumn 1992.
2. This has created something of a moral panic. Applications for media studies were up by 54 percent for 1994-5 with 38,863 students attempting to gain a place on a media course (compared to 26,416 applications for maths and 21,442 for physics). Eighty universities now offer varying types of degrees which fall under the broad title of Media Studies. (*The Observer*, 21 January 1996).
3. Anthony Smith, *Software for the Self*, TS Eliot Memorial Lectures (London: Faber and Faber, 1996) p. 111.
4. In 1996 the British Film Institute published a Report on a longitudinal study of the impact of structural change and technological advances on programme-makers in television. The sample involves around 500 people. Some of the findings indicate that nearly three quarters in the 21 to 30 year-old age group have received higher education and just under a quarter of these did either media studies, film and television studies, or communications studies. British Film Institute, Television Industry Tracking Study, The First Year Interim Report (London: BFI 1996).
5. The BFI survey pointed out that 24 per cent of 21 to 30-years olds in television earn less than £10,000 a year. What may be more significant is that a quarter of the overall sample and a third of freelancers earned less in the year 1994-5 than they did in 1993-4.
6. Professor Alan Smithers in *The Observer*, 24 September 1995.
7. Personal interviews with new recruits to the broadcasting and film industries, teachers and employers in the industry. See Josephine Langham, 2nd ed. *Lights Camera Action* (London: BFI due out in 1997).
8. Anthony Smith, *Software for the Self*, p. 57.
9. Colin MacCabe, 'Tradition Too Has Its Place in Cultural Studies', *The Times Educational Supplement*, 26 May 1995.
10. The new thematic priorities of the Economic and Social Research Council (ESRC) stress the issues which are of fundamental concern to today's media industry. They include: Economic Performance and Development, Globalisation, Regions and Emerging Markets; Human communications and the Social Shaping of Technology, Innovation and the Impact of Technology. The concerns of the industry and the research priorities of the academy are, for once, marching in step.
11. Anthony Smith, *Software for the Self*.
12. Smith's analysis receives some interesting confirmation by someone at the coal face coping with the new digital age. Phil Tippett, a well-known animator who worked on Jurassic Park, has emphasised some of the same themes. Until about two years

ago, he says, the techniques used for special effects have been basically the same since the beginning of film but since then everything has changed. Tippett warns of the potential of digital technology to de-skill; he suggests that in some ways film-making is becoming sloppier. On the set of Jurassic Park one of the grips was caught in shot by accident – smoking a cigarette – but all traces of him were simply removed by computers in post-production editing. See Phil Tippett 'In the Tracks of Jurassic Park' in *Resisting the Virtual Life*, ed. James Brook and Iain A Boale (San Francisco: City Lights 1995), p. 260.

13. Phil Tippett, *Resisting the Virtual Life*, p. 259.
14. *Being Digital*, (London: Hodder and Stoughton, 1995) p.230-231.
15. Colin Sparks suggests that it would be better to refer to the new employees of broadcasting as casual labour rather than freelances. All the worst features of casual labour which made militants of the dockers and the building workers are emerging in the freelance workforce. See his essay, 'Independent Production: Unions and Casualization' in *Behind The Screens, The Structure of British Television in the Nineties*, ed. Stuart Hood (London: Lawrence and Wishart, 1994).
16. Doug Henwood, 'Info Fetishism' in *Resisting the Virtual Life*, p. 170. According to the BFI TV Tracking Study just over a third of the sample worked 60 or more hours a week on average. (Nearly half of the 41-50 years old work 60 or more hours a week.)
17. Copyright is a central issue for the purveyors of the new digital order. At the present time the National Information Infrastructure Bill is before both Houses of Congress in the US. According to an extremely angry John Naughton, while ostensibly this is a bill to update the law on intellectual property rights in an age of electronic communication, in fact it is drawn up by lobbyists for the media industry and it will claw back rights which have been slowly acquired over a century. According to Naughton, the Bill gives extensive rights to copyright owners. It will make it possible for the scanning of a document on the internet to be construed as copying. Digital technology allows the digital documents to report back to their owners their whereabouts so that owners will be able to invoice at will. The Bill will deliver consumers neatly trussed into the clutches of Murdoch, Time-Warner and Disney and all the other multi-media conglomerates who view the information superhighway not as a Jeffersonian tool for liberating mankind but as a firehose down which they can pump their pap and from which none will be allowed to drink for free. *The Observer*, 3 March 1996.
18. Monty Neill, 'Computers, Thinking, and Schools in the New World Order' in *Resisting the Virtual Life*, p. 184.
19. *New York Times*, 31st August, 1994.
20. Monty Neill, 'Computers, Thinking and Schools in the New World Order' in *Resisting the Virtual Life*, p. 184.

Feminising Television, Marketing Feminism

Barbara Crowther
University of Wolverhampton

A general embarrassment seems to hang over the question of television's relationship with feminism. In an increasingly consumer-led market it is seen at worst as a liability, at best a minority interest. For fear of losing audiences, even broadcasters sympathetic to feminism are fighting shy of overtly feminist programmes and series. Few broadcasters have a clear idea (let alone a policy) about what constitutes either a feminist agenda, or definition of what constitutes women's broadcasting, or equal opportunities.[1] Thanks largely to tabloid demonising, feminism is, in general, poorly understood, seen as a threat and ridiculed. The broadcasting industry should not allow itself to contribute to this ignorance and reductionism by the lumpen-laddist audience. Ultimately, the feminist project is about developing a critiquing consciousness that challenges the assumptions, priorities, beliefs and roles imposed upon us all, both women and men, by the ingrained conventions of a patriarchal society. It is also about demonstrating the importance of the difference between the experience of masculinity and femininity in a culture constructed on male perceptions and values.[2]

I want to suggest that broadcasters at all levels should include feminist perspectives and styles in many more areas and by many more processes than are currently seen and that they can do so without sacrificing entertainment value or integrity. No one strategy can by itself be expected to sensitise public consciousness or change attitudes and values. The direct-sell which tackles feminist issues head-on, whether by current affairs programmes or sex-war comedy, is certainly important, but there are also gradualist strategies that can dislodge dominant assumptions around gender and what's valuable in society and that don't actively draw attention to sexual politics. Conventional mainstream products can be feminised from within, in the process of focusing on other matters, and transmit new values by changing the tenor of conventional (male) formats, replacing their perspectives and style for ones that reflect and address the experience of being female.

As my examples will show, the masculine underpinning of television products both reflects and naturalises patriarchal ideology. Because it is unconscious and largely imperceptible in the flow of television, both producers and viewers of programmes may well deny there is a male agenda. However, it becomes more apparent when programmes are subject to the close analytic scrutiny that is usually reserved for literary texts. Academic study is increasingly using television as 'texts' to help explore and understand society. I will use two case studies, from two apparently gender-neutral programmes, to illustrate how deeply the masculine view of the world is embedded in television culture, and how it militates against allowing the feminine – and the feminist – in.

Gendered Reading – adapting Middlemarch

The broad popularity and prestige status of the BBC classic serials (whose recent successes have been bolstered by the insatiable American appetite for Olde England) make them ideal material because they embody contemporary artistic and cultural ideas and values, including attitudes to gender. My analysis of one such adaptation, *Middlemarch*, aims to illustrate how the absence of a feminist perspective has resulted in the reproduction of traditional responses and styles of representation from a pre-feminist age and tends to confirm that the implications of the feminist agenda have barely touched mainstream broadcasting.

The commissioning of a high-budget adaptation of *Middlemarch* by the BBC in 1994 appeared to acknowledge that George Eliot's 1871/2 novel bursts with contemporary relevance. Many of its social concerns echo our own – public health care, housing provision for the poor, political corruption and nepotism, the realignment of political groupings – even the future of the railways. The novel deals with thwarted personal and public ambition, compromised idealism, and is 'about work and the right to work, about the need to discover a vocation which will satisfy the whole self and to be educated to undertake it.'[3] The novel has at its centre an intelligent young woman of independent mind and means, hamstrung by sexist attitudes and the pressure of social opinion and Eliot uses the story to indict a society in which women are prevented from recognising or fulfilling their potential. More than most 19th century novels *Middlemarch* focuses on the often painful and contradictory reality of women's lives, and is full of sensitive and enduring observations about social and marital relations, seen through female eyes. For several years feminist literary scholars have been offering perceptive critical commentaries that complement, and sometimes challenge, the readings of the (largely male) critical tradition. They have explored too some of the novel's points of particular identification for female readers.

However, although this woman-authored text is ideal for a female- focused treatment, the television adaptation had a male producer (Louis Marks), a male director (Anthony Page) and a male screen-writer (Andrew Davies). Nobody questioned this line-up. The notion that a reader's sex may affect their engagement with a text is a live contemporary issue, recognised and debated on many television and radio arts programmes: but, as far as the production of prestige projects is concerned, the question is ignored – and male cultural hegemony is, by default, reinforced.

The historical silencing of women's voices is one of the reasons for the emergence of the study of women's literature. George Eliot herself had to adopt a man's name in order to publish her fiction, and she retained it partly because of the low intellectual esteem accorded to women at the time. In discouraging and undervaluing women, Victorian intellectual prejudice was responsible for a loss to culture. The BBC has applied a modern institutional version of this in failing to recognise that a woman's interpretation of the novel might be valuable in illuminating areas of the text occluded by the male reading tradition.

The television *Middlemarch*, not very surprisingly, reflects a number of masculine interests, and reproduces the preoccupations and perspectives of traditional male literary criticism. Critics such as W.J. Harvey and F.R. Leavis have devoted considerably more attention to the male characters in *Middlemarch*, especially Dr Lydgate and Mr Casaubon, than to Dorothea, the novel's central figure.[4] The TV adaptation followed this model by opening not with Dorothea as the book does, but with Dr Lydgate arriving in *Middlemarch* on the stagecoach, eager to take up his new post at the hospital. Signalled thus as the chief protagonist, the viewer anticipates (correctly) that the narrative momentum will be largely fuelled by his personal and public progress.[5]

Andrew Davies's justification for this re-emphasis is that Dorothea does not set out to stir things up unlike Lydgate: 'It's a bit like a western: a guy rides into town, and thinks, I'm going to clean up this place... oust the bad guys, sort out the health service... One latches on to action characters, not people who suffer and watch'.[6] While this may be good strategy for hooking a television audience, it pushes Dorothea's more contemplative character into the shade. Indeed, Davies's 'suffer-and-watch' reading of Dorothea limits the sympathy afforded her, particularly in relation to her husband, Mr Casaubon. (Interestingly, the only interior monologues used in the production convey Mr Casaubon's feelings of failure and his irritation at his wife's eagerness – a partiality which encourages greater identification with the self-absorbed scholar than the frustrated wife.)

The artistic priorities in Davies's characterisation of Dorothea are evident in the way she is introduced – galloping on horseback with her sister Celia, who pours scorn on Dorothea's distress over a destitute family. While this shows two opposing sides of Dorothea's character – her social compassion and sense of responsibility as well as her delight in sensual pleasure – the scene is visually constructed around the conventional male tendency to sexualise representations of women, to emphasise their physical aspects. Davies admits he wanted to present Dorothea's biological aspect before her intellectual and spiritual side: 'People [sic] will see her red in the face and think, What a girl!'

A more feminist production team might want to avoid privileging her physical appearance and instead seek to integrate her youthful energy with the other aspects of her complex character – intellectual passion, political vision and rebellious spirit. It was disappointing to find the many conflicts Eliot's Dorothea faces (about gender and effective power, divided loyalties and irreconcilable ambitions) are subordinated to a classic romance narrative (her mis-marriage with Casaubon and her obstacle-ridden relationship with Will Ladislaw – the latter, incidentally, cast and photographed as a glamorously Byronic figure to match the physicality of Dorothea). Certainly the romance is a vital element in her story but it dominates the interpretative field of Dorothea's character and prevents a wider exploration of complex tensions in the novel to do with notions of masculinity and femininity, marriage and patriarchal conventions.

Dr Lydgate's wife, Rosamond, is another rich site of gendered tension. Eliot obviously disliked women who were emotionally manipulative and obsessed with material appearances, yet there are clues in the novel (and in her other writings) that she was uneasy about her own negativity towards Rosamond and, indeed, she shows some sympathy towards her. The similarities between Dorothea and Rosamond may in fact be more illuminating than their obvious differences.[7] Both are figures of female rebelliousness, articulating their anger in qualitatively different ways. Eventually, they achieve some intimacy because each is suffering torment alone and finally find, in the other, a safe place to weep providing a cathartic moment of female solidarity, showing gender as a source of alliance rather than competitiveness. It is too easy an option to present them as simplified polarised versions of the feminine.

Many of the other female characters would be receptive to a more radical and generous treatment. The gossip of the community, the network of women's news-exchanges which laces the novel, conveys both the frustrated potential and the rich diversity of women's lives throughout the community. *Middlemarch* is a valuable source of social history about domestic life and attitudes across all classes, and calls into question the authority of the patriarchal figures.[8] The mise-en-scene of the TV-adaptation could have reflected a more female emphasis.

I am not claiming all women share the same interests, but women's different experiential history from men's is significant, and will, especially with encouragement to reflect on it, draw out different points of interest. Giving women the same backing to make prestigious classic drama that well-connected men receive would give the international prime-time viewer a chance to experience the fictional world through imaginative channels developed in critique of the male hegemony of the arts.

Gendered Thinking – popular science

My research on the representation of nature in wildlife programmes (still overwhelmingly made by men) has revealed that the choice and focus of the subject-matter, framing of the stories, language, narration, anthropomorphic imagery, camerawork, and so on provide a particular view of nature, one that privileges the male animal and masculine interests (particularly sexual competition, territorialism, copulation – subjects that provide saleable blood-and-bonking footage). By contrast, the life of a female is reduced more or less to her reproductive role. Furthermore, as feminist scientists have shown, this androcentric bias underlies the conventions of science itself. This has serious implications for the popular understanding of science.[9]

In 1994 I spoke on this theme at the Wildscreen symposium for wildlife filmmakers. Encouraged by a good reception (particularly among women filmmakers who expressed their own long-felt dissatisfactions with the industry) I wrote to Channel 4's Arts Commissioner, proposing this thesis as a topic for the series *J'Accuse*. The idea was enthusiastically accepted and passed on to a male executive producer who gave it to a male producer and a male researcher. The programme was well into production before I actually met with them both[10] and found, to my surprise, that my 'accusation' had already become a demolition job on the whole industry. The proposed programme was to be fronted by 'Douglas', an animated armadillo (the title mascot for Without Walls).[11] The script focused on the genre's obsession with sex and violence – ridiculing it certainly – but nonetheless representing the same male agenda. In its own terms it worked well, but it was not the argument which I was proposing.

Through the contextual framing of 'Douglas's' jokey persona the seriousness of the arguments of the various contributors was undermined; and my original proposition was significantly sidelined. Arguments about the effect of male domination of the industry, the dangers of sociobiological discourse in representing 'the natural', and the challenges of feminist science were lost. My message ultimately failed to reach the production team, sympathetic and pro-feminist as they were. Disappointed in the end result, before transmission I wrote at some length to the Commissioning Editor:

> ... It seems richly ironic that by playing down the centrality of gender the programme thus reinforces the very thesis I hoped it was set up to combat – that natural history programmes marginalise females, and women as a viewing constituency. What this case illustrates, I think, is the issue of vision. By this I mean that those for whom gender poses no personal or social problems are likely to be less attuned to disparities in language, treatment and commonsense assumptions, and less interested in pushing a gendered argument when others are available. Speaking and viewing as a woman is a substantively different experience from that of men; and since a great deal of my research is based on viewing natural history programmes as a woman, and collecting responses from women, a female production team might have taken quite a different line.
>
> I feel that your handing over the project to a male executive, and he to a male producer, suggests a more general assumption that gender doesn't make much difference, and has no significant effect on the product. As part of the wider project of Equal Opportunities, to allow culture to reflect the ideas, experience and talents of female and male equally, it is surely important to recognise cases where this might be most appropriate and to intervene at the point of production and – crucially – in commissioning policy.
>
> I hope you realise I am making no personal criticisms here. I felt motivated to write to you because larger issues are highlighted by this particular case.

The reply, in its entirety, read:

> Thank you for the letter about *J'Accuse Natural History*. As you know, I received your original note and passed it on to the company which makes the series. After that I did not interfere with their choice of producer or director: they have been making programmes for long enough to know what works and what doesn't. Should you be asked to review the film, I'm sure you will enjoy it. It is funny, wry, hard-hitting and rounded.
>
> Yours sincerely,
>
> Waldemar Januszczak.

Both the case studies I have used reflect lost opportunities for expressing and exploring feminist research unpolemically in popular television programmes. Many feminist academics, wary of their research being trivialised or misrepresented, are reticent to hand over control of their work, and steer clear of the broadcast media. Unfortunately broadcasters and feminists hold each other in mutual mistrust yet academics and broadcasters of a feminist outlook should be working together. We share the same desire and objective, to get the unconscious norms of popular thinking feminised, and thereby free both women and men from the restrictions imposed on them by gender-based conventions and habits of thought.

With mainstream broadcasting driven by the need to make saleable products for a public whose tastes are shaped by the men with power (including those with power over the family remote control switch), feminising broadcasting will be a long process. But broadcasting is a potentially transformational medium and necessitates long-term vision. Changing representations of society can influence society's perception of itself. Since the masculine is unconsciously normalised in daily broadcasting there is need for a mechanism within the industry that encourages gender sensitivity throughout the schedules. It should be policy to look for ways of tapping the feminine potential of all material, however unlikely, and policy to monitor and reflect on the effects of the masculine cultural legacy in broadcasting.

Involving more women at all levels of artistic decision-making is certainly necessary, but is not in itself sufficient.[12] Sex equality is not just about head counting but about generating conditions where the expression of different life-experiences becomes part of the norm. Unless, and until, the industry, both in commissioning policy and in small-scale matters, recognises that gender makes a subtle but substantial difference to one's perception of society, and that a programme-maker's sex can affect the product in important ways the positive energies of feminism may well become a casualty in the marketing wars.

Notes and References

1. Women's programmes may run the gamut from polemical consciousness-raising to raucous chat-show babes and include single-issue programmes (on health matters or harassment), day-time magazines or female comedians, but this does not necessarily make them feminist.
2. Masculine culture tends to treat female culture derisorily and, in some cases, men take it upon themselves to speak authoritatively about aspects of female culture. Melvyn Bragg's South Bank Show about Barbara Cartland did not bother to include any feminist scholars or refer to any feminists studies of contemporary romance.
3. Gillian Beer, *George Eliot* (Brighton: Harvester, 1996) p 161-2.
4. Will Ladislaw, however, a very feminised characterisation, is generally seen as weak, and denied serious critical attention. See Gilbert and Gubar, *The Madwoman in the Attic* (London: Yale University Press 1984), p. 528.
5. In the novel there is no male figure comparable to Dorothea's role. Lydgate, whose problems are often paralleled with Dorothea's, is introduced much later, and is not drawn in such sustained psychological depth or with the same sympathy.
6. Andrew Davies's remarks are taken from a public lecture at Warwick University (2 March 1994). According to Davies, Michael Wearing (the executive producer, head of serials, BBC Drama) saw *Middlemarch* as a story as 'about a guy, not girls and who they marry'.
7. 'Oppressed by the gentlewoman's liberty, both are resentful that their husbands perceive them only as graceful yet irrelevant accoutrements and both presumptuously attempt to recreate their respective husbands in their own images'. (Gilbert and Gubar, *The Madwoman in the Attic*, pp 515-8.)

8. Gossip, a singularly female form of discourse, long derided by men, is currently being reclaimed by feminist cultural critics as a site of discursive and social support.
9. Barbara Crowther, 'Towards a Feminist Critique of Television Natural History Programmes' in Penny Florence and Dee Reynolds eds., *Feminist Subjects, Multi-media* (Manchester: Manchester University Press 1994).
10. The specifications of the consultancy were unclear, and it is a mark of my television virginity that I accepted this situation.
11. Nothing indicates the sex of this armadillo until it has gender ascribed to it. It could have been made female for the programme, voiced by a female actor. There was a missed opportunity for playing around self-reflexively with the gender aspects of its own (plasticine) construction to make important points about the politics of anthropomorphic discourse. An armadillo with no markers – male: an armadillo with long eyelashes, breasts or an apron – female.
12. Women, of course, don't always take a feminist approach, and we are all apt to reproduce the values of the profession that trains us. Including women by virtue of their sex does, however, provide the opportunity to think about how their tastes and attitudes differ from men's.

Theory to Practice

Community and Empowerment in Non-Formal Radio Campaigns

Amanda Hayne
Research and Graduate School, University of Manchester

The purpose of development communication is to reach a group of people and change their behaviour. This behaviour change would correspond with some goal or objective which seeks to better a particular aspect of life or improve a group's standard of living. Theorists in this field have attempted to develop knowledge which would improve development communication, to make it more effective and efficient.

Radio is one means of achieving effective and efficient communication. This medium can reach large groups of people at one time. It is inexpensive. It avoids barriers such as illiteracy. In developing countries, these are valid and important issues. However, the radio environment does not exist in a vacuum. For radio messages to be effective, other issues must also be addressed.

The dominant paradigm in development communication is one of these issues. Grassroots participation has arisen from a Marxist critique of the modernization paradigm. In this model, the audience must play an important role in all aspects of development communication.

Social and human development was the foundation of the grassroots paradigm. It examines the participation of the population within all aspects of development, from planning to production to feedback (Rodrigo, 1989). In accordance with the social factors of development, the grassroots paradigm also recognizes that change must be addressed from within. No external source should dictate change necessary for a society to become developed. This prohibition would protect cultural values and beliefs from external ideologies which might be threatening to the cultural well-being of the community (Dissanayake, 1981; Jayaweera, 1987).

There are four main components in the grassroots model, each focusing on the audience: (1) the audience must play a role in the production of a development message; (2) there must be channels of feedback incorporated within the design of the development project; (3) the project itself must be initiated by a group within the state, and not from an external source; (4) the media must be controlled or preferably owned by the audience.

Audience Participation

The problem with many messages in the early stages of development communication was the lack of participation by the audience. Although the relevance of tailoring information towards the audience was recognized as early as Schramm (1964), theorists supporting the grassroots model state that the audience must participate in all levels of producing the message (Berrigan, 1981; Dissanayake,

1981; Hein, 1988; Mody, 1991). This requirement counteracts the belief that producers of information could '(put) the voices of the people on air (to) compensate for the producer's lack of familiarity with the target audience' (Theroux, 1978, p. 31).

Audience participation can occur on a variety of levels. The audience can take part in producing the message. Mody (1991) claims that Western sources and external agents can train individuals within the population to use technical equipment. Sound and video equipment are becoming much more user friendly, hence more accessible to the average person.

Individuals within the population can also assist in the script-writing process. Since development messages can use many formats (such as soap opera, lecture, or music), individuals can write the script reflecting their cultural values. Local communicators would also relate to the audience better than external agents. They could use phrases or words which could capture the mood of the message, words which might not necessarily be known or understood by the external agent. When examining the effectiveness of communication, this component is logical. It is very helpful in the preproduction stage where experts in certain media could refine the audience's initial input in a development message (Mody, 1991).

Feedback is also an important component in any communication process. To ensure that any receiver has acquired the correct message, forms of feedback are incorporated within the design of the message itself. Without reaction, an accurate reception of information is difficult to appraise (Bordenave, 1977).

In interpersonal communication, feedback can be obtained immediately through both verbal and nonverbal indicators. Unfortunately, feedback of this type is difficult to achieve when using the mass media. In development communication, the mass media are preferred to interpersonal communication simply because they have the capacity to immediately reach a great number of people (Hein, 1988). Therefore, one must also incorporate channels of feedback to ensure the message is properly understood.

The concept of feedback was important to grassroots theorists because proper channels of feedback were not seen as essential in prior projects. In rural societies, communication via mass media was one-way. Many of the messages were dispatched from a central unit and disseminated to the public. But this limited the information from rural locations. Because transportation and mail services were slow in these parts of developing states, communication from the target audience to the source was rarely acquired (Berrigan, 1981; Eschenbach, 1977; Magalang, 1976; Wang and Dissanayake, 1982; Webster, 1975).

Feedback ensures that the concerns of the audience are addressed. It also confirms that the audience understands the message. But for feedback to be effective, proper channels must be incorporated within the design of the project itself. A channel which is not accessible to the audience does not nurture feedback (Eschenbach, 1977; Rodrigo, 1989). For example, if the audience is not literate, letters written by audience members might not be an adequate reflection. Instead extension or community workers might provide a more well-rounded evaluation of the effect of the message. It is therefore important to design channels of feedback which are appropriate to the audience.

Project Initiation

One of the key elements in the grassroots approach to development communication is the ability of the audience to develop through their own standards. According to theorists, the only way of reducing the problem of external influence to development was to let the audience decide how they should develop. Development would more likely reflect the attitudes and perceptions of the target audience, since their own concepts would be addressed (Carmen, 1989; Dissanayake, 1981).

Letting the audience decide on development is a potential problem because the target audience might not possess all essential information. The audience may not be able to make a rational decision ensuring the well-being of their future because they lack a broad perspective. Simply stated, an external agent may have to identify problems within developing countries.

Some grassroots theorists have considered this situation. Carmen (1989) claims that a major component of development communication is knowledge empowerment. All individuals have the ability to gain knowledge from communication or discourse. This component of development communication is time-consuming. Yet it does propose a channel for the audience to obtain information to make rational decisions about the well-being of their community.

Monu (1989) claims that one responsibility of development communication is to provide rural communities with information. This information would then give them the power to make rational decisions about the future of their communities. Monu claims, 'meaningful participation depends on the availability of adequately and timely information (especially in more complex technical areas) to make rational decisions in project planning, implementation and evaluation' (p. 10). Monu thus limits his concept of participation. Participation should only be enacted if it is meaningful, if the audience has the information necessary for them to make rational decisions.

Media Ownership

Grassroots theorists believe that the media should be owned by the audience. If this is not feasible, the audience should have some form of control over the broadcasting system. This concern arose because most governments in developing nations were authoritarian. Since this type of government dramatically limits the forum for dissident views, concerns of the audience were not addressed. If development projects do not correspond with government objectives, information might not be disseminated to the target audience (Kasoma, 1990).

The problem of media ownership is not resolved by the capitalist nor the Marxist models. The media in the capitalist model are privately owned. Media owners respond to market demands and broadcast information accordingly. This type of ownership limits educational material, because it is unprofitable. But the Marxist model does not alleviate this problem. If the government controls the media system, they then control the information that will be broadcast. The government would want to maintain the status quo. No information which would threaten this position would be broadcast (Berrigan, 1981; Stephens, 1989). Therefore the only option in an open participatory system is audience-owned media (Kasoma, 1990). The problem with the capitalist and Marxist systems is that they do not encourage the exchange of information dealing with issues important to community members.

Kasoma (1990) believed that the audience could own the media through co-operatives. Information tools such as newspapers, video and posters could be jointly owned by a village or society. Thus individuals could be trained to operate equipment and perform the necessary skills to fulfil this obligation. In this manner, the audience would have control over what issues are addressed as well as the manner in which they are dealt with.

This is an excellent theoretical concept. But Kasoma does limit his theory due to practical reasons. Unless a society has the time, finances, and expertise to achieve a successful system, co-operative media is not a viable solution. One would have to incorporate the time and money to assure proper training of media equipment. Kasoma limits this to feasible media for most developing nations: newspapers, video units and posters. He does not believe that a radio system is economically viable for most developing states.

To conclude, grassroots participation rose from the concerns of previous applications to development. Its purpose was to achieve self-reliance in the audience. The population within developing nations must become decision-makers to assure their cultural, social and economic sovereignty. However, lessons can be learned from this approach regarding the way we, in industrialized countries, view our media. The traditional approach to radio has been hierarchial – a tool to disseminate information from the top downwards. But could radio be used in a different way, by making the audience an integral component in the educational process?

This serves more than simply an ethical perspective as supported by the grassroots model. It has been found that active involvement in the educational process is conducive to success. Zimbardo and Lieppe (1993) state 'When self-persuasion works, it does so because the individual struck some internal chords, generating ideas and arguments that are convincing because they originated in the individual's own system of values, beliefs and knowledge' (p. 181).

Hubley (1993) agrees with the participatory approach in education, specifically regarding health education. He states 'the participants are active and not passive so they are likely to remember what was introduced during the session. They draw from their own experience. They are allowed to discover principles for themselves and can develop problem-solving skills. Participatory learning methods are especially relevant for those who did not do well in school' (p. 75).

Participatory learning, then, becomes a practical issue as well as an ethical one. If the audience could be incorporated in all stages of the design and production of the development message, then messages should be more efficient and effective.

However, in a small pilot study (Hayne, 1993) it was found that while the elements of the grassroots model are practised in part, aspects of the theory were modified to remain true to the intent of the theorists, if not their specific desires.

Theorists want the audience to participate in the design and formulation of the message (Berrigan, 1981; Dissanayake, 1981; Mody, 1991). Practically, this concept may be unfeasible. The audience may not be able to identify the formats and appeals or content which they need for effective communication. In short, they may not be able to tell a designer how to communicate effectively with them.

However, interviews and focus group discussions are means to achieve audience participation. They can be conducted before the initiation of the project or while it is running. Producers can suggest formats and content, and then test the potential message with a sample of audience members. This action does not contradict the principles of the grassroots theorists. The audience still has input.

Grassroots theorists believe that the audience must have accessible channels of feedback to voice their concerns about the development message (Bordenave, 1977; Eschenbach, 1977; Hein, 1988; Magalang, 1976; Mody, 1991; Rodrigo, 1989; Stover, 1984; Wang and Dissanayake, 1982). Audience pretesting again serves as a valuable tool to fulfil this goal. Prior to broadcasting development messages, feedback from the audience can verify that the understand both the purpose of the message and the components needed for change. Pre-testing also increases the effectiveness and efficiency of the development message.

Theorists believe that the audience should initiate development (Bordenave, 1977; Carmen, 1989; Dissanayake, 1981; Hornik, 1988; Mody, 1991; Monu, 1989; Rodrigo, 1989; Stevenson, 1988; Stover, 1984). However, internal community organizations can act on behalf of the target audience. If the audience has no means of obtaining information, or believe that a development issue is necessary, or even exists, than a community organization which works directly with the audience should respond.

Theorists claim that the audience should own and control the media system (Berrigan, 1981; Kasoma, 1990; Stephens, 1989). It would be extremely difficult to practically apply this concept, based on the financial constraints of the audience. In a small study (Hayne, 1993), it was found that no non-formal educational projects used community local radio stations. Instead, communicators had to operate within the system of the particular state which included both public and private stations.

The grassroots model, if modified, can be applied to present day non-formal educational radio campaigns. Not only is it ethical by allowing the audience the opportunity to participate in development, it also encompasses the theory of active involvement.

However, the radio environment does not exist within a vacuum. Communicators must still employ the elements of radio as an effective communicative device. The type of information must be conducive to audience abilities (Crisell, 1986). There should be supplemental information available to the audience, as radio is an ephemeral medium (Bates, 1984). Formats must be used constructively, as the audience's attention must be captured and maintained for the audience to be exposed to the message (Bates, 1984; Reynolds and Anderson, 1992). Finally, and perhaps most importantly, the development message must address the needs of the audience (McAnany, 1979; Hornik, 1988). It is then the responsibility of broadcasters to attempt to create a more conducive environment for audience participation while still remaining true to effective and efficient communication. Radio should not be viewed as dichotomous to the grassroots model. It has simply been used that way.

Bibliography:

Bates, A. (1984) *Broadcasting in Education: An Evaluation*, Binghamton, New York: CSA Publications

Berrigan, F.J. (1981) *Community Communications: The Role of Community Media in Development*, Paris: UNESCO

Bogue, D. (1979) 'Educational Radio Programming: The Radio Forum' In T.D. Peigh, M.J. Maloney, R.C. Higgins & D.J. Bogue (eds) *The Use of Radio in Social Development*, (page 113–127) Chicago: The Community and Family Study Centre, University of Chicago

Bordenave, J.E. (1977) *Communication and Rural Development*, Paris: UNESCO

Burke, R.C. (1992) 'Co-production in Community Development: a Day at the Educational Fair'. in *Educational Media International*, Volume 29, 2, June, 1992, p 91–95

Carmen, R.E.R.M. (1989) 'Development Communication: The Search for a Participatory Paradigm'. *Community Development Journal*, Volume 24, 4, page 264–272

Crisell, A (1986) *Understanding Radio*. London: Methuen

Dissanayake, W. (1981) 'Development and Communication: Four Approaches' in *Media Asia*, Volume 8, 4, page 217–227

Eschenbach, J. (1977) *The Role of Broadcasting in Rural Communication*, Bonn-Bad Godesberg, Germany: Friedrich-Ebert-Stiftung

Hayne, A. (1993) *Can We Practice What They Preach: The Application of Theory in Radio and Development Communication*, Windsor: University of Windsor Press

Hein, K.J. (1988) *Radio Baha'i Equador: A Baha'i Development Project*, Oxford: George Ronald

Hornik, R.C. (1988) *Development Communication: Information, Agriculture and Nutrition in the Third World*. White Plains, New York: Longman

Hubley, J. (1993) *Communicating Health: An Action Guide to Health Education and Health Promotion*, London: MacMillian Press Ltd

Jayaweera, N. & Amunugama, S. (1987) *Rethinking Development Communications*, Singapore: Asian Mass Communications Research and Information Centre

Kasoma , F.P. (1990) 'Media Ownership: Key to Participatory Development'. *Media Asia*, Volume 17, 2,p 79–82

Magalang, D.M. (1976) 'The Comic Book and The Agricultural Approach'. In D.M. Magalang (Ed.) From *The Village to the Medium*, Manila, Phillipines: Communication Foundation for Asia (p 41–64)

Maloney, M (1979) 'Writing and Producing Radio Dramas' In T.D. Peigh, M.J. Maloney, R.C. Higgins & D.J. Bogue (eds) *The Use of Radio in Social Development*, (page 113–127) Chicago: The Community and Family Study Centre, University of Chicago

McAnany, E. (1973) *Radio's Role in Development: 5 Strategies for Use*. (Information Bulletin No. 4). Washington, D.C.: Information Centre for Instructional Technology, Academy for Educational Development

Mody, B. (1991) *Designing Messages for Development Communication*, New Delhi: Sage Publications

Monu, E.D. (1989) 'Delivering Relevant Development Information to the Rural Poor', *Media Asia*, Volume 16, 1, p 10–15

Reynolds, A. & Anderson, R.H. (1992) *Selecting and Developing Media for Instruction*, New York: Van Nostrand Reinhold

Rodrigo, M.L. (1989) 'Communication and Development: Obstacles in Implementing Development Programmes'. *Media Asia*, Volume 16, 4, pages 206–222

Schramm, W. (1964). *Mass Media and National Development: The Role of Information in the Developing Countries*, Stanford, California: Stanford University Press

Stephens, K.D. (1987) 'Alternative Energy for Radio Stations' in *Development Communication Report*, Volume 3, 58, page 13

Stevenson, R.L. (1988) *Communication, Development and the Third World: Global Politics of Information*. New York: Longman

Stover, W. (1984) *Information Technology in the Third World: Can It Lead to Humane National Development?* Bolder, Colorado: Westview Press

Theroux, J.M. (1978) *Techniques for Improving Educational Radio Programmes*, Paris: UNESCO

UNESCO (1962). *Developing Information Media in Africa: Press, Radio, Film, Television*, Paris: UNESCO

Wang, G. & Dissanayake, W. (1982). 'The Study of Indigenous Communication Systems in Development: Phased Out or Phasing In', *Media Asia*, Volume 9, 1, p 3–8

Webster, B.R. (1975). *Access: Technology and Access to Communications Media*, Paris: Unesco

Zimbardo, P.G. and Leippe, M.R. (1991) *The Psychology of Attitude Change and Social Influence*, New York: McGraw-Hill Inc.

Multi-skilling or de-skilling?

New Technologies and the News of the Future

Brent MacGregor
Institute of Communications Studies, University of Leeds

The future

A twenty first-century wired journo-tech receives input on a breaking story in her patch. Remote visual sensors, the descendants of today's surveillance cameras, have recorded a newsworthy real-world event onto a vast visual data bank. The journalist's Knowbot, an expert news 'agent,' consisting of specially trained expert systems software, recognises the importance of the story and draws her attention to it. Instantly the hack can re-view the event and, if dramatic enough, she can code it for instant transmission on Newswatch, the 24 hour surveillance camera channel. A camcopter may be diverted if the story is judged likely to develop significantly and, if it is really big news, a piloted helicopter will be despatched. Otherwise multimedia background information on the story is down loaded to her Personal Information Assistant as the reporter fights her way through the low tech traffic jam in search of the ever elusive exclusive. Arriving at the scene she proceeds to record additional elements of the story, 'filming,' using solid state digital recording equipment — effectively, the equivalent of wearing glasses and a Walkman. If the story is big enough, she can inject live into a global, national or local news network. Otherwise the twenty first century hack shoots the pictures and assembles the story using her Intelligent Recorder and the News templates she has developed over the years. Using these aids, there should be very little need for editing, but should any post production be required the same video goggles which recorded the images become the head up display screens of her virtual edit suite, controlled by the hand held picture pack. The journalist re-composes the visuals and records the voice overs for presentation in various forms. Thus edited, the package need not be sent back to base but can be transmitted straight from the reporter's kit onto a dedicated rolling news service, while a longer premium version is filed on a pay-per-view news-on-demand video server. Marked with her unique digital signature, the story is automatically down loaded to the home servers of all her subscribers who are informed that her story is there. A text-only version is available online for those only possessing antiquated technologies like the World Wide Web and the story will also be available in printed form the next morning on reusable polymer news sheets. There is even a version as ink on dead trees. This genuinely exclusive premium service is available only to those elites lucky enough to be above being merely wired; those who can afford the real value added service of having someone else edit out the news from the incessant information flow and present it to them.

Hype and superhype

Any vaguely aware member of the media-consuming classes today cannot help but have been aware of a flood of digital hype flowing inexorably from the supposedly soon-to-be obsolete but surprisingly hyperactive printing presses of the planet. A subset of the revolutionary claims being made for the new digital technologies are the changes that are prophesied for newsgathering and consumption. The scenario outlined above is a wild exaggeration; a foray into the very risky business of predicting the future. Such visions create either techno-wonder, sceptical amusement or instant dismissal amongst disinterested readers, but the subject is of great concern not just to those who pontificate about the digital revolution. It is a matter of professional life and death to those journalists immediately affected.

VJs and BJs

Lightweight camcorders now make it possible for video journalists or VJs to operate as one-person news-gathering units, unencumbered by the baggage of 'the crew.' Instead of reporter, camera operator, sound recordist and possibly a fixer or producer, it is now possible to despatch one person who, having shot the story, can then return to base and edit the material into a transmittable package. This mode of working is already the norm with two cable news operations in New York and London. Both called Channel One, these twenty four hour rolling local news stations are funded by newspaper industry backers and employ specially trained multi-skilled video journalists instead of specialist reporters, cameramen, recordists and videotape editors. Michael Rosenblum, an American consultant who advised both Channel One operations, describes the new camcorders as being 'the video equivalent of the Leica,'[1] liberating lightweight technology which replaces the labouring beast of the crew with the flexible single person newsgatherer, doing for television news what the 35 mm. stills camera did for photojournalism. He sees the new technologies as giving television news certain advantages that print journalism already has. Roaming unobtrusively, armed only with a notebook computer and mobile phone, the newspaper reporter escapes the logistical limitations that restrict the lumbering television crew. Such a reporter can research, write and file a story unassisted. Soon, with new technologies, television journalists will be able to do the equivalent with equal ease.

There are other advantages, says Rosenblum, demanding that television news should 'introduce the spike.' All too often, the commitment of scarce technical resources means broadcasters have to use the material produced by a reporter and crew whether or not it is up to scratch. There should be no need to air substandard video material just to fill the screen, as suddenly news organisations can have 30 or 40 crews where they once might have had 10 and, given this increased input, it is possible to be much more discerning. New technologies and the working methods that they make possible will give television the same advantages as print in terms of newsgathering flexibility and they will give television news a greater ability to take risks.

There is a certain inevitability about such developments, not because of simple technological determinism, as if the technology somehow foisted itself on the profession, but the result of management-led economic decisions. 'Make no mistake, this is cost driven,' says Ted Taylor, Director of Technology at ITN, who speaks of 'journo-techs' capable of writing copy and editing pictures with equal ease. In his estimation, seven functions in the production process would be removed by such multi-skilling. Chris Cramer, the Head of BBC Television Newsgathering, told assembled hacks in Berlin simply: 'Video journalism will hit you whether you like it or not.' Already BBC World and CBC Newsworld are employing specially equipped and trained VJs or BJs (broadcast journalists) while CNN executives openly talk of 'job compression.' Management, many of whom have never done the jobs in question and who often come from an engineering background, make cost-led decisions about equipment provision which inevitably result in working practices changing radically. What effect such changes have on journalistic output appears to be rarely considered.

In the United States, the revolution is already happening by default. Hard-pressed stations running local news operations on a shoestring are paying poverty wages (c. $13,000 year) to recent communications and journalism school graduates who slave using all too old technology to file two or three stories a day, reporting, shooting and editing alone in the vain hope that such Herculean labour will one day raise them into the realm of such high earners as Peter Jennings, Dan Rather and Christiane Amanpour. The mere mention of such working practices becoming the norm is enough to send many of today's established journalists into an apoplectic sound bite. Martin Bell, whose reporting for the BBC from Bosnia has attracted universal professional acclaim, says with characteristic brevity that he hopes he'll be underground when it arrives as common practice, and his colleague Michael Beurk expresses a concern that 'journalism will suffer.'

One man bands

There is in fact nothing new about single person newsgathering. The BBC's Television Newsreel coverage of the Korean war was conducted first by cameraman Cyril Page and then by Ronnie Noble, both of them working alone.[2] Clockwork Bolex film cameras and small Arriflexes which were literally hand-held, unlike the shoulder-mounted beasts of today, have been around for decades. Such cameras only recorded mute film and, with the demand for synchronous location recorded sound, equipment necessarily became heavier. Nevertheless, news agency staff and many stringers regularly worked alone, capable of recording broadcast quality sound and pictures on 16 millimetre film. Nik Downing, a former SAS soldier, filmed the war in Rhodesia alone and later, with heavier U-matic video equipment, worked without a crew in Afghanistan.

Sue Lloyd-Roberts, working first for ITN and now for the BBC, has been a one woman band recording first on S-VHS, and now Hi-8. She started such work behind the Iron Curtain and has moved on, recently travelling around China with dissident Harry Wu, filming secret forced labour camps. Often questions of access force such working practices on journalists who can hardly film undercover with a full crew. Such notable exceptions certainly prove that it is possible, although to be fair Lloyd-Roberts herself doesn't think the practice should be universal.

Outside of the hurly-burly of news, other areas of programming have employed new video technologies, even going so far as to give the public the equipment.

The BBC's Video Diaries, recorded on Hi-8 video tape, have extended the envelope of what is technically and editorially possible, an example which has been followed by others, including investigative documentaries such as Undercover Britain, filmed with hidden cameras.

There has always been a traditional broadcast standard of technically acceptable picture quality. In the days of film, 16 millimetre was above this threshold but 'amateur' 8 millimetre cine film was not. When videotape arrived as the newsgathering standard, Hi-band U-matic was acceptable while technically inferior lo-band was not. Similarly, Super VHS has been a minimum acceptable standard used by stringers, but domestic VHS has been declared beyond the pale. Cynics suggest that these broadcast standards are merely artificial barriers designed to stem the tide of material streaming into television organisations, and to some extent this is true, but of course anything really unique and vital gets used regardless of the picture quality. The 8mm film of JFK's assassination, the video of Rabin's death[3] and the countless examples of camcorder footage which now appear in everything from the news to light entertainment programming bear witness to this.

Will it work?

Clearly the supposed revolution is to some extent already under way, but what it will mean for the nature of television news is not quite clear. Radio has done single person news gathering and editing for years with reel to reel tape recorders and low tech razor blades and cellotape.[4] Little comment is made about this technologically enabled practice and it would be hard to point to any perceptible decrease in the quality of radio journalism that is attributable to single-person location newsgathering. Television news stringers sent to shoot pictures and natural sound only, often conduct basic interviews with, say, a fire officer or policeman at the scene of an event. Yorkshire Television's news magazine programme, Calendar, has for some years employed a woman stringer working with S-VHS equipment who was originally a journalist. When asked about the shortcomings of such working methods, she replies simply that there is no one to share the driving.

When an orthodox crew is sent abroad, they very often take a spare camera 'channel' in case of what would be very expensive equipment failure. This second camcorder very often gets deployed in the hands of the sound recordist, providing the team with more 'camera power' and, as the team's reporter can clearly only be in one place, this second unit very often becomes a one man band. During the admittedly special circumstances of the Gulf War, ITN cameraman Jim Dutton filmed alone inside Iraq and was then interviewed from London about what he had seen and filmed. Newsnight correspondent Mark Urban and Producer Steve Anderson covered the same conflict, working at times without what they called 'a proper crew.' After this experience Urban says:

> I don't think one should be under any doubt though, that obviously the pro cameraman is going to make a better job of it. ... there's a loss of quality. You have to be able to justify, in terms either of the old thing of being too intrusive, four people with a proper camera on a

tripod and all the rest of it, or some other need to get into some bizarre inaccessible place.[5]

In extreme circumstances, such as Bosnia, overriding security and safety considerations tend to lead to the smallest crew possible, usually two-person teams of reporter and cameraman plus a locally hired interpreter. With a team any smaller, there is not enough support, while with a crew any larger, the risks increase. From a purely pragmatic point of view, it is simply a case of horses for courses.

Teamwork often increases efficiency, with two heads being better than one. A second pair of eyes can often be crucial; it being all too easy for a camera operator to become so engrossed in filming that they simply do not notice something of importance happening just out of shot. Working in a team makes it possible to arrive at a location and split up, with the reporter talking to people and getting a feel for the story before doing any interviews, while the cameraman shoots general views. Once the material is shot and the crew return to base, the picture editor is effectively the first member of the audience, quite ready to question and to dismiss footage regardless of the time and trouble taken to obtain it. While the editor and reporter put the story together, the camera crew are redundant. Oddly enough they rarely look at their own material and there is a case to be made that they should edit it.

Technically speaking, a basic level of multi-skilled operation is not a problem. In my experience undergraduate students can learn to shoot and edit easily enough but they have notable trouble doing the difficult job of creating structure in a time-based visual medium. The human skills needed for the task should not be underestimated. Whatever the technology, there is still a need to have a 'nose for news,' to go to the right place in the first place and negotiate the access needed; a delicate balancing act that no technology will aid. You have to ask the right people the right questions, and possess the background knowledge needed to set the event in context. As input turns to output, as newsgathering becomes broadcasting, the multi-skilled journo tech must be able to write concise copy that complements pictures, have a good broadcasting voice to record those words, possess an appropriate on-screen manner that 'comes through the glass,' not to mention the steady nerves and technical skill required to broadcast live to half the globe while someone is screaming in your ear telling you what to say and some demented zealot is unloading his AK 47 in your general direction.

Great skill in using words and pictures together is not always apparent on our screens today. Few reporters are good film makers and in my experience they certainly don't think of themselves that way. Writing is still the most valued of a reporter's skills.

Will this change with new technologies putting the reporter behind the camera? In terms of professional culture change it is very early days yet and the enabling technologies are likewise in their infancy, regardless of what their proponents claim. Broadcast journalism is constantly evolving. In 1936 when BBC television first went on the air, it would have been a foolish person who would have predicted 24 hour a day global television news networks or indeed even predicted 'the news.'

The 'robo hack'[6] of the future will need to be Robert Fiske, Maggie O'Kane, Martin Bell, Kate Adie, Eammon McCabe and Don Mcullin rolled into one multi-skilled miracle worker we encounter as we surf through the 500 digital channels. But in the uni-skilled world of today Robert Fiske and Martin Bell are exceptions rather than the rule. Equally the huge unionised crews of the 1970s and early 80s didn't automatically lead to good television journalism, with the most important considerations being parking and mass catering. Perhaps the most efficient and socially agreeable solution would be a two person operation of journalistically competent producer and reporter, both of whom could perform the technical tasks of recording and editing pictures and sound. Background research and logistics could be conducted by either and one would present the piece while the other effectively directed it. This would be something very like the current affairs way of working (minus the crew) and could result in a more visually dynamic, medium-appropriate style.

Television will change, offering a wider range of diverse services from raw footage to the polished documentary. This diversity of product will result from an equally diverse range of working methods. The world of the robo hack of the future with which we began is clearly some way off, but if this 21st century descendant of Kate Adie is to do her job properly she will need more than simply the enabling technology. She will need education and training, experience in a supported environment and institutions that care about her, the story and the viewers. Above all, she will need managers who are not just obsessed with trying to keep the cost numbers down and the audience numbers up.

Notes:

1. All quotations are from the proceedings of the News World International Conference, held in Berlin, November 9-12, 1995, unless otherwise noted.
2. Howard Smith, 'The BBC Television Newsreel and the Korean War', *Historical Journal of Film and Television*, Vol 8, No 3, 1988, p.235. Noble's work is described as being 'remarkably imaginative'.
3. This material sold in Britain for £50,000.
4. Audio broadcasting is much more advanced in terms of digital editing and recording. Producers and reporters routinely edit, but equally dedicated editors still exist. Interestingly, new digital technologies have not penetrated all aspects of radio, and in the BBC, news, the most critical kind of programming, is still conducted using tapes and razor blades because it is both faster and more reliable.
5. Interview with the author, 9 July, 1992.
6. A phrase coined by Nick Gowing, then Diplomatic Editor, Channel 4 News.

The Broadcatcher in the Wry

Television, Technology and Consumer Control

John Mundy
University College, Warrington

Turmoil is, of course, a relative experience and one organisation's angst is another's irrelevance. Yet British television in the mid 1990s is faced with a series of unparalleled dilemmas and decisions. Government legislation, actual and intended, issues of size, structure, ownership and remit, the challenges posed or implied by new technologies, tensions between loyalty to the local and the regional combined with aspirations to the global, and the all-too 'here and now' and 'in-yer-face' scramble for market share, would seem sufficient in themselves to guarantee an ongoing game of executive musical chairs. Worse, these dilemmas and decisions take place against a backdrop of seeming ignorance and indifference on the part of the viewing public, who for much of the time appear to remain stubbornly indifferent to the promised cornucopia of digital tv, the liberatory delights of interactive tv, and even – shock, horror – the outcome of the NTL sale.

When public concern does emerge, often fuelled and in part managed by the very antagonisms within the industry which form the substance of that concern, it often focuses on what will come to be seen – if it already isn't – as either bizarre or quaint. Take, for example, the proposed merger between Lord Hollick's MAI and Lord Steven's United News and Media, certainly not a marriage made in any ideological heaven. The unseemly sight of academics throughout the higher education system revisiting their lecture notes is more than matched by the equally unseemly – and perhaps ultimately irrelevant – scramble for 'new media' mergers amongst existing British broadcasters and newspaper groups. As Lisa Buckingham commented in *The Guardian* (February 12, 1996), whatever rhetoric there may be about UK-based 'global players', at the moment 'corporate attention remains focused on extracting the last drops of profit from the domestic media market before far tougher overseas territories are tackled'. Interest in such industry manoeuvrings are, it is true, limited largely to the broadsheet-reading public, and it takes something like BSkyB's decision to charge (again) for the Bruno-Tyson fight to really set us alight, and challenge assumptions about people's willingness to pay for what is marketed as a 'wider choice of programming'. Amidst talk of 'Murdoch's Skyjackers', of 'Skyway robbery' and 'Pay-through-the-nose TV', it's a salutary warning about how far the British public still have to travel if they are to accept what many see as the inevitable and far-reaching shifts implicit in the exercise of 'consumer sovereignty'. And this at a time when well over three million households in the UK have satellite, when Multiple Service Operators (MSO) such as Telewest, Comcast and Nynex are entering not just homes but, to an extent, public consciousness as well, and when, according to the Cable Communications Association, the industry is creating 25 new jobs each day. (Peak 1995). Across Europe, figures for quarterly connections in the fourth chapter of 1995 continue to show a steady rise. (Cable and Satellite Europe, March 1996).

I don't know how the public outcry over this tentative step towards pay-as-you—view TV has been viewed in the boardrooms and managerial offices of the terrestrial broadcasters, but I can imagine. After all, and in spite of developments in multichannel TV, the BBC and ITV still account for 80% of all viewing, and most analysts would agree that ITV retains a firm grasp on TV advertising revenues – perhaps, Channel 4 might argue – in more ways than one. It may be that Andy Allan, Carlton's DP, is justified in believing that ITV will remain the 'country's most popular channel' well into the future. (Television, Jan/Feb. 1996, p 14).

If present market share wasn't sufficient excuse to concentrate executive minds on domestic matters, there's the intriguing spectacle of the House of Lords rallying to the cause with their protective amendment to the Broadcasting Bill, a regulatory ring-fencing of eight major sporting events which are seen to contribute in some manner or means to notions of British national identity, no matter if even the most popular of these events, the Grand National, only manages the same ratings as ITV's Gladiators.

Yet nobody could accuse the UK broadcasting industry of complacency -- far from it. In fact, the pages of the trade and house journals are littered with articles written by luminaries who are acutely aware of the challenges facing the UK television industry. It's just that the road ahead is a difficult one, and there's no authoritative map to guide us in the right direction. Moreover, the situation is more problematic than in the United States where, because broadcasting has always existed within commercial frameworks, public attitudes towards the consumption of cultural production are markedly different. Such attitudes have contributed to an exponential growth of cable services, as the American networks know to their cost, and provide a more receptive context for the claims of people such as TCI's John Malone who, extolling the virtues of digital compression and the 500 channel future, argued that TCI's ultimate goal is 'to give our customers control of their TV service.' (Wasko, 1994).

Here, where the public's relationship to broadcasting has been constructed by notions of public service broadcasting, by the financial structures by which we have paid for our radio and television, and by the relative scarcity of terrestrial broadcasting, the notion of viewing ownership, whether ideological or commercial, is largely alien. It may be that, up to relatively recently, this has favoured established terrestrial broadcasting. What is crystal clear is that this is changing, and all in the name, if not the reality, of consumer choice.

Much has happened since the advocacy in the Peacock Report of broadcasting which was driven by a 'sophisticated market system based on consumer sovereignty', where the exercise of consumer choice would be the quasi-darwinian lubricant which ensured industry sensitivity to what viewers and listeners actually wanted. Government hostility towards Britain's established broadcasting duopoly, coupled with the active encouragement of commercial competitors, expressed through legislation and selective use – or rather non-use

– of powers of monopolistic scrutiny, have certainly made for a difficult decade for both the BBC and the ITV companies. Thames, TV-AM and TVS might want to query the word 'difficult' and even contest the view which regards the determinants which have changed the British broadcasting landscape as the purely, supposedly neutral, 'intrusion of economic analysis into broadcasting'. (Hughes and Vines, 1989). That said, it is clear that the shift from broadcasting to narrowcasting, the growth of dedicated channels delivered by cable and satellite to an increasingly fractured and unpredictable television audience, represents a major shift in power and control within the industry in more ways than one. However, the question remains to what extent this shift in power is confined to within 'the industry', expanding and changing as it is, and to what extent it represents a shift in power to an increasingly active and determining consumer.

Quite apart from the impact upon the established structures, organisations and technologies of British broadcasting, the changes which have occurred during the last ten years have had a profound impact on notions of a coherent, knowable, largely predictable and often taken-for-granted 'television audience'. Ten years ago, it would have been difficult to question industry complacency about the central utility of audience ratings, hard to disagree with the view that 'ratings with their feedback element are the nerve system that largely controls what is broadcast'. (Beville, 1985).

Within the British broadcasting system, two distinct audience paradigms co-exist, the audience-as-public (the BBC and public service broadcasting) and the audience-as-market (the ITV commercial sector). Whilst specific audience data collection reflected this duality, a joint industry approach to audience measurement, firstly through JICTAR and subsequently through BARB research contracts, indicated a common over-riding concern with ratings, with audience size and share, with demographic characteristics. This concern only increased with the launch of Channel 4 and the growth in transmission hours on the other three terrestrial channels during the 1980s. (Kent, 1994). 'Deregulation' (perhaps 're-regulation' is more accurate), the new distribution technologies which have led to a proliferation in viewing choices, together with the impact of wider ownership of a range of new domestic leisure technologies (see Table: Entertainment Equipment in the UK Home 1994) have only increased the desire for more detailed and comprehensive audience measurement data. New technologies of audience measurement – electronic footprinting of rental video cassettes, and refinements to peoplemeters, for example – are a high priority within the audience measurement industry. Significantly, the desire for more information is increasingly dominated by the audience-as-market paradigm. The growing hegemonic power of this conception of the television audience as commodity is something that even the BBC is finding hard to resist.

Whilst many broadcasters might find this shift towards conceptualising the audience as commodity a matter of concern, it actually serves to question many of the cosy illusions which audience measurement has historically engendered. Moreover, it presages one element in the problems facing broadcasting. The very notion of the 'television audience' is a problematic, deeply ideological construct, one which tells us little, in spite of the growing sophistication of the audience measurement industry, about actual, disaggregated, viewers. Audience measurement is, arguably, an important technology of control, and ratings discourse constructs an illusion of control by the industry over viewers which is more symbolic than real (Ang, 1991). At bottom, it refutes the essential nature of broadcasting which is characterised by a 'deep contraction between centralised transmission and privatised consumption'. (Williams, 1974).

What defines broadcasting is its resolutely non-interactive character. The new multi-channel TV environment with its proliferation of dedicated programming, together with ubiquitous VCR technology, invites new audience behaviours such as 'zipping', 'zapping', and time-shifting which are known, cannot be ignored, and cannot be controlled. Just as structural control of the industry is challenged in the shift from broadcasting to narrowcasting, so, too, control over audiences, no matter how notional and symbolic that control has been, is challenged.

Yet, in comparison with what is coming, it may well be that British broadcasting as we know it simply 'ain't seen nothing yet'. As one contemporary commentator puts it: 'The key to the future of television is to stop thinking about television as television'. (Negroponte, 1995).

In its recent (August 1995) consultative document, Beyond The Telephone, The Television and The PC, OFTEL offers some thoughts on 'a new information age' based on converging, interactive technologies. In addition to digital technology producing significant expansion in network capacity at reduced costs to the end user, OFTEL envisages dramatically reduced delivery costs for broadband switched services and, equally if not more significantly, the development of systems which give customer control over the information and services – including their timing and destination – being delivered. The development of 'broadband switched mass-market' (BSM) services means

individual end-users can request the delivery of individually tailored content, in the form of a particular film, ... or through individual access to a database. Full switching produces virtually unlimited capacity – the technological equivalent of opening up unlimited television channels in the language of the 'old' technologies. Instead of broadcasting moving images over a limited number of channels to a largely passive audience, a broadband switched network allows customers to select what and when they receive.

It may be television, Jim, but not as we know it.

Such a vision opens up notions of consumer choice which go beyond anything promised by the still relatively limited changes we have experienced in Britain to date, challenging though these have been. Yet, even this model is some way from the notion of broadcatching, a term coined in 1987 by Steward Brand in America. Interestingly, the OFTEL document notes that, whilst digital broadcasting will inevitably and significantly increase the number of channels available, 'it might not alter the structure of the market'. Significantly, it envisages service providers retaining a gatekeeping capacity, either as owners of a delivery system (cable) or through a 'conditional access system' (satellite and terrestrial broadcasting). Equally significant, the technology will be capable of monitoring consumption of these switched services, and therefore will be able to cost and charge for their consumption.

Genuine interactivity – real broadcatching – may depend on new and ongoing developments in computer technology. With the ability to download digital information, TV liberates itself from most of the real-time constraints demanded from viewers. The ability to digitally 'catch' virtually everything on offer, but determine selectively which information you want to bring up on screen, as well as network with myriad other computers, implies a shift in control radically more pronounced than anything envisaged in Peacock's notion of consumer sovereignty. The convergence of computer technology with television technology threatens, in the eyes of some commentators, the obliteration of the latter as we know it. Gilder (1994) argues that the 'computer industry is converging with the television industry in the same sense that the automobile converged with the horse, the TV converged with the nickelodeon, ... and digital desktop publishing converged with the linotype machine and the letterpress.' The television set, the dumbest piece of electronic equipment in the house, will simply be replaced by ultra-smart 'teleputers', computer nets which offer infinite interactivity, each domestic terminal having the communication capacity of today's broadcast companies.

This vision of an affordable social technology which 'puts the customer in control' may seem a long way off, and as a universal experience, probably is. In the meantime, interactive TV, based on cable technology, is already with us. Innovations in the US, admittedly providing a range of levels of interactivity, are already underway. Yet, it cannot be without significance that these tentative steps towards interactivity are being underwritten by some very familiar names. VCTV (Viewer Controlled Cable Television) in Denver is backed by AT & T and United Artists, the Interactive Network (IN) in northern California by NBC, the Gannet Corporation and (yes) Neilson (*Spectrum*, Summer 1993, p 22). Arguably, in the process, what we are witnessing are attempts to define and 'fix' the ideological and cultural dimensions of interactivity. The involvement of major established entertainment and information corporations inevitably begs questions about notions of viewer control, questions which the British television industry might, at least at one level, find comforting.

The concept of a digitally interactive communicative web, unfettered by control and constraint, is a seductive one for advocates of viewer control. Yet, it may well be that the future will still lie with those who produce and, perhaps more importantly, own software material, whether this material is called 'programming' or some other name. For me, as an outsider from the industry, it often seems significant that I can get access to a studio tour much easier than I can get access to library or archive material. Too often, talk about the technologies of delivery ignore any discussion about the actual material which is to be delivered. While undoubtedly there is a liberatory dimension to the Internet at the moment, which may continue into future interactive technologies, it is hard to foresee anything but an increasing demand for material of all kinds, including that currently produced by corporations which have made huge investments in 'infotainment'.

As I said, the life of a British television executive today is not an easy one. One eye, of course, does need to be kept firmly on those implications and impulses -- decentralisation, globalisation, harmonisation and empowerment -- predicted by Negroponte as the consequences of the digital revolution.

It just may be, however, that in the midst of all the anxieties about changing technologies, about completion within the domestic market, about the ability to take a share of growing world markets, about convergence, interactivity and consumer control, it might be fruitful to keep the other eye on what the industry has done so well for so long, which is to make good television.

Entertainment Equipment in the UK Home 1994
(Source: Television: The Public's View, ITC 1994)

Type of equipment	All Homes	Homes with Children
Video Recorder	83%	94%
Teletext	55%	63%
CD Player	35%	47%
Home Computer	29%	45%
Video games	11%	45%
Satellite TV dish	14%	19%
Video camera	11%	17%
Nicam digital stereo TV	10%	12%
Cable TV	7%	10%
Cable telephone	5%	7%
Widescreen TV	7%	7%
Video disc player	4%	3%

References

Ang, I., *Desperately Seeking The Audience,* (London: Routledge, 1991)

Beville, H. M., *Audience Ratings: Radio, Television, Cable,* (Hillsdale N.J.: Lawrence Erlbaum, 1985)

Gilder, G., *Life After Television: The Coming Transformation of Media and American Life* (New York: Norton, 1994)

Hughes, G. and Vines, D., *Deregulation and the Future of Commercial Television,* Hulme Paper No. 12, (The David Hulme Institute, 1989)

Kent, R., ed. *Measuring Media Audiences,* London: Routledge, 1994)

Negroponte, N., *Being Digital,* (London: Coronet/Hodder and Stoughton, 1995)

Office of Telecommunications (OFTEL) *Beyond the Telephone, the Television and the PC, a Consultative Document,* (London: 1995)

Peak, S., ed. *The Media Guide* 1996, (Fourth Estate, London: Fourth Estate, 1995)

Wasko, J., *Hollywood in the Information Age,* (Oxford: Polity Press, 1994)

Williams, R., *Television: Technology and Cultural Form,* (London: Fontana and Collins, 1974)

Cable and Satellite Europe

Spectrum, The Quarterly magazine of the Independent Television Commission.

Television, The Journal of the Royal Television Society.

Seeking Local Emphasis in the Broadcasting Bill

Dave Rushton

Director, Institute of Local Television, & Lecturer in Communication Policy, Queen Margaret College, Edinburgh

This paper was first presented at The Media Trust Seminar held at Queen Margaret College in Edinburgh on 16th November 1995 on the opportunities for community, voluntary organisations and local broadcasters in the forthcoming Broadcasting Bill.

I used to make programmes for trade unions and community organisations and became dissatisfied with access to broadcasting and the difficulties of getting programmes shown. This dissatisfaction led to research undertaken in Edinburgh in 1989 to assess local programme demands. As might be expected from a capital city, Edinburgh has a rich diversity of material and information, much of which was just not being presented to the city viewers (or beyond) by Scottish Television or the BBC in Scotland. The greatest demand was for a local news service. So here was an opportunity for a city-wide service which might also provide programming that could be distributed to interested viewers living further afield.

So the Institute of Local Television's focus initially was upon the City of Edinburgh, but since then research has been conducted for local authorities and for several enterprise agencies and Arts Associations in other cities. This has confirmed that other city populations share the feeling that they want more information about their own area and that the perception of local area people feel most comfortable with is much, much smaller than the size of a television region.

So we've been trying to explore structures for local TV and promote this smaller scale of local area for TV services since 1989. Our knowledge of regulation and policy in broadcasting has grown bit by bit up to the point where we feel that the wider public needs to be more active, both as community organisations and as individuals, in considering some of the options for future broadcasting as well as thinking about programming.

In the very short space of time that is going to be available after the new Broadcasting Bill is introduced in early December, we need to ensure that the new broadcasting legislation – which will probably be on the statute books unchanged for at least another five or six years – will indeed reflect the real and substantial local interests that we have found to be suppressed, and that, over the last six years, we have tried to represent.

Many community organisations feel they need to have a stake in television, and feel that broadcast television should be made available to benefit these groups.

For the first time new television services are going to be introduced where scarcity of radio spectrum is not an issue. So the arguments that till now have said that television has to be constrained, has to be nationally operated and has to be very highly regulated to avoid duplication or waste in spectrum – because it is such a scarce commodity in analogue form – are no longer quite so relevant and should be less important factors in determining future policy.

Spectrum is going to be as free as water in some parts of the country, and so the new arguments must turn upon why there isn't a broader range of organisations having a stake in its use – not just commercially-focused organisations. And I think how we try to achieve that wider involvement in determining spectrum use for small scale TV services is the point I want to come to at the end of this introduction.

But how have we got to today's position? Cable television has so far not developed as it was intended to in 1980 – to favour local organisations and local services. This local focus was expected when cable was introduced in 1984. At that time, franchises were awarded across the country to cable companies who asked to develop a service in towns they took a fancy to. Figure 1 shows the map of cable as it should have been by 1994 with franchises awarded up till then.

Figure 1

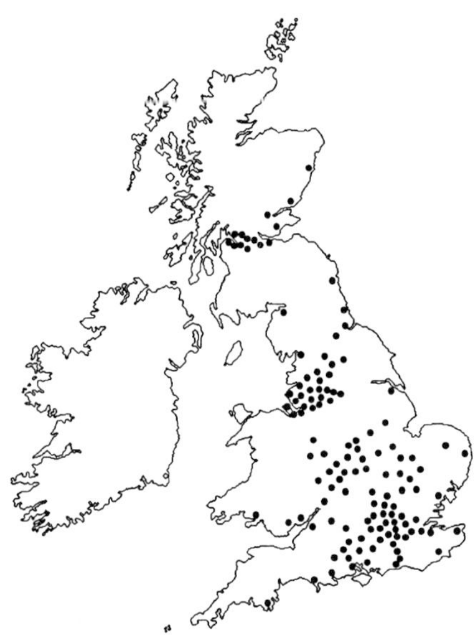

Figure 2

Figure 2 is the map of cable companies actually offering local TV – moving video – services in 1995.

We find there is a cluster of local TV services on cable franchises around London; some emerging in the Midlands; and another cluster in the North West. If you offer TV companies the opportunity to build at will these are really the areas where they want to build. They will obviously build where most people live because then the cable run is shorter, there are more people and there is the chance of selling a range of services to that bigger audience.

One exception where cabling ought to have taken off but hasn't is Glasgow, which has only 10-20,000 homes connected. Cable has really not been a success in Glasgow at all.

So in spite of expectations shared by the Government of the day cable has not offered an opportunity for local organisations - commercial and community - to run news services in particular, which many viewers would like to have at a more local level than regional television.

Figure 3

Figure 4

We get our regional commercial service from the ITV companies and in some areas people have a choice of two or more regional services. The ITV regions cover very large parts of the country, and just to take the Scottish Television example, if someone lives in the South of Mull in Kintyre they are not really going to have a lot of news to share with someone living in North Berwick.

It is very unlikely that they will share the same hospital or that their kids will go to the same school or that the same health trust or educational authority will oversee their local services. And it is very unlikely the people in Mull will go to the same public library as those in North Berwick. So when it comes to empowerment of local communities and to presenting ways of increasing their involvement in their community, the regional TV service does not represent much information that those in each local area can usefully use. You require a more intensive focus on an area, much closer to a five miles radius of where you live, closer to the place where you have some potential responsibility and involvement, for a service to be really relevant. ITV and the equivalent BBC regions are the limitation of a generally available local television service just now – but they are not really local at all.

However, over the last two or three years there have been a number of mergers taking place between companies in the ITV network in the South East of England, the Midlands and the North West, and I think we can expect a dramatic change ahead for television which very few of us have really started to recognise, least of all the academic community which traditionally has been at the forefront of promoting and securing a public space in broadcasting.

If you look at the three areas of the country described above – effectively the London area, the Midlands and the North West – those three areas contain something like 45% of the total UK population and generate 60-70% of its TV advertising revenue.

Figure 5

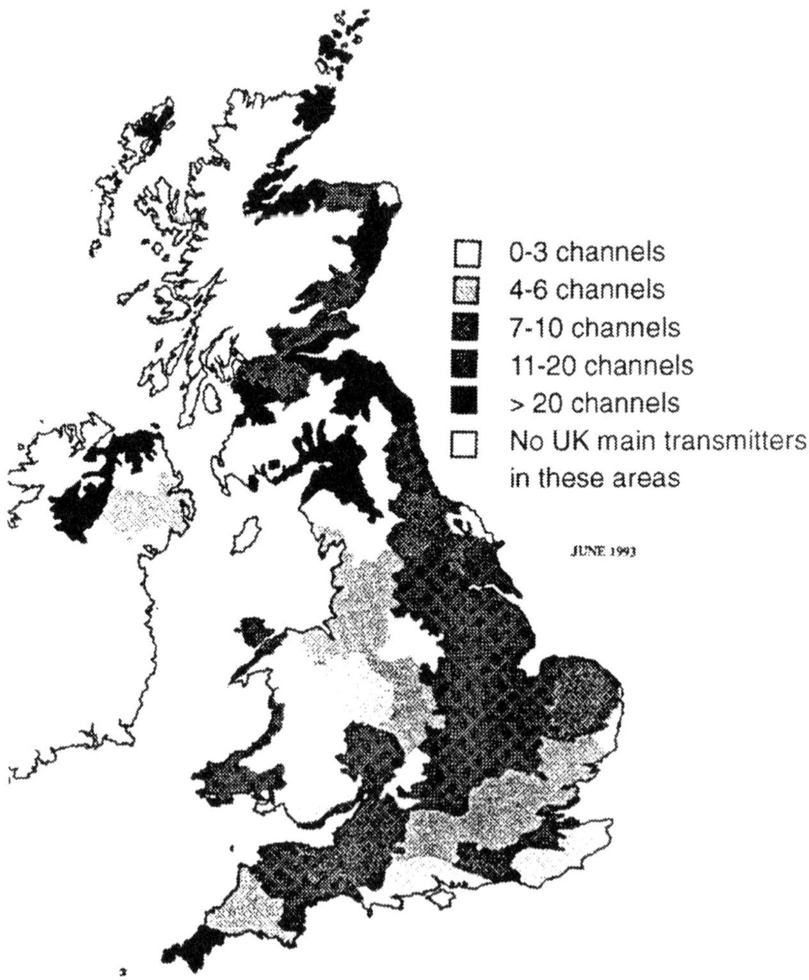

In fact nearly all the viewers in these areas can be reached by broadcasting from just three transmitters: three very tall transmitters, three very powerful transmitters. But it takes another 1170 or so transmitters to reach the balance of the UK population. So if it is possible to achieve up to 70% of the UK TV advertising revenue across just 45% of the audience using basically three transmitters and you have a Government whose policies support the commercial rather than social imperative in the organisation of broadcasting, and encourage financial efficiency and effectiveness over social ambitions, then it strikes me that very soon we shall find ourselves with – if not just the 3 largest transmitters – perhaps (say) 30 or so transmitters which would serve the rump of the present national service as all that was viable.

This suggestion takes us to the model of TV service represented by Channel 5.

Channel 5 is described as a national service. The licence was recently awarded to Channel 5 Broadcasting but the channel can reach only 70% of the country. It is interesting that this 70% of the country can be achieved from just 30 transmitters. Channel 5 doesn't need to use, is not required to use, the additional 1140 transmitters which Channel 4, ITV, BBC1 and BBC2 each need to reach the universal audience.

So just imagine the financial savings there would be in running a TV service without the overheads taken up to power and support a further 1140 transmitters by removing that obligation to reach everyone. Yet the Government persists in calling Channel 5 a public service television operation. That is to say, it will be equal to ITV and the BBC and recognised as the fifth public service channel when the new digital terrestrial channels are allocated.

I suggest that this reduction in the national ambition shows that, in the new legislation, Government is moving towards an acceptance that it is no longer required as part of its national duty to ensure that public services reach everyone in the country and that, in future, services can be both national and public service in character without being national and universal in reach.

And I think that this serious compromise of what is popularly understood to be a national remit in broadcasting (as in other public services) undermines the legitimacy of Government as the exclusive national agency responsible for controlling all television services.

In response, I believe we must secure those channels that are only available in our areas, that have no scope to join together to provide a real national service, and demand the right to regulate and to use them. If local agencies do not do this, people in some parts of the country will not receive new services. And when analogue TV is turned off, these areas will be left without any service at all, because, like Channel 5, the digital plan is not universal in reach.

It is not thought economically feasible or politically necessary to proclaim coverage of the whole country for the next generation of broadcast communications. Nor is this limitation and change in the central remit of Government for universal planning thought worth introducing as a topic for discussion. If central Government is saying that a service retains its national character while reaching only 70% of the country, it is now very important for those who live outside the major media centres to draw attention to the failure to reach 30% of the country.

I believe that we should look at the new Broadcasting Bill from that point of view, and realise that the Government is preparing to introduce services which could withdraw areas from mainstream broadcasting and from a most important means of communication, and that it appears willing to isolate a large element of the population from the new TV services.

Figure 5 indicates the digital proposals which will be the focus of the Broadcasting Bill, alongside the issue of cross- media ownership. (This map, dating from 1993, differs only in degree from the latest version.)

What Figure 6 shows is that people living in London, the Midlands and the North West of England will only receive a limited number of extra channels from digital terrestrial TV. But if you live elsewhere, you could potentially receive several more additional channels, ten or twenty more.

Now while broadcasting remains something that is regulated according to the interests perceived within the central belt – to serve the interests of the people living in these major urban areas of the country, the area where 45% of the population live and where 60–70% of TV advertising can be achieved – there is no incentive to take a blind bit of interest in those ten or more extra channels that would be available outside the major connurbations surrounding London, Manchester and Birmingham. In general, the further you get away from the broadcasting centre in London, then the more spare digital (and analogue) channels become available because where people are spread out fewer channels are required to deliver a service; therefore, more channels remain unused.

With Channel 5 I believe we have seen the move begin from a national, universally available analogue service to a national service which is really a metropolitan service predominantly based around London, the Midlands and the North West and which, on the evidence of Channel 5, will address that metropolitan audience. It seems to me that the next stage on the broadcasting agenda is that we assert in Scotland and in other identifiable countries and regions in the UK the right to control channels and regulate channels that have no national use.

What I am suggesting is something slightly more radical, I suspect, than the Broadcasting Bill is likely to offer. This suggestion is to relocate the centres of regulation and not simply to limit ourselves to services bequeathed locally with a national blessing. I would like to see regional and local agencies deal regionally and locally with broadcasting in their areas.

I have introduced the principle of subsidiarity to describe this. What subsidiarity means is control of services at the lowest feasible level to ensure that the service you want to run can work and function with maximum accountability.

So if you are going to run a really national TV service, then it can be run from London and I have no problems with that (although it need not be London that all national services are run from – the moves to locate Channel 5 north of Watford were a wide-ranging response to the unnecessary centralisation of broadcasting).

But when you start to move away from the national and universal remit and you consider the ten or more extra channels that will be available in several parts of the country outside the existing media centres, I think those channels might be put together like a jigsaw to form a regional or, in Scotland, a Scottish service. And if some of this surplus capacity cannot be used for regional services then it should be regulated even more locally.

The ITC and BBC already have a regional and national structure and might possibly establish that second tier of regulation and organisation. The Broadcasting Bill should devolve regulatory responsibility to those regional bodies to enable them to regulate all frequency and channels in their areas sufficient to support the regional services (and which are not required for the present genuine national services).

On a smaller scale than the region there is the possibility of local regulation. Local foundations in the Netherlands involve charities, voluntary groups, educational organisations, colleges and local council groups. They form the equivalent of a TV Trust. That Trust might oversee channels or frequencies for five years before the local electorate is offered a chance to select another Trust whose remit they might then believe would better fit the local community and its needs (or to return the present Trust if satisfied with its local mix).

This Broadcasting Bill needs to enable local professional services to have autonomy and some security, so as to offer local news, like the service we tried to pilot in the summer in Edinburgh with Scotsman Publications. There's no doubt at all that newspaper groups (Associated Newspapers with Channel One and Mirror Group Newspapers with Live TV) are investing heavily to reach the local audience and, in particular, the young audience who do not read local newspapers. They intend to reach them with lifestyle-type programming and to introduce them to the idea that they can get their news from the Mirror Group or Associated while running a little local opt-out service defined centrally.

The local newspapers are both threatened and enthralled by this process of cross-media development and I think there is an opportunity to involve them and to work with the local newspapers to develop local professional television news services. Beyond the local news interest, for which there is a proven viewer demand, there are opportunities for community news services and community programming to be introduced, for links with colleges, and for training.

Take the Wester Hailes project. This project will make a number of environmental changes to the area over the next three or four years and the project organisers will want to engage the local residents at each stage. There is a lot of programming that could be made about that environmental and employment initiative until its completion in the year 2000, by which time the money will have been raised and spent. But the type of programming required by the community needs to be broadcast as a trickle, dribbling through local news and debate as the project unfolds each week or month, with small topical items letting the city know of progress and of opportunities for involvement.

It's no good just saying, 'Here is our launch video,' as if it were a glossy hand-tooled Bible, so full of exquisite production values that it will be worthy for years until it becomes a museum piece. What is required is for the community in that Wester Hailes project to be involved in making television regularly, just as now people can write letters and reproduce their views in print. It is that level of social programming and that quality of relevance in the local public TV service that digital access will allow. It will only happen in that way, though, if we make our views known about how we want frequency and channels to be used.

To do this we need to establish local regulators, as I have described, and to pull back under local control the cable channels which are largely owned by multi-national companies interested in firstly telephone services and secondly in delivering BSkyB: these companies have made no unique contribution that can justify their access and utility status. For the most part cable does not add anything to communications in the communities it serves.

At the end of the day, our proposal is less radical than it might at first seem. At the moment the Treasury takes £400m per year out of the ITV companies as a mixture of licence fees and as a percentage of advertising revenues. That's £400m of which perhaps some £300m or so was not taken out of programming in 1990 – before the last Broadcasting Act; that transfer of funds to the centre was simply a result of the auction that took place to decide upon the new franchises.

If you think about that money for a moment, it is money redistributed from the advertising gained from each TV region into a central exchequer, to the Treasury. TV advertising costs are reflected in the amount of money that we pay for the goods and services in our area. Put simply, the ITV auction was an indirect form of taxation to take out regional monies for central reallocation.

So what I am suggesting is that this sum be reassigned back to the regions, not to the companies themselves but to the regional ITCs, who should use that money – or part of it – to support smaller scale, more localised public broadcasting services through which community organisations with a public service remit and who want to make programmes can receive benefit.

Any service beamed into each area from the outside which is not a truly national service – such as a film channel or a large sports channel – should in turn provide a percentage of its advertising revenue from each area to the regional regulators who in turn would reallocate these sums towards local services.

This money is drawn from local and regional viewing figures as advertising revenue, and indirectly is a percentage of the sum charged for the advertised goods that are bought by people locally. Some of this should be recycled back into the community as local public service programming.

Cross-subsidy between service suppliers already happens in ITV, so this is not a new idea either. The smaller ITV companies such as Channel, Border and Grampian rely heavily on the cross-subsidy of programme production costs from their bigger colleagues in the ITV network.

What I'm suggesting is establishing the new television regulators on a local and regional basis in a form which can cross-subsidise the introduction of essential local public service programmes, providing relevant and empowering information, local education and entertainment.

Okay, that's my dream. I'd be surprised if it were to emerge in the Broadcasting Bill in December, and I think what's likely to happen is that central controls will not be lifted and may even be tightened. I don't think we're likely to see a radical change, since the agenda is trying to legislate for digital TV quickly, although we've lobbied hard for subsidiarity over the last six months.

At the moment, so long as the Conservatives remain in power, the central controls are likely to remain. I think, however, that there may be some concessions in the form of restricted service licences (RSLs) to enable groups to develop start-up TV operations. The ITC and the Department of National Heritage have both hinted that they want to see this and have recently acknowledged that regional ITV and the cable companies have restricted competition, not opened it up.

The actual cost of the Capital News project we undertook in the summer with *The Scotsman* – as a prototype RSL – was really fairly small, largely because a number of commercial organisations were willing to support and offer equipment in the longer term knowledge that there is a market here to be developed.

For the next three or four years, experiments with TV broadcasting which try out new services will be very heavily subsidised by the manufacturers and sellers of equipment as they will, I'm sure, by the involvement of media students from the colleges.

Both the commercial and educational parties want to see that new, local TV market created and flourishing. At such a point we will find – as we did in the summer – that advertising will be available and, in the longer term, services will be able to be sustained (and equipment bought for full services, and graduates employed). So that's the manufacturers' and the colleges' interests: an alliance between the manufacturers and community organisations – the aristocrats and the peasants perhaps – against the establishment of broadcasters.

I hope there may also be something in the Bill that will introduce some extra local terrestrial services on a permanent basis. These don't need to wait for digital TV to arrive – which will take years to come, and with the need for viewers to purchase set-top converters at £200–300 to translate the signal so their analogue TVs can screen it.

Until then, local frequencies can be offered in analogue form because the planning of digital television is already exposing those analogue frequencies that are not being used, frequencies which have been warehoused by the broadcasters, by the BBC and ITC, who sit on them (or who hide them to prevent competition emerging).

The broadcasters don't need so many surplus channels and the Radiocommunications Agency with its own remit of making frequency pay is trying to claw back those that are not needed. And I am sure frequencies will suddenly be found to have been available for local use if we can succeed in getting a local service defined favourably in the new Bill. And the final point on that, I think that there is going to be further pressure on cable companies to open up their networks. Those pressures have turned on the cable companies following the Labour party announcement that BT should be allowed to deliver entertainment services on their existing networks sooner than expected. Cable really has to develop quickly and exploit its unique selling point, its localness compared with BT and satellite, and it has a limited time to do this.

So watch out for cable companies beginning to solicit for material, seeking ways of building up channels that have a distinct local identity – although many now envisage this being on a regional and not a local basis, as local franchises merge or get taken over by the bigger cable operations.

And finally, I think there will be difficulties even with the Broadcasting Bill in the weaker form I suggest here.

I think we will find that if the length of the local licence is anything like that for radio's restricted service licences (RSLs), which last only a month, even a small trial won't be economic, unless the area concerned is fortunate that each domestic TV aerial is already pointing at the new broadcast transmitter. Because, unlike radio, TV aerial reception is much more directional and no one will put in even a set-top aerial for a short trial. Interestingly, in the last few weeks the Radio Authority has introduced a five year RSL which is almost a semi-permanent restricted service licence – but so far this is only to cover the rural areas.

A five year experiment seems not a bad idea for local TV – it gives a chance for the channel licensee to run a series of weekend services with different parties initially, to try out new partnerships and programme ideas, and to build up experience and to secure an audience gradually. And five years is time in which to recover equipment costs.

The other problem that the Bill might present is the guarantee it might expect of finance for the service. If the full radio licence is adopted as the model for local TV, the licensee has to guarantee the full financing of the service over the licensing period. But as more and more TV channels become available it should become acceptable that say, half a dozen out of perhaps fifteen or so regional and local services might always be in a state of flux, and that compared with big media, little media may thrive on being marginal (and adventurous even if precarious).

One of the things about capitalism is that it gives you the opportunity to fail as well as a chance to succeed. I think that the opportunity to fail is something we should embrace and push forward to the Government. If you make a spectacular mess, then so be it. Everyone else involved in TV is playing it so safe – the local options might find their precariousness a way of life, and seat-of-the-pants TV could be exciting and involving in a way regional and national TV is not.

A further difficulty the Bill might present is the mechanism it chooses to award local licences. If it's anything like the ITV franchise round in 1990, it will be a mockery.

Scottish Television bid £2000.00 for the regional franchise. I have a licence from the ITC entitling my company to broadcast on cable and it cost £375.00. That seems a fair percentage – Scottish Television has 3.2m people in Scotland for its annual £2000.00 and I would settle for access to a cable channel reaching 400,000 people for £375.00. But unfortunately, the licence only regulates the content of my service and does not give me access to a cable channel or any way of broadcasting for that sum. That has to be negotiated with the existing broadcasters (or cable company) and they are not obliged to provide access. That strikes me as being unreasonable.

Open competition presumes a more open access to the broadcasting and cable network than is currently the practice. The Bill must address this bias towards the current service providers who can veto new entrants and establish services built on the regional ITV and larger newspaper revenues.

Before the Bill gets into law, it will also be necessary to reach general agreement on a new, more appropriate definition of quality for the local television services than has so far been applied to the ITV companies in their 'quality threshold'.

If the quality threshold is presumed to be that of regional television then we've got a problem, because revenues will not support (for example) full broadcast specifications in local equipment. So far – in discussions on Channel 5 – the ITC have made no concessions to local broadcasting on the use of (say) Hi-8 or S-VHS equipment.

We've also got quite an interesting discussion to have with the unions, and with each local production sector that's producing programmes at the moment.

Because while we might be willing to make a weekend of programming for £5000 with students over the summer as an experiment, we certainly would not want to establish a benchmark for such programmes were they to be made commercially. We may be willing, up to a point, to be self-exploiting as part of that local process of bringing about empowerment, but not if that undermines employment by reducing an acceptable rate for the job and the quality and editorial integrity of programmes.

Concentration of ownership becomes another issue which may need to be tackled in the local sphere. It isn't just the local newspapers that are showing interest in getting involved in local TV, but if the local newspapers owned the local TV service and maybe the local radio service – wouldn't that reduce plurality, confine democracy, and reduce opportunity for different voices to appear? But would there be a preference for a local newspaper to own the local TV service rather than a national newspaper? To what extent is local ownership, shareholders and stakeholders a preference in defining the local service?

And finally, we really are involved here in a very short consultation time on the Broadcasting Bill, a matter of a few weeks. This Bill is expected to be announced in December and according to the ITC it is expected to have a second reading before Christmas (or early in the New Year).

That is a phenomenally short time-table and to hasten its progress the most contentious item has been stripped from the Bill – the privatisation of the BBC transmitter network has been taken out. So this Bill is likely to be passed without much modification for two reasons: one, there will be nothing in it that's contentious in terms of the present TV landscape and secondly, if there is nothing in it that is contentious there may be nothing in it of interest to us.

So we maybe have to inject into this softly-softly process things that are critical, things that will be uncomfortable for the ITV companies, cable and satellite companies, if we are to succeed in gaining access to spectrum and frequencies and bring regulation under local control.

So the difficulty that I foresee for organisations wishing to take an interest in the Bill in the coming weeks is how community organisations, charities and voluntary agencies as well as local producers can put forward a range of coherent claims to frequency and lobby for access that is convenient to them and that will help them better present their views to the local community.

Acknowledgments

Figures 1, 2, 3 and 4 were compiled by Derek Murray for the Institute of Local Television. Figure 1 is based on cable service data published quarterly by the Independent Television Commission. Figure 2 is based upon a study of local channels on cable conducted by Anja Maaike-Green of Queen Margaret College. Figures 3 and 4 derive from those circulated by the ITC during consultations on Channel 5 to identify areas having frequency options, and this information is provided in tabulated form in The Future of Channel 5, published by the ITC (1993) and in The Application for Channel 5 (April, 1995). Figure 5 was circulated with the ITC's Digital Discussion Document (June, 1993).

The figure for the annual licence payment by STV is from the Scottish Television Annual Report, 1994.

The fee for the Licensable Programme Service Licence for cable is given in the application pack from the ITC.

Who Sets the Agenda?

The New Power of the Consumer in Broadcasting

Brook Sinclair
Adcomm Limited

The consumer is by standard definition a user or receiver of what is produced. The definition implies passivity; as if consumers, divorced from production processes, were powerless. In many commercial fields consumers are vociferous about quality of products and services; each year, some 750,000 serious complaints are registered in Britain.

Consumers as yet have little impact on the UK broadcast industry. Why is this so? To begin with, up till 1990, no statute recognised a consumer's right to receive a broadcast anyway. The role of consumer protection has been assigned to a number of quangos whose job is to promote standards and monitor quality. These bodies have knowledge – and knowledge is power. Their important functions are to regulate the industry on behalf of government, provide a critique of government policy options and, having mainly survived recent broadcast inquiries, to reassert authority.

It is difficult to know where power lies in broadcasting, and necessary to consider the relationships between contenders for power.

Much power once lay with programme producers, but the industry they nurtured was small and elitist. British broadcasting had a good reputation worldwide, but exported only about one tenth of the material traded by the US. Many of the changes to broadcasting were designed to gear the British industry to successful global trading, but thereafter the industry was assigned to the Department of National Heritage, which protects culture, rather than the Department of Trade and Industry, which favours vast exporting companies. British broadcasting is now a battleground for competing forces of cultural inheritors, entertainers and news manipulators. Changes in rules about ownership will make major players in the industry more powerful; but power will be transferred between competing groups, rather than devolve to anyone else.

Broadcasting was once in the hands of people of all-round vision, who mastered the technology of the media. Modern managements are different. A primary objective nowadays is to own as many distribution channels as possible and enjoy the lifestyle of the more prestigious corporation which results. The main danger for broadcasters is there is not enough production to put on these channels. The industry has been assigned to technocrats, who – understanding what makes Mars Bars and Snickers distinctive and likeable – can make television versions available as cheaply as possible; or assigned to managements who make decision making so complicated that they frustrate the creative process beyond belief. The annual expansion of television output is now so low that libraries in future decades must inevitably be empty.

Hundred digital channel television will offer tremendous opportunities for those who cannot now get their versions of Mars Bars on the box. Television has not many styles of programme – the more obvious niche channels already exist – and much output is formulaic. The new creative thinking for an age of abundance may not come essentially from established groups. For consumers who like traditional entertainment and news, the prospect is not so good. The US abundance of choice arrives, programmes have become unmarketable, much output is cheap and non-glossy, and pay TV will be inevitable. One consequence of change is that televisual systems will be abundantly used by people who are not traditional broadcasters; so in the new age, the providers of entertainment will be less powerful.

Who pays the piper? Advertisers – broadcasting's important financial plank – are a powerful force. The advertising industry may not be notably innovative about itself, but its clients may demand a lesser reliance on television which habitually delivers a lot of audiences clients don't want. The new technology will produce more sophisticated forms of marketing. A Sainsbury, armed with virtual reality, turning its stores into a South Sea Island one day and the Garden of Eden the next, may not rely on Carlton. The most likely alternative source of income, pay TV, pay radio and paid-for passwords, are likely to make consumers more influential; this, if nothing else, may stir consumers to seek new forms of representation

The current relationship between television production and audiences is a strange one. For many years, television has been geared to the peer group, to pleasing or displeasing authority, or responding to advertisers because such voices are easily recognised on the line. Television, however, needs audiences. There is a great reliance on extrapolations of sampling, and programme producers often play elaborate games with people they never meet. Broadcasters seem often unhappiest when meeting consumers. Consumer complaint programmes become exhibitions of producers' superior wisdom; they cast articulate journalists to be adversarial about programmes, rather than letting real consumers air their views. As people in the 1990s have begun to make programmes about how television actually works, consumers may someday be perceived to be better informed.

The main power possessed by the consumer is to switch on and off. British viewing figures remain high by international standards, but the real truth is that much of the output is missed. The average person watches about 4% of the output on the four main channels a day. The audience may be in decline; possibly people are losing interest in what is essentially a synthetic medium.

To be entertaining, television packages what appears to be a real world, but with the usual timescales and probability removed. A person's lifetime experiences of birth, marriage, separation, divorce and death are packed into a single soap episode. Highly selective news bulletins present stories fashioned to promote guilt and fear in the spectator. Hence the daily death count, the missing children (presumed dead), the prisoners who might break out and murder us in our beds, and for light relief, the penalty shoot-out (sudden death). Such concoctions do not promote the understanding of issues at all. There is a real world, inhabited by the 99.99% of the population not in jail, but it is never news.

Up to now, organisations formed by broadcasting consumers have tended to be campaign groups. They have campaigned about taste and decency and for the restoration of a kind of broadcasting that ceased to exist twenty years ago. These are legitimate concerns. There have been advisory councils with regional and national representation, but their influence is invisible, and they are, by design, powerless. Broadcasting Standards and Broadcasting Complaints have handled a rising number of specific cases much more visibly, but their remit is limited. There seems a need for a consumer structure which is independent of broadcast managements and which researches broadcasting and its public in the fullest sense. It is reasonable to make the BBC more accountable to licence payers, but an annual report in advance would inevitably be bland and general, particularly if the BBC had to issue expensive updates about changes in plan.

Whilst audience appreciation figures remain high – because few people will admit to continuing to watch a programme they dislike – television producers may feel all is well. Audiences may like television's style but have become wary of its content; but there is nobody to talk to about such general concerns. Overall, the experience may have become less captivating. Television is much watched, anyway, to fill in gaps when there is nothing better to do, and the real world of travel, work, meals, dining out, having friends in, going to the pub, always takes precedence. Is television important? Does broadcasting have much influence? These questions are often raised, but never conclusively answered.

The new broadcasting age will dawn slowly. Only forty countries in the world now have well-developed telephone systems, fifty have a reasonable penetration of television, twenty have better than 35% of households owning a VCR, only one country, Holland, has 25% of households owning a computer. Consumers in many places have none of the basics at all, and billions must be spent to provide them. It will take until 2017 for a pioneering society, the US, to become fully digital. Fully interactive television should flourish from 2020, but the age of virtual reality might not arrive until 2050, when today's children will find themselves somewhat into their middle years.

The desire to possess is what drives the consumer and must be the consumer's greatest power. The perception that many possessions are neither effectively used nor greatly missed in their absence is off-putting. The fact that we may possess 3,000 books, the capability of speaking on the 'phone to two billion people in the world, seven radios, a CD player, a VCR, satellite receivers and a monitor, and make little use of any of them in a normal day fuels one of the major debates of our times. In any country, the urge to possess is very strong. We anticipate that in a more leisured society of the future we might make better use of our possessions. Will there be a more leisured age? There is little sign that people in the 21st century will give up work – real wages should still be rising and it would be economic suicide – so our possessions, like ourselves, must become earners.

Digitalisation will not happen overnight, so in the meantime, addressing other agendas is important. Could broadcasters have a better relationship with consumers, because it is in broadcasting's interest to do so? Can consumers interact more directly with broadcasting, creating a new representative body which researches and communicates? Can power be shared, and shared happily?

Multi-Mediatization and Citizens' Rights

Mark Wheeler
London Guildhall University

Introduction

This paper is concerned with how the Information and Communication Technologies (ICTs) are impacting on citizenship. Therefore I intend to consider the traditional models of citizenship and freedom of information. We will address the potentially liberalizing effects of the new communications technologies and discuss whether market provision is applicable. Further, these reforms to information flow affect democratic structures and may alternatively advance or retard citizenship.

Communications and Citizenship

There are civil, political and social dimensions to citizenship in a democracy. Civil rights, comprising freedom of speech, movement, association and consciousness, should open debate and competition for authority. Personal property rights establish countervailing power centres to the state. Political rights allow individuals to participate through their franchise, occupying public office and juries. Representational assemblies enable citizens to determine laws and distinguish them from being subjects. Social rights ensure the basic living standards through the universal access to information facilities.

Individuals must have access to knowledge to pursue their rights. They should have a broad range of interpretations to debate political decisions, register criticism and propose alternatives. Moreover, they should recognise themselves through the representations on offer. The citizen's access to ideas has been sustained through: the population's universal education to advance knowledge and to discriminate changes in the world; public libraries which are repositories of information; and independent and widespread reporting of local, national and international events by the mass media.

The Multi-Media Revolution

The technological revolution is transforming business and domestic communications. Interactive fibre-optic cable systems are developing alongside the widespread computer and video conferencing. A new generation of networks promotes low-cost broad-band communication. These developments provide access to greater numbers of communication links, permit the distribution of commercial and entertainment material, and advance telephony along the same highways. Moreover, new electronic services located around telecoms, computer and satellites have created a global electronic mail service. International computer and telecommunication networks from universities, companies and the American military, generically entitled the Internet, have grown at a staggering rate connecting 1.3 million computers, 8000 networks and over ten million users[1].

Computers increase data storage, retrieval and transmission. Mass participation technologies which distribute information from a central source to millions are also enhanced. Further, interactive communications flows among individuals and organised groups may be established.[2] There are thousands of on-line Bulletin Board Systems (BBS) and news groups run by computer enthusiasts. Thus, ICTs may have the following effects:

* They explode the limits on the volume of information that can be exchanged.
* They make it possible to exchange information without regard, for all practical purposes, to real time and space.
* They increase the control the consumers have over what messages are received and when.
* They increase the control the senders have over specific audiences who receive the messages.
* They decentralise control over mass communication.
* They bring two way or interactive capacities to television.[3]

Futurists contend that a digital revolution may reform monolithic state edifices, corporations, political parties, schools, workplaces, orthodox economics and popular entertainment. The Internet will increase interactive citizen participation by circumventing the centralized conglomerate and outmoded media structures. The Information Superhighway will provide the electronic landscape, or cyberspace, for a reinvented civil society so that citizens can engage in their civil, political and social rights.[4]

Such interactivity can increase democratic participation through a constant series of referenda. Thus, the technological revolution will enhance freedom of belief, conscience, speech, movement, association and enfranchisement. Governments, regulators and owners will be impotent as millions adopt the interconnecting technology and engage in political discourse. In particular, the Internet offers global communication, in which all citizens can access the same informational and cultural resources. There will be a globalization of citizenship, the decline of nationalism and the reform of archaic political structures.

A Changing Policy Climate

ICTs will change the way people live, work and govern. Labour leader Tony Blair maintains that they will become the key dividing line in British politics. Graham Allen, the Labour spokesperson on the Media, has argued that the Internet, alongside a Bill of Rights and a Freedom of Information Act, will decentralise power and re-build democratic infrastructures. He suggests that local cable television will regenerate politics by opening dialogue between politics and the people.[5] Chris Smith, the former National Heritage spokesperson, was so enthusiastic about the imminent communications revolution that he claimed increases in health provision would occur.[6]

However, it may be suggested that such policy-making is a matter of good public relations. For instance, it is still uncertain what the Information Autobahn means conceptually. Essentially, it refers to telecommunications infra-structures which deliver all kinds of electronic information and communication services. Yet, many possibilities exist:

> In (a traditional telecommunications model of a network) ... traffic goes from a to b using fixed links between locations with switching 'roundabouts' to choose the right roads. Yet the US government's view of the Information Superhighway ... is clearly anchored in the Internet model, which employs a network of networks through which information packets are routed more flexibly using computer-based controls.[7]

In terms of policy implementation, a compromise between state provision and a free market has usually been reached. For instance, an initiative from the G7 countries contends that a global market will exist through the provision of communications technology. Thus, governments must provide minimal legislation to ensure fair competition, private investment, light regulation, open access to networks, universal provision of core services, equality of opportunity, content diversity and the involvement of developing nations. The Labour Party has proposed policies to establish a competitive framework so that the private sector can develop the communications market in exchange for societal provision of hardware.[8] Tony Blair announced that he had struck a deal with British Telecom to furnish every college, school, hospital and library in Britain with free high-band networks in return for full access to cable market.

Electronic Democracy

Alongside policy considerations, telematics, the integration of computing with communications technologies, may transform the democratic process. Previously, citizen participation was undermined by time, size, knowledge and access, and led to elitist or representative models of democracy. Alternatively, a wired world would stem the difficulties of time because communication and participation become instantaneous. Similarly, problems of size are solved because people do not have to be gathered in a single place. Concurrently, the distribution of knowledge is widely available through networks, which in turn removes the difficulty of access.[9] Whilst the capacity of different interactive services to enhance participation varies, they are distinguished from the previous mass media and the information recipients are no longer passive. Thus, teledemocracy becomes a realistic possibility. Direct or communitarian forms of democratic behaviour have been pursued, alongside anarchistic libertarian views to advance citizenship.

For some, true Athenian democracy may be realised. However, Athens was built on slavery and its democratic principles applied to a few. Therefore, will the proliferation of communications networks increase the availability of information? Despite a notional public service commitment, these multimedia developments have been orchestrated by market precepts such as private enterprise and individuals. US Vice-President, Al Gore, warned of a growing disparity between the information rich and poor. An information underclass may emerge to intensify social tensions in advanced and third world countries.[10]

Changes to Political Structures

ICTs could make the representative process more transparent. In Britain, the Internet's open government page has called for an on-line Hansard so that the public will have direct access to Parliamentary debates. In turn, if decision making goes on-line, it will no longer remain the bastion of the civil servants, politicians and vested interests. Moreover, they could reform state secrecy and establish campaigns for open government. The Internet may also be a productive agent for single-issue pressure groups. Charter 88 has provided on-line details of its 'Parliament for our Times', and has established a competition to examine solutions for the future of democracy.

The Liberal Democrats have a speech database on their political opponents to highlight contradictions and inconsistencies over issues. The Labour Party has invested in the American 'Excalibur' database system which, loaded with speeches, policy comments, figures and reports, allows facta to be checked instantaneously. Labour hope to maximise the political mileage of their opponents' errors and also rebut counter productive accusations.[11] Further, they are using databases for fund raising, canvassing, direct mailing, local newsletters, and membership drives. Main-frame and mini-computers have been employed to target supporters and to keep track of elected representatives.

The parties have established 'bulletin boards' on the Internet containing information available for public access. For instance, the Labour Party publishes conference speeches and members are encouraged to subscribe to an e-mail service on Poptel network. They provide on-line links to leadership and officials, 'bulletin boards' and electronic services. Leading political figures such as Paddy Ashdown and Tony Blair have published their e-mail addresses to encourage direct communication with the public. Further, through databases, faxes, press releases and campaign news, the public can access MPs voting records. In future elections, they are hoping that casual voters 'surfing the Internet' will be wooed by their on-screen campaigning. However, ICTs may compound biases in distribution of information to societal groups. Thus, they will augment asymmetries of information and power could be limited to a technocratic elite. Moreover, many users suggest that technological changes will extend to different forms of democracy.

Athenian Electronic Democracy

The plebiscite remains the symbol for true democracy, empowering citizens to make political choices. However, due to the limits of time and physical space it proved to be impractical for registering political preferences. Consequently, representative democratic institutions such as Parliament have been given this power. ICTs can remove these obstacles and direct democracy can become a reality as information is processed to unlimited numbers who may simultaneously participate in debate. Through digital means, voting and public preferences could be directly registered. ICTs can carry opinion polls so that constant referenda may become a reality.

A danger in an electronic, plebiscitary democracy is the focus on speed and numbers. This may undermine discussion and deliberation. Political participation may become a private act of registering one's own pre-conceived bias. The interactive discourse which is a key feature of a developed democracy will be replaced by push button voting. Consequently, as the citizen's knowledge and awareness are subsumed, their ability to make informed and rational decisions is undermined.[12]

Communitarian Electronic Democracy

ICT's may also promote communitarian democracy in which public discourse will encourage the common good. The package of cable television, networked computers and telephones enables two way debate over issues before beliefs are polled. Therefore, more direct forms of voting and opinion giving become available. ICTs also provide new mediums to form communities which previously, due to distance or geographical barriers, had been restricted. To this end, people can use the technology to address social problems. Nonprofit organisations on the neighbourhood, city an regional levels, and Non-Governmental Organisations (NGOs) on the global level, may become modern manifestations of 'civil society'.

Changing the Goalposts in a Modern Political Society

Proponents of certain ICTs, in particular the Internet, claim that the technologies' democratic potential goes beyond reforming political structures or democratic models. Many net users suggest that the Internet provides the forum for public debate. Jon Katz argues that it offers a vast, diverse, passionate, global means for transmitting ideas and opening minds. Net culture provides a medium for individual expression akin to the eighteenth century pamphleteers in colonial America. An electronic agora will exist which, in Thomas Paine's words, means, 'We have it in our power to begin the world over again'.[13]

Thus, new groups and bulletin boards will enhance Paine's arguments for a 'universal society'. Citizens can transcend narrow interests and consider humankind as one entity.[14] As the Internet is the first world-wide medium, people can communicate directly, quickly, personally and reliably. They can form distant but diverse and cohesive communities to send, receive and store vast amounts of information. An advanced use of the Internet was made by the Mexican revolutionary Zapatistas who propagated their views across the world. This usage of the multi-media technology sustained the belief that ICTs could transform the public sphere and advance world-wide communications. Instant global communication will create a global village or community, making plausible Paine's belief in the 'universal citizen'.[15] Everyone can access informational and cultural resources. Moreover, with the plentiful supply of computers, digital communications are nearly uncensorable. We can redefine concepts of political culture, globalize citizenship, challenge normative ideas of objectivity and change identities.

The Net as a Public Sphere?

Currently, Internet newsgroups see themselves as nascent public spheres that will renew democracy.[16] However, these claims dismiss the profound differences between Internet 'cafes' and the agoras of the past. Traditionally, identity has been defined by physical contact. This enforces accountability and enables mutual trust to be developed. Disembodied video text cannot replace face-to-face interchange. Further, it creates shifting forms of identity which undermine political stability.[17] Whereas the public sphere enabled people to interact as equals, online agoras undermine equality by emphasising irrational discourse.

The mass of undigested data misleads the public into believing that they are accessing a great library. However, these data are not information or knowledge. Human understanding, knowledge and wisdom lead to empowerment. The best ideas still go to the journalists and important news stories are sold to media corporations. Therefore, access to limitless data does not enhance participation. It's a very different social 'space' from that of the public sphere:

> ... the net is something entirely new, and its effects on domestic politics can't be predicted using historical precedent. The Internet threatens the government (unmonitorable conversations), mocks private property (the infinite reproducibility of information) and flaunts moral propriety (the dissemination of pornography).[18]

Moreover, dissent on the Net does not lead to consensus. A profusion of views exist without any political co-presence. Individual charisma has no force and compromise, the hallmark of a democracy, evaporates. Since identities are fluid, dissent is encouraged and 'normal' status markers are absent. User groups tend to polarise political opinions.

Critiques of Electronic Democracy

John Gray has argued that the Utopian view of technology is misplaced. Historically, technological reforms have not created new societies, solved intractable difficulties or re-distributed wealth. Instead, they alter the terms for societal or political conflicts as the uses 'to which new technologies are put depend on the distribution of power and access to resources, and on the level of cultural and moral developments in society'.[19] Gray suggests that a quick, technological fix will not empower citizens. Instead, the public's attention is falsely distracted from state and capitalist power.

There are several critiques of electronic democracy. First, democratic decisions are not just based on citizen choice. They are often characterised by the electoral system as no natural majority exists and democracy is no more than a device for registering preferences. Second, information does not necessarily enhance a democracy as many decisions are matters of judgement. A distinction between information and knowledge has to be made. Graham Murdock has commented that cultural rights comprise from entitlements in four main areas: information; knowledge; representation and communication. Information rights enable people to effectively determine personal and political judgements, and analyze the actions of public and private agencies with significant power over their lives. However, as information is of only limited use in its raw state:

> ... it needs to be placed in context, and its implications teased out and debated. Knowledge rights promote these processes by underwriting the public's access to the widest possible range of interpretation, debate and explanation.[20]

As information is not an agency but conditional on those who govern it, our attention returns to a fundamental problem – that the electronic technologies promote the interests of the powerful. This belief partly draws on the gap between promise and practice in the operation of actual systems of electronic participation. It suggests that the problems of access that beset previous democratic forms will be reproduced as similar imbalances and inequality of resources may continue to distort participation. Electronic democracy may serve the ambitions of dominant groups, who depoliticize politics and may transform the citizen into the consumer.

Conclusion

The new information and communications technologies allow for infinite data storage, a wider distribution of information and, most importantly, interactivity. Internet users suggest that the information technologies have the potential to change working habits, decentralize power structures, and reform the public sphere.

Interactivity provides a two-way flow of information and means that the traditional media's power to set the agenda is undermined. The concept of objectivity can be replaced by diversity, so that political issues can be framed and debated. The multi-media will succeed the mass media which has been centralized by the global concentration of ownership.

ICTs have policy and political implications. With regard to industrial policy, the metaphor of the Information Superhighway has been proffered as the future source of wealth and societal benefit. They may determine appropriate democratic models in the near future. They can be used to reform traditional liberal democratic structures such as representational assemblies, political parties and break down official secrets systems. Further, they overcome the problems of time and space which have previously constrained Athenian or communitarian democratic models. Citizens may enjoy greater access to information and consequently attain the knowledge to develop empowerment.

Conversely, it has been suggested that there is a growing divide between an information rich and poor. Governments have let markets orchestrate the development of ICTs. This means that rights of access will be determined by incomes. Those on low incomes will be excluded and omitted. Further, consumerism may replace citizenship, as media moguls make deals with telecommunication and computer entrepreneurs. Therefore, despite the technophile's arguments, the new information technologies do not necessarily enhance democracy. Technology is not an agency, as it may be employed positively or negatively. Consequently, multi-media futurists must ensure that ICTs are governed through appropriate legislation and regulation to realise their democratic potential.

References

1. Flowers, S. (1993) 'Want it? Well Gopher it.' *The Guardian*, 5.8.93.
2. Laudon, K. (1977) *Communication Technology and Democratic Participation*, Praeger Publishers.
3. Horrocks, I. and Pratchett, L. (1995) 'Electronic Democracy: Central Themes and Issues' in Lovenduski, J and Stanyer, J. (ed.), *Contemporary Political Studies*, Volume 3, PSA, University of York, April 18th – 20th 1995, p.1219.

4. Katz, J. (1995) 'Guilty'. *Wired*, September 1995, p. 100.
5. Allen, G. (1995) 'Letter: net corner@guardian.co.uk' *The Guardian*, 16.9.95, p.26.
6. Wintour, P. (1994) 'Blair plans national information grid', *The Guardian*, 28.11.94.
7. Dutton, W., Blumler, J., Garnham, N., Mansell, R., Cornford, J. and Peltu, M. (1994) *The Information Superhighway: Britain's Response, A Forum Discussion*, ESRC Policy Research Paper No. 29, 1994, p.2.
8. Blair, T. (1995) 'Help speed Britain down the superhighway', *The Evening Standard*, 17.7.95, p.9.
9. Street, J. (1995) 'Remote Control: politics, technology and culture', October, 1995, pp.10–11.
10. Arnold, S. (1994) *Internet 2000: The Path to the Total Network, Infonortics in-depth Briefings*, 1994, p. 9.
11. Standage, T. (1996) 'Excalibur revealed', *The Guardian*, On Line Section, 8.2.96, pp.2-3.
12. Martin, J. and Norman, R.D. (1970) *The Computerized Society*, Prentice Hall, pp. 289-9.
13. Paine, T. (1995) quoted from Katz, J. (1995) 'The Age of Paine', *Wired*, May 1995, p.156.
14. *Ibid.*, p.155.
15. *Ibid.*, p.210.
16. Poster, M. (1995) 'The Net as a Public Sphere?', *Wired*, November, 1995, pp. 42 – 43.
17. *Ibid.*, p.42.
18. *Ibid.*, p.43.
19. Gray, J. (1995) 'The sad side of cyberspace', *The Guardian*, 10.4.95, p.18.
20. Murdock, G. (1994) 'Money Talks' in Hood, S. (ed.) (1994) *Behind the Screens: The Structure of British Television in the Nineties*, Lawrence and Wishart, 1994, p. 158.

Review of Papers

Manuel Alvarado

University of Luton and John Libbey Media

Good morning. First of all, I'd like to thank the organisers for inviting me to engage with the papers at this conference and I should like to say just two things. First of all, how interesting they all were in the wide-ranging cover they offer to current issues in broadcasting; and secondly, what an important initiative it is to bring together educators and broadcasters in this way. It's interesting that, although all the papers were written by people working in higher education, they nevertheless deal with serious broadcasting issues – issues with which broadcasters themselves will very much want to engage.

Okay, I didn't really know how to discuss the papers because they were so wide ranging, whether to summarise or just to make observations – or what have you. I've had to make some rather detailed references so please excuse me if I start burrowing through, trying to find a quotation or something I want to make an observation on. What I'd like to do is the following. First of all, I've made my own artificial list to give structure. I've tried to do that on the basis of trying to move through the classic stages of commodity existence. I've moved from those papers which seem to have addressed questions of production through distribution and ending up on consumption. The exception is the last paper which, although it starts off in the first sentence with consumption, gets us back into production. Now I've done that, not because I like running round in circles much but because the last paper allows me to go into the final section of what I would like to say this morning. This is to make some of my own observations as a way of setting perhaps some agendas for future research. It also helps me to draw upon a number of points from a range of papers which I wouldn't have done as I went through them individually. I won't necessarily speak about each paper by the way. It depends on how the time goes and how we proceed. Are there any questions about that before I start. No? Okay.

I'd like to start with Jo Langham's paper because in fact I said I was going to start with production but it seems to me that she starts with pre-production, not in the technical sense but in an educational sense. She raises the question: Where do people come from who are going to work in broadcasting?

Jo writes: 'However, it would seem that when computers can play moving pictures and television sets can carry computing functions, the distinction between them dissolves. This has important consequences because when computer and television screens converge notions about the separateness of entertainment, knowledge and information could disappear also.' Well, that's an interesting, and perhaps provocative, observation. Maybe that will be the case. However, it seems to me that while there is an increasing convergence of entertainment, education and information this relates rather more to programme production strategies than to technological change. I rather fancy that in the future people will not predominantly be watching TV sitting at a desk or using a computer, lying on the sofa. I think in consumption terms they don't converge at all.

The second observation I would make about Jo's paper is that she moves into the area of telecommunications which I think is very important and draws on the wider sphere of television and broadcasting and radio. Clearly there is a convergence of all the technologies which is the buzz word of the moment. I also thought it was interesting that she made certain assumptions about the movement from, if you like, coaxial cable to fibre optic cable and the significance of that. I think that's interesting simply because recently I was reading about the Gambia and the Gambia doesn't really have a conventional telephone system. But it does have a national telephone system based on satellite technology rather than cable. I think it's a potentially interesting phenomenon in third world countries where, in fact, cabling will not be possible. It won't be a question of what sort of cable we lay but rather we can't really afford to lay cable at all. However, what we can do is to use satellites to engage in telephone conversations. I think, in fact, certain third world countries are going to leapfrog, to jump over the sort of debates that are taking place within Western Europe or North America.

And then the third point I'd like to make in Jo's papers was her observations about copyright and intellectual property abuse. Personally I must admit that I've always been rather uninterested in misuse of copyright. It seems to me that Jo reveals what I have always suspected, that copyright law has little to do with protecting the rights of authors but is treated with much seriousness by the major conglomerates because it is really about protecting the possessions of the major broadcasting companies and the major organisations of the world. So it's interesting the way that Jo points that out.

I'd like to move on briefly to Brent McGregor's very interesting paper and again I'd just like to make two observations, I suppose. I think that in the future scenario he outlines there is a very important concluding observation. I quote: 'This genuinely exclusive premium service' that is Newswatch, the 24 hour surveillance camera channel that he outlines, is available only to 'those élites lucky enough to be above being merely wired, who can afford the real value-added service of having someone else edit out the news from the incessant information flow, and present it to them'. Now I think that is a very interesting observation because it runs through a number of the papers. One has a sense in reading them that there is a mass of information flowing 24 hours a day, 7 days a week in 180 countries of the world, or however many there are of them. The problem is: Well, how does one process that? How does one engage in all this activity? When I recently signed up to Screen L on my domestic e-mail service system, I thought: 'Oh this is interesting, an academic set of discussions about film that takes place in North America. I'd like to see what they're talking about.' I don't think I have ever read one message. I get something like thirty every day and, on top of everything else I am doing, it's information overload. Potentially interesting things may be going on there – I have no idea.

The second observation of Brent's I'd like to pick up on is really to ask a very simple straightforward question which is: Why does the technological future imply the following danger and I quote: 'the danger is not that news will change but that it will one day be the only kind of factual television.' All I'm saying here is that I'd like you at some point, either here or in writing, to actually flesh that out and explains what that means because it isn't clear from the argument that that is necessarily the case.

Moving on to Dave Rushton's paper. David's broad project is to explore the structures of local television and promote small-scale, local area TV services. This has required him to scrutinise carefully broadcasting regulations and policy. He indicates the slow development of cable and the lack of opportunities for community cable development which is even more striking if one thinks back to Canada in the 60s and the UK in the 70s when, of course, these sort of cable experiments were taking place. Very little, as he indicates, has been achieved by 1996. What he then does is compare cable development to transmitter coverage, taken in the context of the introduction of Channel 5 which he identifies as a national service but which is really a metropolitan service. Dave argues for a different regulatory model. I would like to quote two paragraphs from Dave.

He writes: 'What I am suggesting is something slightly more radical than the Broadcasting Bill is likely to offer. The suggestion is to relocate the centres of regulation and simply to limit ourselves to services bequeathed locally with the national blessing. I would like regional and local agencies to deal regionally and locally with broadcasting in the areas.' He then goes on to say: 'What I'm suggesting is establishing new television regulators on a local and regional basis in a form which can cross-subsidise the introduction of essential local public service programmes providing relevant and empowering information, local education and entertainment.' This last phrase I think is key. These are obviously important and worthy aims. I feel that what is missing here and what isn't addressed in fact in any of the papers, with one exception, is the question of television drama, i.e. the most expensive area of TV production and also probably the most important area of programming for most audiences. I will return to this issue in my summary conclusions.

I would just perhaps ask Dave one final question: I like the following statement and I quote: 'I think we can expect a dramatic change ahead for television which very few of us have really started to recognise, least of all the academic community which traditionally,' and this is the most important bit, 'has been at the forefront of promoting and securing a public space in broadcasting.' Well, I wish that were true Dave, wherever you're sitting. I hope you'll tell me who's been at the forefront in education. I don't want to sound cynical but I suppose I was a little surprised by those fine words.

Okay, watching the time, I just want to skim over the other papers, not because they're not interesting but because clearly I have too much material in terms of the questions and the observations I would like to make. I would like to come on in fact to the final paper that I wish to address which is Barbara's paper which, as I say, shouldn't really come at the end because it's not really about consumption. It's only the first sentence which is concerned with the consumer. What Barbara does is to start by focusing on the consumer and the power, or the lack of power, for the feminist female audience. She places that audience within the broader context of the lack of policy within the industry about equal opportunities. What Barbara then does, in a sort of circular way as far as the presentation here is concerned, is offer a fascinating account of the production of *Middlemarch* and an edition of *J'Accuse*. I won't comment on either account because it seems to me they strike a depressingly exemplary analysis of broadcasting in the UK.

But I'd like to use the opportunity of her analysis of *Middlemarch* to offer some concluding remarks of my own which, as I say, I think relates to a number of points made through all the papers. In his paper John Mundy quotes Lisa Buckingham of the *Guardian* who writes that, whatever the rhetoric there may be about the UK-based, global players and I quote: 'corporate attention remains focused on extracting the last drop of profit from the domestic media market before far tougher overseas territories are tackled.' Now I quote this because I'm afraid I disagree with this analysis and I'd like to explain in the last few moments why I don't agree with it.

I said at the beginning of this session that the papers at this conference covered a wide range of media issues within the production, distribution, consumption and new technologies orbit. They do. However, there seems to me to be two disparate but connected areas of media analysis which are generally under-researched and under published about and don't really feature here. The first is the lack of precise economic analysis of the distribution of television programmes, the financing the Internet, and so on, in conventional economic cost and value terms. The second absence, with the exception of Barbara's paper, is a discussion of television drama. This also relates to John Mundy's observations where he writes: 'Talk about the technology's delivery, ignore any discussion about the actual material which is to be delivered.'

Now the two are connected for the following reasons. In my view television programmes are unique objects in the capitalist world,. They're the only commodity whose value is determined by what the purchaser can afford to pay and not for a price economically determined by the producer. Is it because in the UK the costs of production are written off after first transmission? This means that the programme has no marginal unit cost of production. If you take for example a TV set. A TV set cannot be sold for less that the cost of the raw material of its production, Obviously so. A television programme can. I think this holds true for all other products and commodities we buy. Only TV programmes can be sold for less than their costs of production. So, for example, an episode of *Inspector Morse* may fetch £100,000 in the USA but be sold to Burkina Faso for £100. That is what those countries can afford, given the size of their relative populations and the size of their economies. In which case, it seems to me, that Lisa Buckingham is wrong. Profit is not necessarily made for the domestic media markets at all but zero costs of production are achieved in the domestic markets in order to enable the United Kingdom's programmes to be highly competitive internationally.

Which brings me to *Middlemarch* and TV drama generally. Incidentally there are in fact a couple of small disagreements I have with Barbara. One is where she writes, 'television adaptations of classic novels have enjoyed startling success recently in Britain and on the export market.' My disagreement here is that such classic novels have always enjoyed great success in Britain and overseas, particularly with PBS in the States. All that has happened recently is that the BBC has run out of ideas and courage and, instead of engaging in more dangerous contemporary drama, has fallen back, in my view, on boring adaptations of the classics, knowing that the American will love them. No, the point is all drama, and costume drama in particular, is the most expensive area of TV production and an extremely conventional and popular area of TV production.

Secondly, I would say that what is depressing about the situation is that only a dozen or so countries in the world can afford to make drama because only they have large enough populations from which to extract a licence fee or to attract advertisers and so enable them to take the risk of producing such costly productions. There are only five countries in Europe, in fact, which can engage in such drama production – the UK, Germany, France, Italy, Spain; and in the Americas you have – the USA, Mexico, Brazil; in South East Asia you have – India, China, Japan; in Africa, Nigeria, and so on. Now the implications of this situation, where only a dozen countries in the world can produce what one would call, I suppose as a shorthand, 'quality' drama – expensive quality drama – are depressingly clear for all small countries and for regional, local and community television. I commented on the fact that most of the papers were referring to news and the new technologies and community initiatives. All of these things offer exciting possibilities. What unfortunately they don't do, or address, is the possibilities of very different types of drama from what we've normally experienced and enjoyed on television. In terms of the most popular area of programming worldwide, I can't see the picture changing very much for the next fifty years.

Thank you. Are there any questions or observations? Right, time for the next session.

Jo Langham: Can you just expand on what you said about copyright?

Manuel Alvarado: Well I can't just instantly locate where you write about it but it seems to me you demonstrate the problem. You see what I've never understood about copyright is that people and academics get very very worried about getting copyright on their work but as someone who has had quite a lot of work copyrighted over the years I must have earned 10p from it. It seems to me that the people who are concerned about copyright are not the authors but the publishers. It is my publishers who have been worried about copyright because it's they who lose the money while copyright is always being argued as being important in protecting authors' rights. It doesn't protect authors' rights at all

Jo Langham: That was the point I was arguing.

Manuel Alvarado: I was saying that you brought that point out rather well. I'm sorry I didn't express myself clearly at that point. You made the point much more clearly that I ever have done. That is what I was saying.

John Gray: You've had an interesting series of papers today all by academics. Is there a danger of too much, dare I say it, 'navel gazing'? Is this really helping us to integrate the new culture whatever this may be.

Manuel Alvarado: I think we're moving in that direction but we're not there yet. I think two things. There has got to be ever closer relations between broadcasters and academics; academics should stop being academics in that sense. I would like to see them engaging more intellectually and productively in work terms with people in broadcasting. The reason I feel very positive is that at least three or four of the papers, although they were written by people working in education, were written by people with extensive broadcasting experience. I think the quality of the papers reflected that. All that I would say is that I hope more broadcasters will begin to write papers and even go and teach on a part-time basis in educational institutions. I also hope that broadcasters will increasingly welcome educators and academics to come and work with them in their studio complexes. I don't think it is fully happening yet but I do think it is improving. The situation is far better than it was ten years ago John.

John Gray: In publishing, is there a niche for a new kind of book, bridging the gap between the people who study the media and those who work in it?

Manuel Alvarado: I hope so, and that's what we particularly try to achieve. I'll just give you one example of a difficulty. I'm very keen to develop a more extensive series of titles about journalism. It seems to me that journalism has not been well served by publishers and publishing over the years. But, if you take the case of a journal we publish called the *British Journalism Review*, the editorial board are all working journalists and they all complain that they have very few journalists who subscribe to *British Journalism Review*. I say 'Yes, because journalists expect things for free.' They expect things on the basis as if they were reviewing them. That seems to be one of the difficulties on the professional side. The professionals working in the media don't expect to buy these things. Sorry to be cynical.

Jo Langham: Can I just endorse what you are saying about the industry and academia. I've noticed a vast difference between America and Britain and I've worked in both countries. Two anecdotes. When I first came here I worked for the BBC and it just so happens that the BBC newsroom overlooked the UMIST car park and the journalists used to stand, watch and comment pejoratively on academics leaving work at 5.00 pm – not counting the research and writing that went on at home in the evening and weekends. Then you go into academia from the media and the academics say, 'Of course, you know nothing about research.' The isolation between the two professional groups in Britain is classic.

Manuel Alvarado: Yes I think the difference is interesting, I've just been at the University of Texas, Austin. The Communications Broadcasting Department of the University is so huge and the studio complex is so massive that they actually lease out a section of it to the local PBS stations. That is fascinating because it means they are working with each other all the time. It makes a huge difference.

Questioner: With the pressure on costs wouldn't it be a good idea for industry and academia to pool their ideas? For the industry to go to academics for their research?

Manuel Alvarado: I think that is interesting. What was quite frightening in a couple of papers – Jo's and someone else's commented on the fact that young graduates in their late twenties were working for very little money in the broadcasting industries which traditionally have been very well paid. Now one side of me thinks, 'Yes, well, broadcasters were always overpaid, it's about time they woke up to the real world.' On the other hand, if there is that downward spiral towards increasing exploitation of young people going into the industry, that has very worrying implications.

I'm sorry we have to end there. Thank you.

Appendix

The Broadcasting Bill: BECTU's views on key issues

This paper was to have been presented by Tony Lennon, President of BECTU, at one of the Paper Sessions. Unfortunately, he was unable to do this, and the paper is hereby included as an appendix.

DIGITAL TERRESTRIAL BROADCASTING (DTB)

Public Service Broadcasting and DTB

1. BECTU believes in a programme-driven approach, placing public service broadcasters at the heart of the transition to DTB.
2. We therefore welcome the aspects of the Bill consistent with our own proposals:
- BBC to operate its own multiplex
- ITV/C4 to share a multiplex
- C5 to have a half share on a multiplex extra bandwidth allowing the public service broadcasters to run new services
- a requirement for 100% simulcasting of existing analogue services, free-to-air.

Switch-off Date for Analogue

3. We believe that the commitment only to 'review' the switch-off date for analogue is unsatisfactory and that a specific date should be set, taking into account on the one hand the need to encourage broadcasters to make the transition to DTB and on the other hand to ensure that viewers (especially those with limited resources) are not compelled to purchase new receiving equipment before they are ready and able to do so.

Transmission

4. We believe that the most effective switchover to DTB will be achieved in respect of the BBC and ITV/C4 multiplexes if the existing transmission arrangements remain in place ie:
- BBC Transmission to undertake the transmission for the BBC multiplex,
- NTL to undertake transmission for the C3/C4 multiplex.

S4C

5. We believe that increased digital capacity is necessary for S4C in order to allow the channel to pursue the add-on services (e.g. widescreen) that may be necessary to encourage viewers to transfer to DTB. We support the overall aim of both S4C and Channel 4 offering full and separate services across Wales, with sufficient capacity for additional services as described above.

Payments to the Exchequer

6. We oppose any system of financial bidding for broadcasting licences and there-

fore welcome the absence of cash bids for multiplex licences, and the absence of payments to the Exchequer during the initial licence period.

Programming and Technical Standards

7. We are concerned at the absence of strong and specific programme standards requirements. We believe that the following essential criteria should be included in digital programme licences:
- a requirement for a wide range of high quality programming;
- a requirement for a proper proportion of regional programming (made in the relevant nation/regions);
- a requirement for a proper proportion of original programming (as opposed to a sole reliance on transferred analogue programming, repeats and imports).

8. Programme standards should be reinforced by clear and consistent technical standards, with the presumption that programming will be provided to the highest feasible technical quality.

Staffing Issues

9. We welcome the requirement to include, within programme licence applications, proposals for training and retraining. We note, however, the absence of any other significant reference to staffing matters in licence applications. We believe that all licence applicants should be required to have full regard to working conditions, crewing levels, job security, health and safety, equal opportunities and training within their proposals to the ITC.

Conditional Access

10. We believe it should be a mandatory and strongly enforceable requirement that there should be common, fair and non-discriminatory encryption and subscription management systems. We are not satisfied that the Bill provisions are adequate in this respect. [Nor do we believe this can be left to a separate licencing system to be introduced via a European directive.]

Ownership

11. We believe that the Bill contains no adequate protection against concentration of ownership in DTB. We take the view that there should be a specific prohibition on newspaper groups controlling either digital television channels or multiplexes.

12. On the particular issue of the control of multiplexes, we oppose the raising of the maximum holding from 2 to 3 multiplexes since this would allow one company to control 50% of the market – an unhealthy degree of concentration.

Radio: Digital Audio Broadcasting – (DAB)

13. We continue to support the proposals to reserve digital capacity for BBC national, national/regional and local radio services.

14. We continue to support the reservation of digital capacity for INR.

15. While recognising the encouragement given to ILR stations to invest in digital broadcasting, we believe that stronger guarantees on digital access are

required, together with consideration of assistance in the transition to DAB, especially for smaller stations with fragile finances.

OWNERSHIP

Licence Limits

16. BECTU believes that the maximum holding of two ITV licences should be retained and we therefore strongly oppose the lifting of the limit and its replacement with a looser maximum of 15% of the total television audience.
17. We believe that this will inevitably lead to an excessive concentration of ownership within the ITV network. We fear that the widespread speculation that ITV will consolidate into 3 or 4 companies during 1996 is unfortunately accurate.
18. As well as the general and familiar arguments against concentration of ownership in the media on political and cultural grounds, we believe that the government's proposals are based on a fallacy. Just as with the previous wave of mergers in ITV (Carlton/Central, Granada/LWT, MAI/Meridian/Anglia, Yorkshire/Tyne Tees) the government appears to have accepted the argument that British media companies require a large domestic base in order to compete internationally. In practice none of the companies already involved in mergers has been noticeably more successful than before in exporting programmes, nor in international co-productions and joint ventures. The real benefit has been in terms of domestic economies of scale and market share – often at the expense of the job security and conditions of broadcasting workers. Such transparently narrow and self-serving arguments should not, in our view, continue to be rewarded in terms of government policy.

Cross-Ownership

19. BECTU is equally strongly opposed to the relaxing of cross-ownership limits, thus allowing national newspaper groups to control ITV or C5 licences. We believe that the current 20% cross-holding limit should be retained (and we therefore welcome the proposal that this should continue to apply to News International and the Mirror Group).
20. The political and cultural arguments against concentration of ownership within ITV apply with even more force to the prospect of increased concentration across the media as a whole. A major incursion by national newspapers and publishing groups into television presents a real problem for any society that claims to be pluralist and democratic.

The Regional Nature of ITV

21. A defining characteristic of ITV, since its very inception, has been the regional character of the licence-holders – with a significant proportion of programming made in the region, by regionally-based staff, and with a regional orientation. The recent trend towards concentration in ITV has already seriously eroded the regional character and regional production base of ITV companies. Further concentration, and particularly the incursion of national newspaper groups with strong national corporate priorities can only accelerate this process.
22. We have no confidence, in the face of the proposed relaxation in the owner-

ship regime, that the proposed new licence conditions to protect regional programmes and production will be in any way adequate, devoid as they are of any specific targets for regional production and staffing levels.

Cable/Satellite/DTB
23. We note the absence of restrictions on newspaper control of cable, satellite and DTB licences, subject only to the overall 15% audience limit. We reiterate our view that strong ownership and cross-ownership controls should be applied in all these sectors; that News International should not continue to be allowed to own both major newspaper and satellite interests; and that, as indicated above, national newspapers should not be allowed to control either digital television channels or multiplexes.

Long-Term Proposals
24. We note the abandonment of the consideration of longer-term proposals on media ownership, about which we expressed a number of serious concerns. We believe that longer-term proposals will still need to be developed, but, we would hope, on a basis closer to our own views.

BBC
BBC Transmission
25. BECTU is totally opposed to the sell-off, on any basis, of BBC Transmission. Full briefings are available separately on this issue.

BBC Commercial Services
26. We question the need for the ITC's proposed new role in licensing BBC commercial services. Such services are already regulated and monitored in the public interest by the BBC Board of Governors and ultimately by the government and Department of National Heritage. We question the need for a confusing extra tier of regulation, especially from a body whose experience and *raison d'être* is in the wholly-commercial broadcasting sector.

S4C FUNDING
27. We believe that in amending the S4C funding formula it will be essential to build in a new and sufficiently higher base figure to account for the channel's proposed new digital responsibilities, including not just transmission costs but other programming and marketing factors.

BROADCASTING STANDARDS COUNCIL
28. BECTU opposed the creation of the BSC in the Broadcasting Act 1990 as an unnecessary, unwelcome and confusing addition to broadcasting regulation. We continue to urge its abolition rather than the merger of its functions with the BCC.